Collins e

Italian
Conversation

Ciao!

Come va?

Published by Collins
An imprint of HarperCollins Publishers
Westerhill Road
Bishopbriggs
Glasgow G64 2QT

Second Edition 2015

10 9 8 7 6 5 4 3 2

© HarperCollins Publishers 2006, 2015

ISBN 978-0-00-811199-1

www.collinsdictionary.com
www.collins.co.uk/languagesupport

Typeset by Davidson Publishing
Solutions, Glasgow

Printed in Italy by GRAFICA VENETA S.p.A.

A catalogue record for this book is
available from the British Library.

If you would like to comment on any
aspect of this book, please contact us at
the given address or online.
E-mail: dictionaries@harpercollins.co.uk
 www.facebook.com/collinsdictionary
 @collinsdict

Acknowledgements
We would like to thank those authors and
publishers who kindly gave permission
for copyright material to be used in
the Collins Corpus. We would also like
to thank Times Newspapers Ltd for
providing valuable data.

MANAGING EDITOR
Janice McNeillie

CONTRIBUTOR
Mirella Alessio

FOR THE PUBLISHER
Gerry Breslin
Hannah Dove

Introduction

What is it?

Collins Easy Learning Italian Conversation is a book for learners of Italian of all ages. It will increase your confidence in holding a conversation in Italian, whether you are just starting to learn Italian, studying at school or at an evening class, or brushing up your language skills. You may be going on holiday or planning to go travelling in Italy, go there on business, or live there. Whatever your situation, you'll want to be able to communicate effectively and naturally in Italian.

Why do you need it?

Becoming proficient in a foreign language means being able to use and understand a number of different aspects – vocabulary, grammar, pronunciation, and so on. However, it takes a while to be able to put all these elements together and be sure that what you are saying sounds like natural Italian. The *Easy Learning Italian Conversation* has been carefully designed to bring these aspects together and give you language structures which you can use in conversation with confidence, knowing that you will be speaking Italian as spoken by Italian speakers.

How is it structured?

Collins Easy Learning Italian Conversation is made up of 12 units, each illustrating the language used in a particular situation, followed by a summary which brings together the key language covered throughout the units. You'll also find the One-stop phrase shop – a unit which contains all the important expressions and turns of phrase that help you to sound more natural in Italian.

A short grammar and verbs supplement gives you additional language support, ensuring that you have everything at your fingertips. Finally, the English-Italian glossary covers the most important vocabulary you may need to personalize your conversation.

How does it work?

Language allows us to express ourselves and interact with others. In any given situation, we perform different language tasks, such as asking for information, agreeing and disagreeing, complaining, making suggestions and so forth. To do this, we use linguistic structures (*How...?, When...?, Could I...?, I'd like...* and so on) which can be used in a variety of contexts. Each unit in *Collins Easy Learning Italian Conversation* gives you all the phrases you might need in a given situation, grouped by structure. English headings help you navigate through the structures to enable you to find what you want quickly and easily. Throughout the units, there are also tips headed Buono a sapersi! which highlight important differences in the way English and Italian work.

A conversation, by definition, is a two-way process. It is as important to understand what is being said to you as it is to be able to respond. At the end of each unit, there is a section headed Listen out for. Each of these sections gives you a variety of the most typical phrases which you might hear in a given situation. Becoming familiar with these will allow you to have a successful conversation with a Italian speaker. For further help with pronunciation, a free download with all the important structures recorded is available on **www.collins.co.uk/easylearningresources**.

Communicating effectively in Italian isn't just about linguistic competence – it's also about cultural knowledge. For you to feel confident in Italy, it is also useful to know more about Italian culture and lifestyle. At the end of each unit, the Lifestyle Tips will give you the information you need to gain a deeper insight into the language, the country and its people.

Why choose *Collins Easy Learning Italian Conversation*?

- **easy to use** all the key language structures you need to give you the confidence to hold a conversation in natural Italian

- **easy to read** a clear, modern layout which allows you to find what you need quickly and easily

- **easy to understand** the language you may hear from Italian speakers in a given situation

- **easy to speak** free audio download available on **www.collins.co.uk/easylearningresources**

The *Collins Easy Learning* range

The *Collins Easy Learning Italian Conversation* is part of the best-selling *Collins Easy Learning* range, which includes the highly acclaimed *Collins Easy Learning Italian Dictionary. Collins Easy Learning Italian Grammar* and *Collins Easy Learning Italian Verbs* support you with all your grammatical needs. The *Collins Easy Learning* series is the ideal language reference range to help you learn Italian.

Italian pronunciation

Italian pronunciation is not very difficult. Words are written pretty much as they sound, so when you see a word written down you can generally pronounce it with no problem, and when you hear a new word you know immediately how to spell it. There are no sounds in Italian that are very different from English. Below we give some tips to help you speak natural-sounding Italian.

Italian vowels

In English, vowels we don't emphasize often sound like "uh", so the *e* in *mother* and the *a* in *central* sound just the same. Sometimes vowels don't get pronounced at all, as is the case with the first *e* in *interesting*. In Italian this never happens. Italian vowels are always clearly pronounced.

Italian vowels are generally pronounced as follows:

a	– like the *a* in *apple*
e	– like the *e* in *set*
i	– like the *ee* in *sheep*
o	– like the *o* in *orange*
u	– like the *oo* in *soon*

Italian consonants

Most Italian consonants are pronounced the same as English ones, except that double consonants are two distinct sounds, so that the **tt** in **tutto** is pronounced as in *hat trick* and not as in *fitted*.

The following are Italian consonants that differ from English:

c	– before **e** and **i** is pronounced *tch* (cento, cinema, cioccolato)
ch	– is pronounced like *k* in *kettle* (chiesa, chilometro)
g	– before **e** and **i** is pronounced like *j* in *jet* (gelato, gennaio, giorno, giacca)

gh	– is pronounced like *g* in *get* (g̲hiaccio, lag̲hi)
gl	– before **i** is normally pronounced like *ll* in *million* (meg̲lio, mig̲liaio)
gn	– is pronounced like the *ny* in *canyon* (g̲n̲occhi, cog̲n̲ome)
sc	– before **e** and **i** is pronounced *sh* (sc̲ena, sc̲endere, las̲c̲iare, s̲c̲ienza)
z	– is pronounced *ds* or *ts* (z̲ucchini, z̲ucchero, mez̲z̲o, z̲ia)

Which syllable to emphasize

To make your Italian sound more fluent and natural you need to stress the right syllable. Here are some guidelines:

• Two-syllable words always stress the first syllable, unless the final vowel has an accent:

ca̲sa (*house*)	gior̲no (*day*)
bel̲la (*beautiful*)	du̲e (*two*)
so̲no (*I am*)	spes̲so (*often*)
lu̲i (*he*)	og̲gi (*today*)

• Words with three or more syllables generally have the stress on the next to the last syllable:

ingle̲se (*English*)	fini̲to (*finished*)
anda̲re (*to go*)	andre̲sti (*you'd go*)
veni̲re (*to come*)	supermerca̲to (*supermarket*)
settima̲na (*week*)	straordinariame̲nte (*extraordinarily*)

• If a word has an accent on the final vowel, it is stressed on the final syllable.

età̲ (*age*)	metà̲ (*half*)
così̲ (*like this*)	perché̲ (*why, because*)

Words of this type include many nouns that end in **–ty** in English

università̲ (*university*)	curiosità̲ (*curiosity*)
città̲ (*city*)	crudeltà̲ (*cruelty*)

- Two future tense forms always have an accent (*I* and *he/she/it/You*):

farò (*I'll do*)   aspetterò (*I'll wait*)
sarà (*it will be*)   si divertirà (*she'll enjoy herself*)

- Some words have the stress on a syllable which is not the last, or the next to the last. In this book we use italics to show when an unexpected syllable is stressed, to help you learn the correct pronunciation.

*u*tile (*useful*)   *nu*mero (*number*)
*ma*cchina (*car*)   *ca*mera (*room*)
*su*bito (*suddenly*)   *com*pito (*homework*)
diffi*ci*le (*difficult*)   por*ta*tile (*portable*)

- It's specially important to notice which syllable you should emphasize when pronouncing infinitives ending in **–ere**, because they vary. Some, such as **avere** (*to have*) and **vedere** (*to see*) have normal stress, on the next to the last syllable.

However, there are many important exceptions, for example:

*es*sere (*to be*)   *ven*dere (*to sell*)
*scen*dere (*to get off*)   di*vi*dere (*to divide*)
*sce*gliere (*to choose*)   *chiu*dere (*to close*)

BUONO A SAPERSI!
Past participles such as **finito** and **partito** always have the stress on the next to last syllable, but similar-looking words such as **subito** and **compito** sometimes have the stress on a syllable you wouldn't expect.

Small talk

Come va? – How are things?

Whether you're going to be working in Italy or you're going to spend some time with your Italian-speaking friends, you'll want to be able to chat with people and get to know them better. The phrases in this unit will help you talk naturally to friends, family and colleagues in a number of everyday situations.

GREETINGS

Just as in English, there are several ways of greeting people in Italian, depending on who you are addressing, and whether you want to be formal or not. Say **buongiorno** (*good morning*) or **buonasera** (*good afternoon/good evening*), if you want to sound polite.

Hello...

Buongiorno.	**Hello**.
Buongiorno signora Rossi.	**Good morning**, Mrs Rossi.
Buongiorno Francesco, come va?	**Good afternoon** Francesco, how are you?
Buonasera.	**Good evening**.

BUONO A SAPERSI!
buon pomeriggio (*good afternoon*) exists in Italian. However it is only used on the radio or television, for example by newscasters. It would sound a bit odd if you greeted people saying **buon pomeriggio**: stick to **buongiorno** or, later on in the day, **buonasera**. Remember to say **buongiorno** or **buonasera** as you enter a shop or a restaurant.

Use **salve** (*hi*) if you wish to sound a bit more informal, whether you know the people you are greeting or not. If you're on friendly terms with someone or if you are addressing somebody young, you can say **ciao** (*hi*).

Hi...

Salve, cerco Matteo.	**Hi**, I'm looking for Matteo.
Salve, come va?	**Hi**, how are things?
Ciao ragazzi, come va?	**Hi** there, how are things?

Use **arrivederci** to say goodbye to people you don't know well. You can just say **ciao** to people you know or to somebody young. **buongiorno** and **buonasera** are also often used to say goodbye.

Goodbye...

Arrivederci.	**Goodbye**.
Arrivederci, signora Clari!	**Goodbye**, Mrs Clari!
Ciao, ci vediamo domani.	**Bye**, see you tomorrow.
Allora io vado, **buonasera** a tutti.	I'm off, **goodnight** everybody.

BUONO A SAPERSI!
Remember to say in Italian **arrivederci** when you leave a shop or restaurant.

While in English you can use *goodnight* to mean 'goodbye' or to wish somebody a good night's sleep, in Italian you use **buonanotte** (*goodnight*) only before going to bed.

Goodnight...

Meglio domire adesso. **Buonanotte**!	Better go to sleep now. **Goodnight**!
Vado a dormire, sono proprio stanca. **Buonanotte** a tutti.	I'm going to bed, I'm really tired. **Goodnight** everybody.
Buonanotte e sogni d'oro!	**Goodnight** and sweet dreams!

See you...

A domani!	**See you** tomorrow!
A lunedì!	**See you** on Monday!
Ci vediamo!	**See you** later!
Allora **a più tardi**, ciao!	**See you** later!

INTRODUCING PEOPLE

You may want to introduce people you know to one another. The simplest way is by saying **questo** (or **questa**) è (*this is*) when introducing a person. You can also use **ti presento** (*I'd like you to meet*) when addressing someone you know well, or **le presento** to be more formal. When speaking to several people use **vi presento**.

This is...

Questo è mio marito David.	**This is** my husband, David.
Questi sono i miei figli Andrew, Gordon e Emma.	**These are** my children, Andrew, Gordon and Emma.
Ti presento Lara.	**I'd like you to meet** Lara.
Mi permetta di presentarle Richard, il mio compagno.	**Let me introduce You to** Richard, my partner.
Vi presento James, il fratello di Kate.	**I'd like <u>you</u> all to meet** James, Kate's brother.

When you're introduced to someone, you'll want to know how to react. Just say **piacere** (*nice to meet you*) or **molto piacere** (*how do you do?*). You can also say **piacere di conoscerla**, or **conoscerti** to somebody younger. You can then introduce yourself, by saying your name. In more formal situations, Italians quite often give their surname rather than their first name.

Nice to meet you...

Piacere, Emma.	**Nice to meet you**, I'm Emma.
Piacere, io sono Anna e questo è Kevin.	**Nice to meet you**, I'm Anna and this is Kevin.
Molto piacere, Sinclair.	**How do you do**, my name's Sinclair.
E tu sei Maria? **Piacere di conoscerti**.	Are you Maria? **Nice to meet you**.
Piacere di conoscerla, avvocato Martini.	**Nice to meet You**, Mr. Martini.

BUONO A SAPERSI!

Italians often use titles like **avvocato** (*lawyer*), **ingegnere** (*engineer*), **architetto** (*architect*) when addressing professionals, even without the name of the person, for example **Buongiorno architetto!**, in the same way as we would address a doctor.

If you want to introduce yourself to somebody, you can say **Piacere...** and your name. A more formal way is to use **Mi permetta di presentarmi,...** (*May I introduce myself,...*).

Hello, I'm...

Piacere, sono Kate Brooks.	**Hello**, I'm Kate Brooks.
Piacere, Peter.	**Hello**, I'm Peter.
Salve, sono il fratello di Jane.	**Hi**, I'm Jane's brother.
Mi permetta di presentarmi, mi chiamo Thomas Baxter.	**May I introduce myself**, I'm Thomas Baxter.

BUONO A SAPERSI!

If you have missed an introduction but you are keen to meet somebody you can say:
Mi scusi, non ci siamo presentati, io sono Catherine. Lei è...?
(*Excuse me, we haven't been introduced, I'm Catherine, You're...?*).

In order to get the conversation going, you'll want to be able to talk about yourself – what your name is, what you do and so on. To say what your name is in Italian, you use **mi chiamo** which literally means *I call myself*, from the verb **chiamarsi** (*to be called*). Alternatively, like in English, you can simply say **sono** (*I am*), from the verb *essere* (*to be*). For more information on the verbs **chiamare** and *essere*, see pages 275 and 282.

My name is...

Mi chiamo Jonathan Jones.	**My name is** Jonathan Jones.
Ciao, **mi chiamo** Danielle.	Hi, **my name is** Danielle.
Ci chiamiamo John e Francis.	**We are** John and Francis.
Salve, **io sono** Liam.	Hi, **I'm** Liam.
Piacere, **noi siamo** Christine e Peter.	Nice to meet you, **we are** Christine and Peter.

If you want to say how old you are, use **ho** followed by your age and **anni** (literally *I have ... years*). **ho** comes from the verb **avere** (*to have*). For more information on **avere**, see page 279.

I'm... years old

Ho trentasette **anni**.	**I'm** thirty-seven **years old**.
Ho ventidue **anni**.	**I'm** twenty-two.
Mio figlio **ha** otto **anni**.	My son**'s** eight.
Quanti anni **hai**?	How **old are you**?

BUONO A SAPERSI!

If you have to ask **Quanti anni ha?** (*How old are You?*) you can always add **se non sono indiscreto** (or **indiscreta**) (*if You don't mind my asking*).

To talk about who you are and what you do, use **sono** (*I am*), **ho** (*I have*) and **faccio** (*I do*). These come from the verbs **essere** (*to be*), **avere** (*to have*) and **fare** (*to do*). For more information on these verbs, see pages 282, 279 and 283.

I'm...

Sono il fratello di Ben.	**I'm** Ben's brother.
Sono un'amica di Paul.	**I'm** a friend of Paul's.
Non **sono** sposata.	**I'm** not married.
Avevo una ragazza ma adesso **sono** single.	I had a girlfriend but **I'm** single now.
Siamo amiche di Helen.	**We are** Helen's friends.

When you say what you do in Italian, you use the verb **fare** (*to do*): *I'm a baker* is **faccio il panettiere**. The verb **essere** (*to be*) can also be used, but it is less common.

I'm a ...

Faccio l'insegnante.	**I'm** a teacher.
Faccio il medico.	**I'm** a doctor.
Faccio il programmatore presso un'azienda inglese.	**I work as** a programmer for a British company.
Sono avvocato.	**I'm** a lawer.
Siamo studentesse.	**We are** students.

BUONO A SAPERSI!
Remember that when talking about people's jobs, *a* in English is often translated by the definite article (**il**, **la** and so on) in Italian.

I have...

Ho due sorelle.	**I have** two sisters.
Ho un figlio e una figlia.	**I have** one son and one daughter.
Abbiamo parenti nel sud Italia.	**We have** relatives in southern Italy.

I live...

Abito nel Galles.	**I live** in Wales.
Abito da sola.	**I live** alone.
Abitiamo in un appartamento.	**We live** in a flat.
Adesso **vivo** in Italia.	**I live** in Italy now.

I'm staying...

Sto all'Hotel Belvedere.	**I'm staying** at the Hotel Belvedere.
Sto da amici.	**I'm staying** with friends.
Mi fermo a Milano per una settimana.	**I'm staying** in Milan for a week.

To say that you've done something for a given length of time, use **da** (*for*) with the present tense. Another common way of talking about things you've been doing for a while is to use **sono... che...**.

I have been... for...

Faccio l'infermiera **da** cinque anni.	**I've been** a nurse **for** five years.
Vivo in Italia **da** dieci anni.	**I've been living** in Italy **for** ten years.
Sono a Ravenna **da** due settimane.	**I've been** in Ravenna **for** two weeks.
Sono sei mesi **che** studio l'italiano.	**I've been** learning Italian **for** 6 months.
Sono tre mesi **che** insegno inglese in Italia.	**I've been** teaching English in Italy **for** 3 months.

When you're chatting socially, you will want to ask any number of questions. One simple way of finding out information from someone is to say **mi parli di** (*tell me about*) to someone you don't know very well, or **parlami di** to someone younger. These come from the verb **parlare** (*to speak*). For more information on this verb, see page 275.

Tell me about...

Mi parli della sua famiglia.	**Tell me about** Your family.
Mi parli un po' **di** lei.	**Tell me** a bit **about** Yourself.
Parlami del tuo nuovo ragazzo.	**Tell me about** your new boyfriend.
Dimmi in che consiste il tuo lavoro.	**Tell me** what your job involves.
Ma basta parlare di me. **Dimmi di** te, adesso.	Enough about me. Now **tell me about** you.

Another common way of asking for information in spoken Italian is to use question words: **Come...?** (*How...?*), **Cosa...?** (*What...?*), **Dove...?** (*Where...?*), **Quando...?** (*When...?*) and so on.

How...?

Come va?	**How** are things?
Come sta?	**How** are You?
Come stai, Marco?	**How** are you, Marco?
Volevo chiederti, **com**'è andata la vacanza?	I meant to ask, **how** was your holiday?
Come va con l'università?	**How**'s university going?

What...?

Cosa fai nella vita?	**What** do you do?
Cosa le piace fare nel tempo libero?	**What** do You enjoy doing in your free time?
Cosa farai quando finisci l'università?	**What** are you going to do when you finish university?

What's your name?

Come si chiama?	**What's Your name**?
Ciao! E tu **come ti chiami**?	Hi! **What's your name**?
Come si chiama sua moglie?	**What's** Your wife's **name**?
Come vi chiamate?	What are <u>your</u> names?

Where...?

Dove *a*bita?	**Where** do You live?
Dove lavora?	**Where** do You work?
Dov'è il suo ufficio?	**Where** is Your office?
Di dove sei?	**Where** do you come **from**?

When...?

Quando arrivi?	**When** will you get here?
Quando parte?	**When** are You leaving?
Quando ci troviamo?	**What time** are we meeting?
Quand'è il tuo compleanno?	**When** is your birthday?

If you want to ask how long someone has been doing something, use **Da quanto tempo...?** or just **Da quanto...?** (*How long ... for?*) followed by the present tense. For more information on the present tense, see page 271.

How long have...?

Da quanto tempo lavori qui?	**How long have** you been working here?
Da quanto tempo è sposata?	**How long have** You been married?
Da quanto stai in It*a*lia?	**How long have** you been in Italy?

Sometimes you'll want to ask why a friend or acquaintance did or didn't do something. You can use **Perché...?** (*Why...?*) and the past tense to ask. For more information on the past tense, see page 272.

Why...?

Perché hai cambiato casa?	**Why** did you move house?
Perché si è licenziata?	**Why** did You quit your job?
Perché non mi hai telefonato?	**Why** did**n't** you call me?
Perché non c'è andata?	**Why** did**n't** You go?

SAYING WHAT YOU WANT TO DO

When you're talking to friends or colleagues you will often need to be able to talk about what you would like to do. To say what you want to do, use **vorrei** (*I'd like*). **vorrei** comes from the verb **volere** (*to want*). For more information on **volere**, see page 285.

I'd like to...

Vorrei ringraziarla dell'aiuto.	**I'd like to** thank You for your help.
Vorrei parlare con la signora Martini, per favore.	**I'd like to** speak to Mrs Martini, please.
Vorremmo invitarvi a bere qualcosa.	**We'd like to** take <u>you</u> out for a drink.
Vorremmo presentarle un amico.	**We'd like** You **to** meet a friend of ours.

You can also use **voglio** (*I want*) to talk about what you want to do. If you want to say that you want someone to do something, you use **voglio che** followed by the subjunctive. For more information on the subjunctive, see page 273.

I want to...

Voglio organizzare una festa.	**I want to** organize a party.
Voglio invitare un po' di amici per il mio compleanno.	**I want to** have a few friends over for my birthday.
Voglio che tu venga con me.	**I want** you **to** come with me.
Voglio che la serata vada bene.	**I want** the evening **to** be a success.

MAKING SUGGESTIONS

One easy way of making suggestions to your friends and colleagues is to use **si potrebbe** (*we could*) followed by the verb in the infinitive. **potrebbe** comes from the verb **potere** (*to be able*). For more information on **potere**, see page 284.

We could...

Si potrebbe chiedere a Paul di venire con noi.	**We could** ask Paul to join us.
Si potrebbe uscire a bere qualcosa insieme.	**We could** go out for a drink.
Ci si potrebbe incontrare un'altra volta.	**We could** meet another time.
Ci si potrebbe trovare al Caffè San Marco.	**We could** meet at the Caffè San Marco.

Just as in English you can make a suggestion by simply asking **Perché non ...?** (*Why don't ...?*).

Why don't...?

Perché non ci troviamo uno di questi giorni?	**Why don't** we get together sometime?
Perché non invitiamo Fabio e la sua ragazza?	**Why don't** we invite Fabio and his girlfriend?
Perché non li chiami?	**Why don't** you phone them?
Perché non viene a pranzo con me?	**Why not** meet me for lunch?

You can also make a suggestion using the Italian phrase **E se...?** (*How about...?*) which is followed by a verb in the imperfect subjunctive. For more information on the subjunctive, see page 273.

How about...?

E se li invitassimo a cena?	**How about** asking them round for dinner?
E se venisse con noi?	**How about** if You came with us?
E se passassi a prenderti la mattina?	**How about** if I picked you up in the morning?

Use **Dovrei...?** (*Should I...?*) followed by the verb in the infinitive to ask if you should do something. **dovrei** comes from the verb **dovere** (*to have to*). For more information on **dovere**, see page 281.

Should I...?

Dovrei invitare Anna?	**Should I** invite Anna?
Dovrei richiamarla?	**Should I** call her back?
Dovrei scusarmi?	**Should I** apologize?

EXPRESSING OPINIONS

When talking to people in a social or work situation, you may wish to express your opinion of something. In Italian you can use **credo** or **penso** (*I think*). When you use **credere** and **pensare** with **che**, the verb which follows is in the subjunctive. For more information on the subjunctive, see page 273.

I think...

Penso che sia una splendida idea.	**I think** it's a great idea.
Penso proprio **che** sia troppo tardi per andare al cinema.	**I think** it's really too late to go to the cinema.
Credo che Sonia abbia ragione.	**I think** Sonia's right.
Non credo proprio **che** sia così.	**I don't think** that's the case at all.
Non credo che sia una buona idea rivederci.	**I don't think** it's a good idea for us to see each other again.

In my opinion...

Secondo me è una buona idea.	**In my opinion**, it's a good idea.
Secondo me ci creerà problemi.	**In my opinion**, it will cause us problems.
Secondo me è la decisione giusta.	**In my opinion**, it's the right decision.
Per me non è vero.	**In my opinion**, it's not true.

If you want to ask other people what they think of something, use **Che ne pensa di...?** (*What do You think of...?*). Use **Che ne pensi di...?** if you are talking to somebody you know well or to somebody young.

What do you think of...?

Che ne pensa del suo ultimo film?	**What do You think of** his latest movie?
Che ne pensa di questo ristorante?	**What do You think of** this restaurant?
Che ne pensi di questa idea?	**What do you think of** this idea?
Che ne pensa?	**What do You think?**

To agree or disagree with what other people say, use **sono d'accordo** or **non sono d'accordo**.

I agree...

Sono d'accordo.	**I agree.**
Sono d'accordo con Nigel.	**I agree with** Nigel.
Sono completamente **d'accordo con** lei!	I entirely **agree with** You!
Non sono del tutto **d'accordo con** Giovanni.	**I don't** altogether **agree with** Giovanni.
Non condivido questa decisione.	**I don't agree with** this decision.

Where we use the verb *to be* in English in the phrases *to be right* and *to be wrong*, Italian speakers use **avere** (*to have*): **avere ragione** (*to be right*), **avere torto** (*to be wrong*).

You're right...

Hai ragione!	**You're right!**
Secondo me **ha ragione**.	I think **You're right**.
Ha ragione Matteo.	Matteo**'s right**.
Credo che **abbiate ragione** voi.	I think **you're right**.
Per me Marina **ha torto**.	I think Marina **is wrong**.
Fai male a non ascoltarla.	**You're wrong not to** listen to her.

TALKING ABOUT YOUR PLANS

When talking to your colleagues and friends you will want to
tell them about your plans. In Italian, as in English, the present
is very often used to talk about plans, especially for things
that have been arranged and that are definite. For more on the
present tense, see page 271.

I'm...

Vedo Gianni giovedì.	**I'm seeing** Gianni on Thursday.
La **vedo** questo pomeriggio.	**I'm seeing** her this afternoon.
Andiamo al cinema stasera.	**We're going** to the cinema tonight.
Pranziamo insieme venerdì prossimo.	**We're going for lunch** next Friday.

In English, when we talk about the future we often say *I'm going to*.
In Italian you can either use the future or the present tense
(see page 271).

I'm going to...

Gli **telefonerò**.	**I'm going to phone** him.
Lo **avvertirò** che non posso venire.	**I'm going to let** him **know** I can't come.
Dirò loro **di** venire un po' più tardi.	**I'm going to tell** them to come a bit later.
Usciamo a cena domani sera.	**We're going to go out** for dinner tomorrow night.
Andiamo a trovarli lunedì.	**We're going to go** and see them on Monday.

Are you going to...?

Glielo **dici** oggi?	**Are you going to tell** him the news today?
Pensi di rivederlo?	**Are you going to** see him again?
Lei ci **va a** questa festa?	**Are You going to go to** this party?
Comprerà una casa?	**Are You going to buy** a house?

When talking about what you intend to do, you can use **ho intenzione di** (*I intend to*) followed by a verb in the infinitive.

I intend to...

Ho intenzione di invitarla a bere qualcosa.	**I intend to** ask her out for a drink.
Ho intenzione di andarli a trovare quest'estate.	**I intend to** go and see them this summer.
Abbiamo intenzione di invitarlo durante la vacanze.	**We intend to** invite him over during the holidays.
Intendo sistemare la questione prima possibile.	**I intend to** sort out this problem as soon as possible.

Do you intend to...?

Hai intenzione di andare al matrimonio di Carlo e Mariella?	**Do you intend to** go to Carlo and Mariella's wedding?
Ha intenzione di contattarli?	**Do You intend to** get in touch with them?
Cosa **hai intenzione di** dire?	What **do you intend to** say?
Intende restare in questa zona?	**Do You intend to** stay in this area?
Come **intendi** dargli la notizia?	How **do you intend to** tell him the news?

MAKING ARRANGEMENTS

When making arrangements with someone, use **Le va bene...?** or, more informally, **Ti va bene...?** (*Is it okay by you if...?*) to ask someone if something suits them. **va** comes from the verb **andare**. For more information on **andare**, see page 278.

Is it okay by you if...?

Le va bene cenare alle nove?	**Is it okay by You if** we have dinner at nine?
Le va bene alle due?	**Is** two o'clock **okay by You**?
Ti va bene se ti telefono la settimana prossima?	**Will it be okay if** I phone you next week?
Vi va bene se restiamo d'accordo così?	**Would** this arrangement be **okay by you**?

To ask somebody if they would prefer something, use
Preferisce…? or, more informally, **Preferisci…?** (*Would you prefer it…?*) which are from the present tense of the verb **preferire**. You can also use the conditional **Preferirebbe…** or **Preferiresti…**. For more information on –**ire** verbs like **preferire** and on the conditional, see pages 268 and 274.

Would you prefer it if…?

Preferisci che ci incontriamo in centro?	**Would you prefer it if** we met in town?
Preferisce che ci troviamo al ristorante?	**Would You prefer it if** we met at the restaurant?
Preferite che vi passi a prendere?	**Would you prefer** me to come and collect you?
Preferirebbe andare allo spettacolo dopo?	**Would You prefer it if** we went to the later show?

Is it better to…?

È meglio invitare anche sua moglie?	**Is it better to** invite his wife as well?
È meglio se ti chiamo di sera?	**Is it better to** ring you in the evening?
È meglio se l'avvisiamo prima di venire?	**Is it better to** let You know before we drop in?

If you want to confirm an arrangement with somebody, you can use **Siamo d'accordo…?** or **Allora d'accordo…?** (*Are we agreed…?*).

Are we agreed on…?

Siamo d'accordo per la data?	**Are we agreed on** the date?
Siamo d'accordo su dove trovarci?	**Are we agreed on** where to meet?
D'accordo, signora?	**Are we agreed**, madam?
Allora **d'accordo**?	**Are we agreed**, then?
D'accordo.	**Agreed!**

BUONO A SAPERSI!
D'accordo is used to accept offers or to agree: **Ci andiamo insieme? – D'accordo!** (*Shall we go together? – OK!*).

SAYING WHAT YOU HAVE TO DO

When you want to say that you have to do something in Italian, you use **devo** (*I have to*) followed by the infinitive. **devo** comes from the verb **dovere** (*to have to*). For more information on **dovere**, see page 281.

I have to...

Devo fare una telefonata.	**I have to** make a phone call.
Devo stare a casa stasera.	**I have to** stay in tonight.
Devo andare a cena con i colleghi.	**I have to** go out to dinner with my colleagues.
Dobbiamo essere là alle otto in punto.	**We have to** be there at eight o'clock sharp.

I must...

Devo finire prima delle due.	**I must** finish before two o'clock.
Adesso **devo** proprio andare.	I really **must** go now.
Devo telefonare a mia moglie.	**I must** call my wife.

Do you have to...?

Devi dargli una risposta oggi?	**Do you have to** give him an answer today?
Deve andare subito?	**Do You have to** go right now?
Dobbiamo portare qualcosa?	**Do we have to** bring something?

When you want to say that you should or ought to do something, use **dovrei** (*I should*) and then the verb in the infinitive. To find out more about the infinitive, see page 267.

I should...

Dovrei chiamare Anne.	**I should** call Anne.
Dovrei darle il mio numero di cellulare.	**I should** give You my mobile number.
Dovreste venire a trovarci.	**You should** come and see us.

To ask what someone has to do or when or why they have to do it, put **cosa** (*what*), **quando** (*when*) or **perché** (*why*) at the beginning of the sentence, before **deve** or, more informally, **devi** (*do you have to?*). **deve** and **devi** come from the verb **dovere** (*to have to*). For more information on **dovere**, see page 281.

What do you have to...?

Cosa deve fare?	**What do You have to** do?
Quando devi partire?	**When do you have to** go?
Perché dovete rientrare così presto?	**Why do <u>you</u> have to** go back so soon?

To say that you don't have to do something, you can use **non sono obbligato** (or **obbligata**) **a** (*I'm not obliged to*).

I don't have to...

Non sono obbligato a restare in albergo.	**I don't have to** stay at the hotel.
Non sono obbligata a invitarli da me, se è tardi.	**I don't have to** invite them back, if it's late.
Non siamo obbligati a coinvolgere tutta la famiglia.	**We don't have to** involve the whole family.

To say what you mustn't do, you can use **non devo** (*I mustn't*) and then the verb in the infinitive.

I mustn't...

Non devo fare tardi anche stasera.	**I mustn't** be late again tonight.
Non devo perdere il suo numero.	**I mustn't** lose his number.
Non dobbiamo vederci più.	**We mustn't** see each other again.

LISTEN OUT FOR

Here are some key phrases which you are likely to hear in conversation.

Salve, come va?	Hi, how are you?
Ci conosciamo?	Have we met before?
È qua con amici?	Are You here with friends?
Di dove sei?	Where are you from?
Quanto vi fermate a Catania?	How long are <u>you</u> staying in Catania?
Da quanto studia l'italiano?	How long have You been learning Italian?
Riesce a seguire la conversazione?	Are You following the conversation?
Veramente, parli un ottimo italiano.	Your Italian is really very good.
Parlo troppo veloce?	Am I speaking too fast?
Preferisce se parlo inglese?	Would You prefer it if I spoke English?
Vuole che ripeta?	Would You like me to say it again?
Vuole che parli più piano?	Do You want me to speak more slowly?
Capisce il dialetto?	Do You understand dialect?
Mi scusi, ma parlo un pessimo inglese.	I'm sorry, but my English is really bad.
Mi può dare del tu.	You can call me *tu*.
Potremmo darci del tu.	Shall we call each other *tu*?
È sposata?	Are You married?
Avete figli?	Have <u>you</u> got any children?
Vieni qua spesso?	Do you come here often?
Mi piacerebbe rivederti.	I'd like to see you again.

Lifestyle Tips

• The polite *you* (**lei**) is used to address people whom you don't know. It's also a way of showing respect to someone who's older than you, or to someone who's senior to you at work. People who work together on a daily basis usually say **tu** to each other (**darsi del tu** – *to say* **tu** *to each other*), but it is safer to wait a little before taking that step. Many people do not like to be addressed as **lei**, because they think it's too formal. They will usually suggest you call them **tu,** saying **mi puoi dare del tu** or **possiamo darci del tu**. You can make the first move and ask **Ci diamo del tu?**, if you think that the other person will be more comfortable using the **tu** form.

• Like *sir* in English, **signore** is a formal way of addressing a man. **signora**, however, is used much more in Italian than *madam* is in English. You can use it to address any woman you call **lei**, even if you know her well.

• When meeting someone for the first time, you usually shake hands (**darsi la mano**), whether it's a man or a woman. In the world of business, in meetings or in negotiations, shaking hands is very common. Men who are on friendly terms usually shake hands, while women kiss each other on both cheeks. Men kiss female friends and also male relatives. Young men on friendly terms might hug or slap each other on the shoulder if they haven't seen each other in a long time. Bear in mind that habits may be different depending on where you are in Italy, as well as on the age group and formality of the situation.

• The words **ragazzo** and **ragazza** can either mean *boy/girl* or *boyfriend/girlfriend*. If someone says **il mio ragazzo**, they are talking about their boyfriend. However, you stop using **ragazzo/ragazza** when you get older, perhaps after the age of 25. To say *my partner*, use **il mio compagno** for a man and **la mia compagna** for a woman.

• Italian people socialize in cafés, bars and restaurants as British people do. Italian bars serve both coffee and alcoholic drinks, so you can go to a bar both **a prendere un caffè** or **a prendere l'aperitivo** (a drink before lunch or dinner, which also includes a great selection of finger food).

Getting there

Buon viaggio! – Have a good trip!

If you're going to be travelling to and around Italy, the phrases in this unit will help you ask for directions, find out how to get to places and talk to fellow travellers in everyday Italian.

TALKING ABOUT YOUR PLANS

When you're travelling around, you will probably want to talk about what you're going to do. You can use the future tense or the present tense to talk about your plans. For more information about the future and the present tenses, see page 271.

I'll...

Passerò una settimana a Roma.	**I'll spend** a week in Rome.
Raggiungerò degli amici a Ferrara.	**I'll be joining** some friends in Ferrara.
Torneremo a Milano per il fine settimana.	**We'll get back** to Milan for the weekend.
E poi **vado** a Pisa.	Then **I'll go** to Pisa.
Torniamo a Napoli dopo una settimana.	**We'll go back** to Naples a week later.
Ci **fermiamo** qui fino alla fine del mese.	**We'll be staying** here till the end of the month.

When you're talking about what you intend to do, you can use
ho intenzione di (*I intend to*) followed by a verb in the infinitive.

I intend to...

Ho intenzione di prendere il treno delle sette.	**I intend to** get the seven o'clock train.
Ho intenzione di passare la giornata a Catania.	**I'm going to** spend the day in Catania.
E poi **abbiamo intenzione di** andare a Palermo.	Then **we're going** to go to Palermo.
Abbiamo intenzione di fare la strada costiera.	**We intend to** drive along the coast.

I'm planning to...

Ho in programma di noleggiare una macchina.	**I'm planning to** hire a car.
Ho in programma di andare in Sicilia.	**I'm planning to** go to Sicily.
Conto di passare due giorni a Cortina.	**I plan to** spend two days in Cortina.

I hope to...

Spero di andare in Toscana quest'anno.	**I hope to** go to Tuscany this year.
Spero di visitare gli Uffizi.	**I hope to** visit the Uffizi.
Speriamo di riuscire a vedere tutto.	**We hope** we can see everything.

Use **salvo imprevisti** or **se tutto va bene** (*if all goes to plan*) at
the beginning of a sentence to talk about a plan that might have
to be changed.

If all goes to plan...

Salvo imprevisti arrivo entro venerdì.	**If all goes to plan**, I'll be there by Friday.
Se tutto va bene, ci fermiamo prima a Taormina.	**If all goes to plan**, we're going to stop in Taormina first.

SAYING WHAT YOU HAVE TO DO

If you want to say that you have to do something in Italian, such as buy a ticket, catch a train and so on, you use **devo** (*I have to*) or **dovrei** (*I ought to*) followed by the infinitive. These are from the verb **dovere** (*to have to*). For more information on **dovere**, see page 281.

I have to...

Domani **devo** comprare il biglietto per il traghetto.	**I have to** buy my ticket for the ferry tomorrow.
Devo prima prendere il treno per Parma.	**I have to** get the train to Parma first.
Devo andare a prendere la macchina entro le tre.	**I have to** pick up the car before three.
Deve presentare la patente.	**You have to** show your driving licence.

I ought to...

Dovrei fare ancora benzina.	**I ought to** get some more petrol.
Dovrei confermare il volo.	**I ought to** confirm my flight.
Dovremmo essere in stazione alle sette.	**We ought to** be at the station at seven.

Another way of saying what you must do is to use **bisogna che** (*it is necessary that*) followed by the subjunctive. For more information about the subjunctive, see page 273.

I must...

Adesso **bisogna** proprio **che** vada in stazione.	I really **must** go to the station now.
Bisogna che lo chiamiamo domani mattina.	We **must** call him tomorrow morning.
Bisogna che ritiri i biglietti in agenzia.	I **must** pick up the tickets from the travel agent's.

SAYING WHAT YOU WANT TO DO

When you are travelling, you may want to say what you would
like to do in Italian. You can use **vorrei** (*I'd like*) or **voglio** (*I want*)
with the infinitive. They both come from the verb **volere** (*to
want*). For more information on **volere**, see page 285.

I want to...

Voglio andare a Torino.	**I want to** go to Turin.
Voglio scendere a Verona.	**I want to** get off at Verona.
Voglio cambiare il biglietto.	**I want to** change my ticket.
Vogliamo partire domani mattina.	**We want to** leave tomorrow morning.

I don't want to...

Non voglio viaggiare in prima classe.	**I don't want to** travel first class.
Non voglio andare fin là a piedi.	**I don't want to** walk all the way there.
Non voglio perdere la coincidenza.	**I don't want to** miss my connection.

I'd like to...

Vorrei noleggiare una bici.	**I'd like to** hire a bike.
Vorrei andarci in barca.	**I'd like to** go by boat.
Il mio amico **vorrebbe** denunciare lo smarrimento del bagaglio.	My friend **would like to** report his luggage missing.

You can also use **desidero** (*I would like*), which is slightly more
formal. This comes from **desiderare** (*to want*). For more
information on **-are** verbs like **desiderare**, see page 268.

I would like...

Desidero un biglietto di sola andata in prima classe.	**I would like** a single ticket, first class, please.
Desideriamo prenotare un tavolo al vagone ristorante.	**We would like to** reserve a table in the dining car, please.

If you want to say that you feel like doing something, say **ho voglia di** or **mi va di** (*I feel like*). **ho** comes from the verb **avere** and **va** comes from **andare**. For more information on **avere** and **andare,** see pages 279 and 278.

I feel like...

Ho voglia di passare per Fiesole.	**I feel like** going via Fiesole.
Ho proprio voglia di andare a Portofino.	**I quite fancy** going to Portofino.
Non ho nessuna voglia di passare sei ore in treno.	**I really don't feel like** spending six hours on the train.
Mi va di spezzare il viaggio.	**I feel like** breaking the journey.
Non mi va di passare un'altra notte qua.	**I don't feel like** spending another night here.

MAKING SUGGESTIONS

You may wish to make a suggestion to your colleagues or friends in Italian. One way of doing this is to use **potremmo** (*we could*), or **si potrebbe** (*one could*). Both come from the verb **potere** (*to be able*). For more information on **potere**, see page 284.

We could...

Potremmo andare domani.	**We could** go there tomorrow.
Potremmo fare tappa a Siena.	**We could** break our journey in Siena.
Si potrebbe andare a piedi, se preferisci.	**We could** walk, if you prefer.

If you want to ask someone if they would like to do something, you can generally use the verb **volere** (*to want*). An alternative is **ti piacerebbe** or, to somebody you know less well, **le piacerebbe**, from the verb **piacere**. For more information on **volere**, see page 285.

Would you like to...?

Vuoi andare in acqua?	**Would you like to** go for a swim?
Vuoi riposare un po'?	**Would you like to** have a little rest?
Vuoi guidare?	**Would you like to** drive?
Vuole fermarsi qui?	**Would You like to** stop here?
Ti piacerebbe andarci a piedi?	**Would you like to** walk there?
Le piacerebbe visitare il museo?	**Would You like to** go to the museum?

Just as in English, you can make a suggestion by simply asking **Perché non...?** (*Why don't...?*).

Why don't...?

Perché non noleggiamo una macchina?	**Why don't** we hire a car?
Perché non prendiamo la metropolitana?	**Why don't** we take the underground?
Perché non chiediamo al conducente?	**Why don't** we ask the driver?

You can make a suggestion using **E se...?** (*How about...?*) which is followed by a verb in the imperfect subjunctive. For more information on the subjunctive, see page 273.

How about...?

E se prendessimo l'autostrada?	**How about** going on the motorway?
E se ci andassimo in traghetto?	**How about** taking the ferry?
E se passassimo per Riccione?	**How about** going via Riccione?

...if you like

Ti posso dare un pass**a**ggio, **se vuoi**.	I can give you a lift, **if you like**.
Possiamo chi**e**dere al controllore, **se vuole**.	We can ask the ticket inspector, **if You like**.
Se vuole possiamo dividere un taxi per l'aeroporto.	We can share a taxi to the airport, **if You like**.

ASKING FOR INFORMATION

When you are travelling around in Italy, you will often need some information to help you get to where you want to go. When you are asking for information you may need to get someone's attention in order to ask them a question. To do this you can use **Scusi...** or **Mi scusi...**, if addressing an adult, or **Scusa...**, if you're addressing somebody younger.

Excuse me...

Scusi, cerco la stazione.	**Excuse me**, I'm looking for the station.
Scusi, cerco il munic**i**pio.	**Excuse me**, I'm looking for the town hall.
Mi scusi, cerco la piazza principale.	**Excuse me**, I'm looking for the main square.

If you want to ask a general question, you can use **È...?** (*Is it...?*).

Is it...?

È di qua?	**Is it** this way?
È vicino?	**Is it** near here?
È lontano?	**Is it** far?
È questo il treno per Lecce?	**Is** this the train for Lecce?
È questa la fermata per il museo?	**Is** this the stop for the museum?
È l**i**bero questo posto?	**Is** this seat free?

Is there...?

C'è un distributore nei paraggi, per favore?	**Is there** a petrol station near here, please?
C'è una stazione della metropolitana qui vicino?	**Is there** an underground station near here?
C'è una riduzione per studenti?	**Is there** a student discount?
Ci sono ristoranti in questa zona?	**Are there** any restaurants around here?

In order to get more specific information, you may want to ask, for example, **Dove...?** (*Where...?*), **Quale...?** (*Which...?*), or **A che ora...?** (*What time...?*).

Where...?

Dov'è il deposito bagagli?	**Where**'s the left-luggage office?
Dov'è il più vicino posteggio di taxi, per favore?	**Where**'s the nearest taxi rank, please?
Dove sono le toilettes?	**Where** are the public toilets?

Which...?

Quale linea devo prendere, per favore?	**Which** line do I take, please?
Quali autobus vanno in centro?	**Which** buses go to the town centre?
Da quale binario parte il treno per Pisa?	**Which** platform does the train for Pisa go **from**?
Scusi, **in che direzione** è Treviso, per favore?	Excuse me, **which way** do I go for Treviso, please?
In che direzione è l'Arena, per favore?	**Which way is it to** the Arena, please?

What time...?

A che ora è l'imbarco?	**What time** do we board?
A che ora parte il treno?	**What time** does the train leave?
A che ora arriviamo a Bologna?	**What time** do we get to Bologna?

How often...?

Con quale frequenza partono le corriere per Trento?	**How often** is there a bus for Trento?
Con quale frequenza partono i voli per Londra?	**How often** is there a flight to London?
Ogni quanti chilometri bisogna fare il pieno?	**How often** do you have to fill up?
Quante soste facciamo per strada?	**How often** do we stop on the way?

How long...?

Quanto ci si mette?	**How long does it take**?
Quanto ci si mette per arrivare in stazione?	**How long does it take** to get to the railway station?
Quanto ci si mette per andare da Rovigo a Verona?	**How long does it take** to get from Rovigo to Verona?
Quanto ci mettiamo per arrivare?	**How long will it take us** to get there?

How much is...?

Quanto costa un biglietto per Cagliari?	**How much is** a ticket to Cagliari?
Quanto si paga di autostrada da Milano a Pisa?	**How much is** the motorway toll between Milan and Pisa?
Quanto costa lasciare la valigia al deposito bagagli?	**How much does it cost** to leave a suitcase in left-luggage?
Quanto costerebbe affittare una macchina per due giorni?	**How much would it cost** to hire a car for two days?

Use **Posso...?** (*Can I...?*) or **Si può...?** (*Can you...?*) to ask whether you can do something, or if something is generally possible.
These are from the verb **potere** (*to be able*). For more information on **potere**, see page 284.

Can I...?

Posso noleggiare una macchina per una giornata?	**Can I** hire a car for one day?
Possiamo cambiare il biglietto in Internet?	**Can we** change our tickets online?
Ci **si può** andare a piedi?	**Can you** walk there?
Si può fumare in treno?	**Can you** smoke on the train?
Si può pagare con la carta di credito?	**Is it possible to** pay by credit card?

ASKING FOR THINGS

When asking for something, you can use **Mi dà...?** (*Can I have...?*) or **Potrebbe darmi...?** (*Could I have...?*). These come from the verb **dare** (*to give*). For more information on **dare**, see page 280.

Can I have...?

Mi dà una piantina della metropolitana, per favore?	**Can I have** a map of the underground, please?
Mi dà un abbonamento settimanale, per favore?	**Can I have** a weekly pass, please?
Potrebbe darmi l'orario ferroviario, per favore?	**Could I have** a train timetable, please?

Often, just as in English, you can leave out **Mi dà...?** or **Potrebbe darmi...?** and just ask directly for what you need.

A..., please

Un biglietto di sola andata, **per favore**.	**A** single, **please**.
Un posto vicino al finestrino, **per favore**.	**A** window seat, **please**.
Una cabina per 2 persone, **per favore**.	**A** cabin for two, **please**.
Tre biglietti andata e ritorno per Como.	**Three** returns to Como.

When you want to find out if something is available, or if someone has something, use **Ha...?** (*Have you got...?*) or, more informally, **Hai...?**. Use **Avete..?** if you are asking more than one person. These come from the verb **avere** (*to have*). For more information on **avere**, see page 279.

Have you got...?

Ha l'orario degli *au*tobus?	**Have You got** the bus timetable?
Ha una cartina che mostra come arrivarci, per favore?	**Have You got** a map that shows how to get there, please?
Hai l'ora, per favore?	**Have you got** the time, please?
Avete l'orario dei traghetti?	**Have you got** the timetable for the ferry, please?

If you are asking someone if they can do something for you, you should use **Può...?** (*Can you...?*), although **può** can also be left out.

Can you...?

Mi **può** avvisare quando stiamo per arrivare alla fermata per il museo?	**Can You** tell me when we're near the museum stop?
Mi **può** lasciare qui, per favore?	**Can You** drop me here, please?
Ci **può** portare all'Hotel Duomo, per favore?	**Can You** take us to Hotel Duomo, please?
Ci mostra dov'è sulla piantina?	**Can You show us** where it is on the map?

Would you mind...?

Le dispiacerebbe scrivere l'indirizzo?	**Would You mind** writing down the address?
Le dispiacerebbe lasciarmi all'albergo?	**Would You mind** dropping me at my hotel?
Le dispiacerebbe mostrarci dov'è?	**Would You mind** showing us where it is?

SAYING WHAT YOU LIKE, DISLIKE, PREFER

You will want to be able to discuss what you like and dislike with your Italian-speaking acquaintances. To say what you like, use **mi piace** (*I like*) with singular nouns and **mi piacciono** with plural nouns. To say what you don't like, use **non mi piace** or **non mi piacciono** (*I don't like*) These come from the verb **piacere**.

I like...

Mi piace viaggiare in treno.	**I like** travelling by train.
Mi piacciono queste stradine di campagna.	**I like** these country roads.
Mi piace molto viaggiare in nave.	**I really like** travelling by boat.
Mi piace tantíssimo viaggiare in aereo.	**I love** flying.

I don't like...

Non mi piace guidare sulla destra.	**I don't like** driving on the right.
Non mi piace guidare di notte.	**I don't like** driving at night.
Non mi piacciono le macchine col cambio automatico.	**I don't like** automatics.

I hate...

Odio i motorini.	**I hate** scooters.
Odio le cartine!	**I hate** maps!
Detesto dover chiedere indicazioni.	**I hate** having to ask for directions.

Do you like...?

Ti piace viaggiare in aereo?	**Do you like** flying?
Ti piace viaggiare da sola?	**Do you like** travelling by yourself?
Le piace questa regione?	**Do You like** this area?
Le piacciono i viaggi organizzati?	**Do You like** organized tours?

If you want to say what you prefer, use **preferisco** (*I prefer*) or **preferirei** (*I'd prefer*). These come from the verb **preferire** (*to prefer*). For more information on **-ire** verbs like **preferire**, see page 268.

I prefer to...

Preferisco viaggiare in aereo.	**I prefer to** fly.
Preferisco prendere l'autostrada.	**I prefer to** go on the
motorway.	

I'd rather...

Preferirei viaggiare col bel tempo.	**I'd rather** make the journey in good weather.
Preferirei sedermi vicino al finestrino.	**I'd rather** sit next to the window.
Preferirei non lasciare qui la mia macchina.	**I'd rather** not leave my car here.
Preferiremmo guidare di giorno.	**We'd rather** drive in the daytime.

LISTEN OUT FOR

Here are some key phrases which you are likely to hear when you're travelling about.

Prossima fermata: ...	Next stop: ...
Il treno diretto per Bologna centrale parte dal binario tre.	The train for Bologna centrale leaves from platform three.
Si deve convalidare il biglietto in stazione.	You must stamp your ticket at the station.
Biglietto, prego.	Ticket, please.
Le dispiace se mi siedo qui?	Do you mind if I sit here?
Continui dritto fino al semaforo.	Go straight on till You get to the traffic lights.
Prenda la seconda a sinistra.	Take the second turning on the left.
È difronte alla cattedrale.	It's opposite the cathedral.
È vicinissimo.	It's very near.
Ha sbagliato strada.	You've gone the wrong way.
Ci si può andare a piedi.	It's within walking distance.
È fra tre fermate.	It's three stops from here.
Imbarco immediato, uscita 3.	Now boarding at gate 3.

Lifestyle Tips

• If you're behind the wheel of a car, be ready to produce your driving licence if asked for it by the police. If you haven't got it with you, you may well be fined. The police officer might ask you: **patente, prego** (*your driving licence, please*). Italian drivers also have to be able to produce their **libretto di circolazione** (*registration document*) and their **assicurazione** (*insurance certificate*).

• Motorways are not free in Italy. When you go onto the motorway, you get a **biglietto**. When you come off the motorway this will show how many kilometres you've driven and how much you have to pay (**il pedaggio**). **Telepass** is an electronic toll collection system used to collect **il pedaggio** and gives access to reserved lanes.

• If you're asked to produce your **biglietto** on the bus, the train or the underground, it means that you have to show your ticket to the inspector.

• Generally, you have to buy your ticket before getting on a bus. Once on board the bus, you date-stamp the ticket by punching it in a machine. You can buy tickets at newsagents and many tobacconists. If you are staying in a place for some time, it may be worth buying an **abbonamento**, which will last a week or a month from when it is first stamped.

• Train tickets need to be punched before you get on a train. Tickets are only valid if date-stamped, so if you have forgotten to do this, it is advisable to go and see **il controllore** (*the ticket inspector*) as soon as possible, or you might be fined.

• If you're in a hurry, you can hop on the train and buy a ticket directly from a ticket inspector. This will cost you more, however. If you contact the inspector as soon as you get on the train or before the first stop the fine is around 5 €; otherwise you'll be faced with a more expensive fine of 60 € or more.

• Queues tend to be informal in Italy. So if you're trying to get to an information desk and don't know if it's your turn, just ask **Tocca a me?**. If you want to let someone in before you, you can say **prego, dopo di lei** (*after you*).

Home
from home

Buonanotte! – Sleep well!

If you're going to stay in Italy, the phrases in this unit will provide you with the language you need to help you find the sort of accommodation you want and ensure everything is to your satisfaction when you're there. We'll also give you a few tips on what the receptionist or your landlord or landlady may say to you.

ASKING FOR THINGS

To say what kind of accommodation you want in Italian, use **vorrei** (*I'd like*), or, if you want to be slightly more direct, **voglio** (*I want*). These come from the verb **volere** (*to want*). For more information on **volere**, see page 285.

I'd like...

Vorrei una stanza con balcone.	**I'd like** a room with a balcony.
Vorrei prenotare una camera doppia per due notti.	**I'd like** to book a double room for two nights.
Vorrei fermarmi tre notti.	**I'd like** to stay three nights.
Vorrei prenotare una stanza nel vostro agriturismo per due settimane.	**I'd like** to book a room in your agriturismo for two weeks.

I want...

Voglio un appartamento luminoso.	**I want** a flat with plenty of light.
Voglio cambiare stanza; quella che mi avete dato è troppo rumorosa.	**I want to** change rooms; the one you gave me is too noisy.
Voglio un rimborso.	**I want** a refund.
Non vogliamo una stanza che dia sulla strada.	**We don't want** a room overlooking the road.

When you want to find out if something is available, use
Avete...? (*Do you have...?*) or **Avreste...?** (*Would you have...?*).
These come from the verb **avere** (*to have*). For more information
on **avere**, see page 279.

Do you have...?

Avete informazioni su dove alloggiare?	**Do you have** any information about accommodation?
Avete camere libere?	**Have you got** any rooms free?
Avreste degli asciugamani, per favore?	**Would you have** any towels, please?
C'è accesso ad Internet?	**Have you got** internet access?

If you want to ask for something, you can use **Mi dà..?** (*Can I have...?*).

Can I have...?

Mi dà la chiave della stanza, per favore?	**Can I have** the key to my room, please?
Mi dà una ricevuta, per favore?	**Can I have** a receipt, please?
Ci dà una lista degli alloggi disponibili?	**Can we have** a list of available accommodation?
Mi potrebbe dare ancora due asciugamani?	**Could I have** two more towels?

If you are asking someone whether they can do something for
you, use **Può...?** (*Can You...?*) and **Potrebbe...?** (*Could You...?*) or,
more informally, **Puoi...?** or **Potresti...?**. They all come from the
verb **potere** (*to be able*). For more information on **potere**, see
page 284.

Can you...?

Può darmi conferma della prenotazione per posta elettronica?	**Can You** confirm the booking by email?
Mi può svegliare alle sette, per favore?	**Can You** give me an alarm call at seven o'clock, please?
Potrebbe cambiare gli asciugamani, per favore?	**Could You** change the towels, please?
Potrebbe farmi vedere la stanza, per favore?	**Could You** show me the room, please?

Would you mind...?

Le dispiacerebbe mostrarmi come funziona il forno?	**Would You mind** showing me how the oven works?
Le dispiacerebbe chiamarmi un taxi?	**Would You mind** calling a taxi for me?
Le dispiacerebbe portarmi la valigia in camera?	**Would You mind** taking my suitcases up to my room?

TALKING ABOUT YOURSELF

When you are enquiring about somewhere to stay you will need to give information about yourself. Use **sono** (*I am*) to talk about yourself and **siamo** (*we are*) to include the people who are with you. These come from the verb **essere** (*to be*). For more information on **essere**, see page 282.

I'm...

Sono una studentessa.	**I'm** a student.
Sono canadese.	**I'm** Canadian.
Sono del sud dell'Inghilterra.	**I'm** from the south of England.
Siamo in vacanza.	**We're** on holiday.
Siamo i proprietari.	**We're** the owners.

My name is...

Mi chiamo Brian Gallagher.	**My name is** Brian Gallagher.
Mi chiamo Olivia Green.	**My name is** Olivia Green.
Sono la signora Smith. Ho prenotato una stanza doppia per questa notte.	**My name is** Mrs Smith. I've booked a double room for tonight.
Il cognome è Morris...	**My surname is** Morris...
...e **il nome è** Emma.	...and **my first name is** Emma.
Si scrive M-O-R-R-I-S.	**It's spelt** M-O-R-R-I-S.

BUONO A SAPERSI!
Remember that the Italian alphabet is pronounced differently from the English alphabet. For more information on how to say letters of the alphabet in Italian, see page 204.

ASKING FOR INFORMATION

When you want to find something out about your accommodation, an easy way to ask questions is just to put **È...?** (*Is...?*) before what you want to know. Alternatively, you can simply make your voice go up at the end of the sentence.

Is it...?

È caro?	**Is it** expensive?
È un hotel moderno?	**Is it** a modern hotel?
È lontano?	**Is it** far?
La colazione **è** compresa nel prezzo?	**Is** breakfast included in the price?
Le spese **sono** comprese nell'affitto?	**Are** bills included in the rent?

You can use **C'è...?** in Italian to ask *Is there...?* and **Ci sono...?** to ask *Are there...?*.

Is there...?

C'è un posto per mangiare qualcosa qui vicino?	**Is there** anywhere near here where we can get something to eat?
C'è un ascensore?	**Is there** a lift?
C'è un balcone?	**Is there** a balcony?
Ci sono toilettes per disabili?	**Are there** disabled toilets?

Use **cerco** (*I'm looking for*) or **cerchiamo** (*we're looking for*) to ask where something is. **cerco** comes from the verb **cercare** (*to look for*).

I'm looking for...

Scusi, **cerco** il campeggio.	Excuse me, **I'm looking for** the campsite.
Cerco una pensione per stanotte.	**I'm looking for** a B&B for tonight.
Cerchiamo l'Hotel Bellini.	**We're looking for** the Hotel Bellini.

To get more specific information, you may need to ask **Quale...?** (*What...?*), **Dove...?** (*Where...?*) or **A che ora...?** (*What time...?*).

What...?

Qual è l'indirizzo del proprietario?	**What's** the landlord's address?
Qual è il numero dell'agenzia immobiliare?	**What's** the number for the letting agency?
Quale mi raccomanda?	**Which** one would You recommend?
Quali stanze hanno vista mare?	**Which** rooms have a sea view?

> **BUONO A SAPERSI!**
> **quale** works for all singular nouns, whether masculine or feminine. It becomes **qual** before a word beginning with a vowel, as in **Qual è...?** (*What's...?*).

Where...?

Dov'è il bar?	**Where's** the bar?
Dov'è la palestra?	**Where's** the gym?
Dove sono gli ascensori?	**Where** are the lifts?
Dove trovo una presa per il portatile?	**Where** can I plug in my laptop?

What time...?

A che ora è servita la cena?	**What time's** dinner?
A che ora chiudete il portone la sera?	**What time** do <u>you</u> lock the doors at night?
Entro che ora bisogna liberare la stanza?	**What time** do we have to vacate the room **by**?
Fino a che ora è servita la colazione?	**What time** do you serve breakfast **till**?

How much...?

Quanto viene una camera doppia a notte?	**How much is** a double room per night?
Quanto viene la pensione completa?	**How much is** full board?
Quanto verrebbe affittare un appartamento per tutto luglio?	**How much would it be** to rent an apartment for the whole of July?

How many...?

Quante camere con bagno vi sono rimaste?	**How many** en-suite rooms have you got left?
Quanti letti ci sono nella camera famigliare?	**How many** beds are there in the family room?

ASKING FOR PERMISSION

Often when you are staying in a hotel or other accommodation you will need to be able to ask whether you can do something. Use **Posso...?** (*Can I ...?*) or **Possiamo...?** (*Can we...?*) to ask if you can do something. These come from the verb **potere** (*to be able*). For more information on **potere**, see page 284.

Can I...?

Posso vedere la stanza?	**Can I** see the room?
Posso lasciare le valigie qui per cinque minuti?	**Can I** leave my suitcases here for five minutes?
Possiamo usare la piscina?	**Can we** use the pool?
Possiamo piantare la tenda qui?	**Can we** camp here?

You can use **Si può...?** to ask if something is okay, or possible.

Is it okay to...?

Si può parcheggiare qui?	**Is it okay to** park here?
Si può fumare in camera?	**Is it okay to** smoke in the room?
Si può mangiare fuori?	**Is it possible to** eat outside?

Do you mind if...?

Le dispiace se parcheggio la macchina qui fuori per un minuto?	**Do You mind if** I park my car outside for a moment?
Le dispiace se pago con la carta di credito?	**Do You mind if** I pay by credit card?
Le dispiace se prendiamo la camera al piano di sopra?	**Do you mind if** we take the room on the next floor?

If you want to ask someone if you may do something, you can also use **È permesso..?** *(Am I allowed to...?)* followed by the infinitive.

Am I allowed to...?

È permesso ricevere ospiti?	**Am I allowed to** have guests?
È permesso usare la griglia?	**Are we allowed to** use the barbecue?
È permesso usare il telefono?	**May we** use the phone?
Ci è permesso portare il cane?	**Are we allowed to** bring our dog?

SAYING WHAT YOU LIKE, DISLIKE, PREFER

When talking about what you like, use **mi piace** *(I like)* with singular nouns and **mi piacciono** with plural nouns. To say what you don't like, use **non mi piace** or **non mi piacciono**. These come from the verb **piacere**.

I like...

Mi piace cenare all'aperto.	**I like** having dinner outside.
Mi piacciono gli alberghi piccoli.	**I like** small hotels.
Mi piacciono i campeggi in montagna.	**I like** campsites in the mountains.
Mi piace tantissimo questa pensione.	**I love** this guest house.

I don't like...

Non mi piace questo albergo.	**I don't like** this hotel.
Non mi piace viaggiare in traghetto.	**I don't like** going on the ferry.
Non ci piace pianificare tutto in anticipo.	**We don't like** to plan everything in advance.

I hate...

Odio questo arredamento.	**I hate** this decor.
Odio le grandi catene alberghiere.	**I hate** big chain hotels.
Detesto non avere il bagno.	**I hate** not having a bathroom.

If you want to say what you prefer, use **preferisco** (*I prefer*) or **preferirei** (*I'd prefer*). These come from the verb **preferire**. For more information on **-ire** verbs like **preferire**, see page 268.

I prefer...

Preferisco questo hotel.	**I prefer** this hotel.
Preferisco stare presso una famiglia.	**I prefer** to stay with a family.
Preferiamo gli ostelli **ai** campeggi.	**We prefer** youth hostels **to** camp sites.

I'd rather...

Preferirei stare in centro.	**I'd rather** be in the town centre.
Preferiremmo abitare in campagna.	**We'd rather** live in the country.
Preferirei non dover far file.	**I'd rather not** have to queue.
Preferirei dividere un appartamento **piuttosto che** abitare da sola.	**I'd rather** share a flat **than** live on my own.

EXPRESSING OPINIONS

You may well be asked what you think of your accommodation. Whether it's perfect or not up to scratch, to say what you think you can use **penso che** (*I think*) or **trovo che** (*I find*) followed by the subjunctive. These come from the verbs **pensare** (*to think*) and **trovare** (*to find*). For more information on **-are** verbs, see page 268, and for the use of the subjunctive, see page 273.

I think...

Penso che la camera sia un po' piccola.	**I think** the bedroom's a bit small.
Penso che la casa sia molto accogliente.	**I think** the house is very welcoming.
Trovo che ci sia troppo rumore la notte.	**I find** there's too much noise at night.
Ho trovato il servizio eccellente.	**I found** the service excellent.

In my opinion...

A mio avviso, costa troppo per quello che è.	**In my opinion**, it costs too much for what it is.
Secondo me, fa proprio per noi.	**In my opinion**, it's just what we want.
Secondo me, la stanza è troppo piccola.	**In my opinion**, the room is too small.
A mio avviso, è completamente inaccettabile.	**In my view**, it's totally unacceptable.

If you would like to suggest that you do something, use **posso** (*I can*) followed by the infinitive and **se vuole** (*if You like*) – or **se vuoi** for a person you know well – at the end. **posso** comes from the verb **potere** (*to be able*). For more information on **potere**, see page 284.

I can..., if you like.

Posso darle conferma delle date domani, **se vuole**.	**I can** confirm the dates tomorrow, **if You like**.
Posso mandarle un acconto, **se vuole**.	**I can** send You a deposit, **if You like**.
Possiamo cercare un altro albergo, **se vuoi**.	**We can** look for another hotel, **if you like**.

If you wish to ask what someone would like you to do, you can use **Vuole che...?** (*Would You like me to...?*) or, more informally, **Vuoi che...?**, followed by a verb in the subjunctive, which you can find out more about on page 273.

Would you like me to...?

Vuole che paghi in contanti?	**Would You like me to** pay cash?
Vuole che le mostri la prenotazione?	**Would You like me to** show you my booking?
Vuoi che ti aiuti con le borse?	**Would you like me to** help you with your bags?
Vuole tenere i passaporti?	**Would You like to** keep our passports?

ASKING FOR SUGGESTIONS

You may want to ask for advice or a recommendation concerning your accommodation. To ask for advice, use **Mi consiglia...?** (*Would You advise me to...?*). This comes from the verb **consigliare** (*to advise*).

Would you advise me to...?

Mi consiglia di prenotare in anticipo?	**Would You advise me to** book in advance?
Mi consiglia di portare qualcosa da mangiare?	**Would You advise me to** bring something to eat?
Ci consiglia di portare dei sacchi a pelo?	**Would You advise us to** bring sleeping bags?

Would you recommend...?

Mi consiglierebbe questo hotel?	**Would You recommend** this hotel?
Mi consiglierebbe questa agenzia immobiliare?	**Would You recommend** this estate agency?
Ci consiglierebbe di affittare settimanalmente?	**Would You recommend that we** rent by the week?
Ci consiglierebbe di prendere un appartamento in città?	**Would You recommend us to** take a flat in town?

SAYING WHAT YOU HAVE TO DO

If you want to say that you have to do something with regard to your accommodation in Italian, you use **devo** (*I have to*) or **dovrei** (*I ought to*), from the verb **dovere** (*to have to*). For more information on **dovere**, see page 281.

I have to...

Devo prendere nota dell'indirizzo dell'albergo.	**I have to** write down the address of the hotel.
Devo passare alla reception per pagare.	**I have to** go to reception to pay.
Dobbiamo partire domattina alle sei.	**We have to** leave at six tomorrow morning.

BUONO A SAPERSI!
The word **domattina** is a contraction of **domani** (*tomorrow*) and **mattina** (*morning*).

I ought to...

Dovrei scaricare la macchina.	**I ought to** unpack the car.
Dovrei fare il bucato.	**I ought to** do a load of washing.
Dovremmo alzarci entro le sette di mattina.	**We ought to** be up by seven am.
Dovremmo avere un doppione delle chiavi.	**We ought to** have a spare set of keys.

In Italian you can tell somebody what you need by using **ho bisogno di** (*I need*).

I need...

Ho bisogno di una culla.	**I need** a cot.
Ho bisogno di telefonare al mio ufficio a Londra.	**I need** to call my office in London.
Abbiamo bisogno di una camera al piano terra.	**We need** a room on the ground floor.

You can use **Devo ...?** (*Do I have to...?*) followed by the infinitive, or **Bisogna che...?** (*Do I need to...?*) followed by the verb in the subjunctive to ask about what you have to do. For more information about the subjunctive, see page 273.

Do I have to...?

Devo lasciare la chiave alla reception quando esco?	**Do I have to** leave the key at reception when I go out?
Devo passare alla reception per pagare?	**Do I have to** go to reception to pay?
Dobbiamo avvertirvi quando lasciamo l'albergo?	**Do we have to** let <u>you</u> know when we leave the hotel?

Do I need to...?

Bisogna prenotare?	**Do I need to** book?
Bisogna che faccia le pulizie nell'appartamento prima di partire?	**Do I need to** clean the flat before leaving?
Bisogna che portiamo dei sacchi a pelo?	**Do we need to** bring sleeping bags?
Quando bisogna liberare la camera?	**When do I have to** vacate the room?

TALKING ABOUT YOUR PLANS

When you are talking about your plans to stay somewhere, you can use the future tense or the present tense in Italian. For more information on the future and present tenses, see page 271.

I'll...

Affitterò un appartamento per le prime tre settimane.	**I'll rent** a flat for the first three weeks.
Arriverò al campeggio di sera.	**I'll arrive** at the campsite in the evening.
Trovo un albergo quando sono là.	**I'll find** a hotel when I get there.

I'm going to...

Mi fermo a Parma.	**I'm going to stay** in Parma.
Affitterò uno chalet in montagna.	**I'm going to rent** a chalet in the mountains.
Faremo campeggio.	**We're going to camp**.

I'm staying...

Sto in un ostello per la prima settimana.	**I'm staying** in a youth hostel the first week.
Poi **sto** in un albergo.	After that **I'm staying** in a hotel.
Sono ospite presso una famiglia la prima notte.	**I'm staying** with a host family the first night.

If you want to say that you intend to do something, you can use **ho intenzione di** or **conto di** (*I intend to*).

I intend to...

Ho intenzione di prendere un appartamento in affitto.	**I intend to** rent a flat.
Ho intenzione di trovare un agriturismo.	**I intend to** find an agriturismo.
Conto di fermarmi fino a venerdì.	**I intend to** stay until Friday.
Contiamo di partire domani dopo colazione.	**We intend to** leave after breakfast tomorrow.

COMPLAINING

Unfortunately the service you get in your accommodation may not always be perfect. A very simple way of complaining is to say what the problem is using **c'è** (*there is*) and **ci sono** (*there are*), or **non c'è** (*there isn't*) and **non ci sono** (*there aren't*).

There's...

C'è troppo rumore.	**There's** too much noise.
C'è uno spandimento sul soffitto.	**There's** a leak in the ceiling.
Ci sono scarafaggi nell'appartamento.	**There are** cockroaches in the flat.

There isn't...

Non c'è acqua calda.	**There isn't** any hot water.
Non ci sono asciugamani puliti in camera.	**There aren't** any clean towels in the room.
La stanza **non ha** un balcone.	The room **doesn't have** a balcony.
L'appartamento **non ha** l'aria condizionata.	The flat **doesn't have** air-conditioning.

You can also use the verb **essere** (*to be*) to describe what the problem is.

It's...

L'appartamento **è** sporco.	The flat**'s** dirty.
L'hotel **è** troppo rumoroso.	This hotel**'s** too noisy.
L'acqua della piscina **non è** molto pulita.	The water in the swimming pool **isn't** very clean.
Qua **fa** troppo caldo.	**It's** too hot in here.

BUONO A SAPERSI!
Remember that with most expressions such as *it's hot* or *it's cold* in Italian, you should use the verb **fare** (*to do*), not **essere** (*to be*).

LISTEN OUT FOR

Here are some key phrases which you are likely to hear when you're looking for somewhere to stay.

Che tipo di alloggio cercate?	What type of accommodation are you looking for?
A che nome è la prenotazione?	Whose name is the booking in?
Per quante notti?	For how many nights?
Per quante persone?	For how many people?
La colazione è compresa nel prezzo.	Breakfast is included in the price.
Mi fa vedere il passaporto, per favore?	Can I see your passport, please?
Siamo al completo.	We're full.
Va pagata una cauzione di 300 euro.	There's a 300 euro deposit.
Mi date un recapito telefonico?	What number can we contact you on?
Non sono ammessi i cani.	We don't allow dogs.
Come desidera pagare?	How would You like to pay?
Compili questo modulo, per cortesia.	Please fill in this form.
Una firma qui, prego.	Please sign here.
Come si scrive il suo nome, per favore?	How do you spell your name, please?

Lifestyle Tips

• If you are renting a property for a longish period, but haven't moved to Italy in any kind of permanent way, you are likely to be offered a **contratto per non residenti** (*contract for non-residents*).

• Short-term rented property is normally furnished (**ammobiliato**), while long-term rented accommodation is usually unfurnished (**non ammobiliato**).

• It is less common in Italy to share a flat with other tenants, unless you are a student. However, it is possible to rent **una camera ammobiliata** (*a furnished room*) in a flat or a house.

• Properties are described by size in square metres and number of rooms, for example **appartamento ammobiliato di 80 m², salotto, cucina abitabile, camera da letto, cameretta, bagno con doccia, balcone, cantina** (*80 m² furnished flat, sitting room, dining kitchen, double bedroom, single bedroom, bathroom with shower, balcony, storage cellar*).

• A studio apartment is called **un monolocale** in Italian, literally *a one-room flat*, with sleeping and cooking facilities in the one room. They can be quite smart, and are often rented by professionals who need to be in a town from time to time, or by visitors who prefer them to hotels.

• If a flat is described as being in a **stabile d'epoca**, it means it is in a period building.

• If you are looking to rent for a longer period, you will find adverts in local papers and on websites, as well as signs on doors of buildings with contact phone numbers. You could also contact the local **agenzie immobiliari** (*estate agents*), who will normally charge a commission.

• As a tourist, you may be staying in **un hotel** or **albergo**, **una pensione**, **un bed&breakfast** (now quite common), **un agriturismo** (where guests eat the farm's own produce), **un appartamento**, **una villa** or **un residence** (very often a luxurious option, with serviced furnished flats of different sizes, fitness area, pool, conference rooms, etc.).

Wining and dining

Buon appetito! – Enjoy your meal!

If you're going out for a meal in Italy either in a local trattoria or in a fancy restaurant, the phrases in this unit will give you the confidence to talk to the waiter and chat with your Italian friends in easy, natural Italian. We'll also give you some tips on getting advice about what to order, and a few key phrases waiters are likely to use.

MAKING ARRANGEMENTS

If you want to make arrangements such as where and when to meet when you go out for a meal with Italian-speaking people, you can start by asking **Dove...?** (*Where...?*) and **A che ora...?** (*What time...?*).

Where...?

Dove andiamo a mangiare?	**Where** shall we go to eat?
Dove ci troviamo?	**Where** shall we meet?
Dove volete che vi venga a prendere?	**Where** do <u>you</u> want me to pick <u>you</u> up?

What time...?

A che ora ci troviamo?	**What time** shall we meet?
A che ora arriva Giulia?	**What time** is Giulia going to get here?
Per che ora hai prenotato il tavolo?	**What time** did you book the table **for**?

If you want to check that the arrangements suit your friends or colleagues, you can use **Va bene se...?** (*Does it suit you if...?*).

Does it suit you if...?

Va bene se andiamo fuori a cena domani sera?	**Does it suit you if** we go out for a meal tomorrow night?
Va bene se ci troviamo alle sette?	**Does it suit you if** we meet up at seven?
Va bene se ci incontriamo là?	**Does is suit you if** we meet there?
Vi andrebbe meglio sabato sera?	**Would** Saturday evening **suit you better**?

It would suit me best to...

Per me andrebbe meglio incontrarci là.	**It would suit me best to** meet there.
Per me andrebbe meglio andarci per le otto.	**It'd suit me best to** be there for eight.
Per noi andrebbe meglio andarci in macchina.	**It'd suit us better to** go there by car.

To check what is the best thing to do for others, use **È meglio...?** (*Had we better...?*).

Had we better...?

È meglio prenotare?	**Had we better** book?
È meglio arrivare presto?	**Had we better** arrive early?
Sarebbe meglio cambiare la prenotazione?	**Had we better** change our reservation?

ASKING FOR INFORMATION

When you're going out for a meal you'll need to ask for various pieces of information, such as where things are and how much they cost. **Dove...?** (*Where...?*), **A che ora...?** (*What time...?*) and **Quanto viene...?** (*How much...?*) are very useful to know.

Where is...?

Dov'è il ristorante?	**Where is** the restaurant?
Scusi, **dov'è** la cassa?	Excuse me, **where is** the till?
Scusi, **dov'è** il bagno?	Excuse me, **where is** the toilet?

What time...?

A che ora aprite?	**What time** do <u>you</u> open?
A che ora chiudete?	**What time** do <u>you</u> close?
Fino a che ora si può mangiare?	**What time** do <u>you</u> serve **till**?

How much is...?

Quanto viene una bottiglia di vino locale?	**How much is** a bottle of local wine?
Quanto viene un'insalata?	**How much is** a side salad?
Quant'è il menù turistico?	**How much is** the set menu?

What is...?

Cosa c'è nella 'ribollita'?	**What's** a 'ribollita' made of?
Con cosa è servito?	**What does** it come **with**?
Che c'è come dessert?	**What is** there for dessert?

Many of the questions you will be asking can be answered by *yes* or *no*. To ask this kind of question, you can either put **è** before what you want to know or alternatively you can raise the tone of your voice at the end of the sentence.

Is it...?

È caro come ristorante?	**Is it** an expensive restaurant?
È un piatto tipico regionale?	**Is it** a traditional local dish?
È un piatto vegetariano?	**Is it** a vegetarian dish?
È compreso nel menù da 15 euro?	**Is it** included in the 15 € set menu?
È aperto di domenica questo ristorante?	**Is** this restaurant open on Sundays?

ASKING FOR THINGS

When you're out in a restaurant you will need to be able to ask for what you want. If you want to ask for something in Italian, use **vorrei** (*I'd like*) or **vorremmo** (*we'd like*). **vorrei** and **vorremmo** come from the verb **volere** (*to want*). For more information on **volere**, see page 285.

I'd like...

Vorrei del pane, per favore.	**I'd like** some bread, please.
Vorrei una caraffa d'acqua, per favore.	**I'd like** a jug of water, please.
Vorremmo ordinare, per favore.	**We'd like** to order, please.
Ancora del pane, per favore.	**We'd like** some more bread, please.
Un tavolo per due, per favore.	A table for two, please.
Il conto, per favore.	The bill, please.

> **BUONO A SAPERSI!**
> When the waiter approaches and you want to say that you're not ready to order, use **Ci** (or **Mi**) **dà ancora un minuto, per favore?** (*Can we* (or *I*) *have another minute, please?*). Alternatively, if your order has already been taken, you can say **abbiamo** (or **ho**) **già ordinato, grazie** (*someone's already taken our* (or *my*) *order, thanks*).

To talk about what you want to order, use **prendo** (*I'll have*). **prendo** comes from the verb **prendere**.

I'll have...

Come antipasto, **prendo** il prosciutto crudo.	As a starter, **I'll have** the Parma ham, please.
Come dolce, **prendo** la mousse di cioccolato.	For dessert, **I'll have** the chocolate mousse.
Da bere **prendiamo** dell'acqua minerale frizzante.	**We'll have** sparkling water to drink.
Non so cosa **prendere**.	I don't know what **to have**.
E per secondo, la cotoletta alla milanese.	And for my main course, **I'll have** the cotoletta alla milanese.
Per me lo stesso.	**I'll have** the same.

When you want to find out if something is available, use **Avete...?** (*Have you got...?*). **avete** comes from the verb **avere** (*to have*). For more information on **avere**, see page 279.

Have you got...?

Avete un menù per bambini?	**Have you got** a children's menu?
Avete un seggiolone?	**Have you got** a high chair?
Avete un tavolo all'aperto?	**Do you have** a table outside?
Avete la carta dei vini?	**Do you have** a wine list?

If you want to ask someone, for example the waiter, for something in Italian, use **Mi porta...?** (*Can I have ...?*) or **Mi porterebbe...?** (*Could I have ...?*). **porta** and **porterebbe** come from the verb **portare**. For more information on **-are** verbs like **portare**, see page 268.

Can I have...?

Mi porta un'altra forchetta, per cortesia?	**Can I have** another fork, please?
Mi porta la lista dei dolci, per favore?	**Can I have** the dessert menu, please?
Mi porterebbe dell'olio d'oliva, per favore?	**Could I have** some olive oil, please?
Ci porterebbe del pane, per favore?	**Could we have** some bread, please?
Mi fa il conto, per favore.	**Can I have** the bill, please?

If you want to ask the waiter to do something for you, use
Potrebbe...? If you want to ask someone such as a friend or a
close colleague to do something for you, use **Potresti...?** (*Could
you ...?*) instead. **potrebbe** and **potresti** come from the verb
potere. For more information on **potere**, see page 284.

Could you...?

Potrebbe portarmi del pane, per favore?	**Could You** bring me some bread, please?
Potrebbe portarci i caffè?	**Could You** bring us our coffee, please?
Potrebbe magari tornare tra cinque minuti?	**Could You** possibly come back in five minutes?
Potresti passarmi il sale, per favore?	**Could you** pass me the salt, please?
Le posate sono sporche. Ce le cambia, per favore?	The knives and forks are dirty. **Could You** change them, please?

Would you mind...?

Le spiace chiudere la finestra?	**Would You mind** closing the window?
Le spiace se mi siedo qui?	**Would You mind** if I sit here?
Ti dispiace se ci scambiamo di posto?	**Would you mind** swapping seats with me?
Le dispiace se le do i cappotti?	**Would You mind** taking our coats?

SAYING WHAT YOU WANT TO DO

If you want to say what you'd like to do when you're eating out,
use **vorrei** (*I'd like*) followed by the infinitive. **vorrei** comes from the
verb **volere** (*to want*). For more information on **volere** see
page 285.

I'd like...

Vorrei ordinare, per favore.	**I'd like** to order, please.
Vorrei vedere la lista dei dolci.	**I'd like** to see the dessert menu.
Vorrei riservare un tavolo, per favore.	**I'd like** to book a table, please.
Vorremmo ordinare del vino, per favore.	**We'd like** to order some wine, please.
Vorremmo pagare con la carta di credito.	**We'd like** to pay by credit card.

You can also say what you fancy having in Italian by using **ho voglia di** (*I fancy*), followed by the infinitives **prendere** (*to have*) or **mangiare** (*to eat*).

I fancy...

Ho voglia di prendere la grigliata mista.	**I fancy** the mixed grill.
Ho voglia di mangiare cinese, per cambiare.	**I fancy** Chinese food for a change.
Non ho voglia di prendere l'antipasto.	**I don't really feel like** a starter.

SAYING WHAT YOU LIKE, DISLIKE, PREFER

When you're out wining and dining you will probably want to talk about what you like or dislike, especially when it comes to food. To say what you like, you can use **mi piace** (*I like*) with singular nouns and **mi piacciono** with plural nouns. If you want to say that you don't like something, you can use **non mi piace** or **non mi piacciono**.

I like...

Mi piace il formaggio.	**I like** cheese.
Mi piacciono gli asparagi.	**I like** asparagus.
Mi piacciono tantissimo i frutti di mare.	**I love** seafood.
Ti piacciono i carciofi?	**Do you like** artichokes?
Le piace la cucina cinese?	**Do You like** Chinese food?

I don't like...

Non mi piace il whisky.	**I don't like** whisky.
Non mi piacciono le olive.	**I don't like** olives.
Non mi piace tanto la cucina messicana.	**I'm not too keen on** Mexican food.
Non le piacciono i funghi?	**Don't You like** mushrooms?
Odio la trippa.	**I can't stand** tripe.

If you want to say what you prefer, use **preferisco** (*I prefer*). This comes from the verb **preferire** (*to prefer*). For more information on **-ire** verbs like **preferire**, see page 268.

I'd rather...

Preferisco assaggiare una specialità locale.	**I'd rather** try a local dish.
Preferisco se facciamo alla romana.	**I'd rather** we split the bill.
Preferisco prendere un antipasto **piuttosto che** il dolce.	**I'd rather** have a starter **than** a dessert.
Preferiresti andare da un'altra parte?	**Would you rather** go somewhere else?

If you have special dietary needs, you can mention them by using **sono** (*I'm*).

I'm...

Sono allergico alle uova.	**I'm** allergic to eggs.
Sono vegetariana.	**I'm** a vegetarian.

ASKING FOR SUGGESTIONS

If you want to ask the waiter to recommend something, you can use **Cosa mi consiglia?** (*What do You recommend?*). If you are asking a friend or a colleague, you can say **Cosa mi consigli?**.

What do you recommend...?

Cosa mi consiglia come antipasto?	**What do You recommend** as a starter?
Cosa mi consigli di prendere?	**What do you recommend** I have?
Che vino **ci consiglia**?	**Which** wine **do You recommend**?
Ci consiglia una specialità del posto?	**Can You recommend** a local dish?

If you want to ask whether you should do something, use **Crede che dovrei...?** or, more informally, **Credi che dovrei...?** (*Do you think I should...?*).

Do you think I should...?

Credi che dovrei prendere la torta?	**Do you think I should** have the cake?
Credi che dovrei assaggiare l'anguilla?	**Do you think I should** try the eel?
Crede che dovrei prendere del vino rosso con questo piatto?	**Do You think I should** have red wine with this dish?
Credi che dovrei lasciare la mancia?	**Do you think I should** leave a tip?

You may wish to make a suggestion to your colleagues or friends in Italian. One way of doing this is to use **potremmo** (*we could*). This comes from the verb **potere**. For more information on **potere**, see page 284.

We could...

Potremmo sederci qui.	**We could** sit here.
Potremmo prendere solo un'insalata.	**We could** just have a salad.
Potremmo sederci fuori, **se preferite**.	**We could** sit outside, **if you prefer**.

If you want to make a suggestion using *let's*, you can use the **noi** form of the imperative in Italian. For more information on the imperative, see page 273.

Let's...

Sediamoci fuori.	**Let's sit** outside.
Prendiamo le tagliatelle.	**Let's have** the tagliatelle.
Saltiamo gli antipasti.	**Let's not bother with** a starter.

If you are asking someone whether they feel like having or doing something, use **Che ne dici di...?** or, if don't know them well, **Che ne dice di...?** (*Do You fancy...?*). If you are talking to more than one person use **Che ne dite di...?**. You can also use **Ti va...?**, **Le va...?** or **Vi va...?**.

Do you fancy...?

Che ne dice di un caffè?	**Do You fancy** a coffee?
Che ne dice di ordinare ancora una bottiglia?	**Do You fancy** ordering another bottle?
Che ne dite di prendere due porzioni in quattro?	**Do you fancy** sharing two portions between the four of us?
Ti va di provare la minestra?	**Do you fancy** trying the soup?
Vi va di prendere un dolce?	**Do you fancy** a dessert?

You can have...

Può prendere un antipasto, **se vuole**.	**You can have** a starter, **if you like.**
Può prendere un digestivo, **se vuole**.	**You can have** a liqueur, **if you like**.
Può prendere il menù a 20 euro, **se vuole**.	**You can have** the €20 set menu, **if you like**.

Another very simple way of making suggestions is to ask a question using the verb in the present tense followed by a question mark. For more information on the present tense, see page 271.

Shall we...?

Prendiamo prima un aperitivo?	**Shall we have** a drink first?
Ordiniamo ancora una bottiglia?	**Shall we order** another bottle?
Chiediamo il conto?	**Shall we ask** for the bill?

COMPLAINING

You may wish to complain if the service or the food are not to your satisfaction. You can do this by saying **Scusi, ma...** (*Sorry but...*).

Sorry, but...

Scusi, ma la mia minestra è fredda.	**Sorry, but** my soup is cold.
Scusi, ma c'è carne nel sugo. Io sono vegetariano.	**Sorry, but** there's meat in the sauce. I'm vegetarian.
Scusi, ma non è quello che avevo ordinato.	**I'm afraid** that's not what I ordered.
Scusi, ma ce l'ha messo in conto due volte.	**I'm afraid** You've charged us twice for it.
Mi scusi, ma il vino sa di tappo.	**I'm sorry, but** the wine is corked.

LISTEN OUT FOR

Here are some key phrases which you are likely to hear when you're eating out.

Sei libera sabato?	Are you free on Saturday?
Passo a prenderti?	Do you want me to pick you up?
Avete prenotato?	Have you got a reservation?
Mi dispiace, siamo al completo.	Sorry, we're full.
Di qua, prego.	This way please.
Se mi vuole seguire.	Follow me please.
Ecco la lista dei vini.	Here's the wine list.
Il piatto del giorno è sulla tabella.	Today's special is on the board.
Vi consiglio gli asparagi.	I'd recommend the asparagus.
È una specialità della zona.	It's a local speciality.
Volete ordinare?	Are you ready to order?
Volete prima un aperitivo?	Would you like a drink first?
Cosa bevete?	What will you have to drink?
Vi porto una mezza porzione?	Shall I bring you a half portion?
Il pesce è appena pescato.	The fish is really fresh.
Desidera del formaggio o un dolce?	Would You like the cheese board or a dessert?
Purtroppo l'abbiamo finito.	I'm afraid there's none left.
È il dolce della casa.	This dessert is our speciality.
Desidera qualcos'altro?	Would You like anything else?
Arrivo subito.	I'll be right with you.
Lo porto subito.	I'll bring it right away.
Siete miei ospiti.	It's on me.
Offre la casa.	This is on the house.

Lifestyle Tips

• To attract the waiter's attention, you just need to say **Scusi?**, **Cameriere!** (Waiter!) or **Cameriera!** (Waitress!).

• Unless you're having a pizza, you'll always be given **del pane** (*bread*) with your meal. You'll be charged for it as part of **il coperto** (*the cover charge*). Most Italian people wouldn't contemplate having a meal without bread.

• Dishes such as spaghetti, lasagne and risotto come under the heading **Primi** (*First courses*) on restaurant menus. Meat and fish come under **Secondi** (*Mains*). These don't usually come with much in the way of vegetables – these have to be ordered separately. They come under **Contorni** (*Side dishes*).

• While service charges are usually included on restaurant bills, it is still very common to leave **una mancia** (*a tip*) of between five and ten per cent, especially if the service has been good. In bars, people tend to leave a few **centesimi** (*cents*) as a tip.

• Children are welcome in Italian restaurants, even in the evening. If you need a high chair, you can ask **Avete un seggiolone?**

• If someone says **Buon appetito!** (*Enjoy your meal!*) the correct response is: **Grazie, altrettanto!** (*The same to you!*).

Hitting
the town

Buon divertimento! – Have a good time!

The phrases in this unit will help you to feel confident in all kinds of social situations in Italian. Whether you are going to a concert, the theatre or cinema, going to watch a sports match, going to a bar, or giving or being invited to a party, these phrases will ensure that your Italian sounds natural.

MAKING SUGGESTIONS

When you're planning to go out with Italian-speaking friends or colleagues you may want to suggest what you could do. One good way of making a suggestion is to use **possiamo** (*we can*) or **potremmo** (*we could*) followed by **se vuoi** or, more formally, **se vuole** (*if You like*). These are from the verb **potere** (*to be able*). For more information on **potere**, see page 284.

We can...

Possiamo andare a bere qualcosa, **se vuoi**.	**We can** go and have a drink, **if you like**.
Possiamo andare a teatro, **se vuole**.	**We can** go to the theatre, **if You like**.
Potremmo andare a un concerto, **se vuoi**.	**We could** go to a concert, **if you like**.

Another way of making a suggestion in Italian is by using the imperative. For more information about the imperative, see page 273.

Let's...

Andiamo a bere qualcosa.	**Let's go out** for a drink.
Vediamo se riusciamo a trovare biglietti per la partita di sabato.	**Let's see** if we can get tickets for the match on Saturday.
Sediamoci qui.	**Let's sit** here.
Ordiniamo ancora una bottiglia di vino?	**Shall we order** another bottle of wine?

You can also ask someone what they would like to do by asking **Vuoi...?** or, more formally, **Vuole...?** (*Do You want to...?*).

Do you want to...?

Vuoi andare a prendere un caffè sabato pomeriggio?	**Do you want to** go for a coffee on Saturday afternoon?
Vuoi andare al bar dopo il cinema?	**Do you want to** go to a bar after the film?
Faccio una festa. **Vuoi** venire?	I'm having a party. **Do you want to** come?
Volete che ci vediamo al bar domani sera?	**Do you want to** meet in the bar tomorrow night?
Vuole cenare da noi domani sera?	**Would You like to** come for dinner tomorrow night?
Volete passare la notte da noi?	**Do you want to** stay the night with us?

BUONO A SAPERSI!
When talking about *tonight* and *tomorrow night*, use **questa sera** or **stasera** and **domani sera**. The word **notte** (*night*) is only used to refer to very late at night.

Do you fancy...?

Ti va di venire al concerto?	**Do you fancy** coming to the concert?
Ti va di prendere un caffè da qualche parte?	**Do you fancy** going for a coffee somewhere?
Hai voglia di andare a bere qualcosa stasera?	**Do you fancy** going for a drink tonight?
Avete voglia di andare al cinema?	**Do you fancy** going to the cinema?

TALKING ABOUT YOUR PLANS

If you want to talk about the plans you've made for social activities, you can use the future tense or the present tense. For information about these tenses, see page 271.

I'm going to...

Inviterò degli amici per il mio compleanno.	**I'm going to invite** some friends over for my birthday.
Vado alla festa di Lorenzo sabato prossimo.	**I'm going to** Lorenzo's party next Saturday.
Ceniamo dai nostri amici stasera.	**We're going to have dinner** at our friends' house tonight.

Are you going to...?

Inviterai tanta gente?	**Are you going to invite** many people?
Va alla festa di Susie?	**Are You going to go** to Susie's party?
Quando **riuscite a** venire?	When **will <u>you</u> be able to** come?

If your plans are not yet fixed, you can use **forse** (perhaps).

Perhaps...

Forse ci andrò.	**Perhaps** I'll go.
Forse bevo ancora qualcosa.	**Perhaps** I'll have another drink.
Forse faccio una festa.	I **may** have a party.

ASKING FOR INFORMATION

When you're planning to go out socially, you will need to ask for some information about what's available or what's on. You can use **C'è...?** (*Is there...?*) or **Ci sono...?** (*Are there...?*).

Is there... ?

C'è un cinema qui?	**Is there** a cinema here?
C'è una partita di calcio oggi pomeriggio?	**Is there** a football match on this afternoon?
Ci sono concerti gratuiti questo fine settimana?	**Are there** any free concerts on this weekend?

To ask someone whether they have something, for example, in a bar or at the theatre, use **Avete...?** (*Do you have...?*).

Do you have...?

Avete due posti in platea?	**Do you have** two seats in the stalls?
Avete un programma?	**Do you have** any programmes?
Avete birra alla spina?	**Do you have** draught beer?

To obtain specific information, for example, what time something starts or finishes or how much it costs, you can use phrases such as **A che ora...?** (*What time...?*), **Quanto costa...?** (*How much...?*) and **Quanto...?** (*How long...?*).

What time...?

A che ora comincia il film?	**What time** does the film start?
A che ora finisce il concerto?	**What time** does the concert finish?
Per che ora è prenotato il taxi?	**What time** is the taxi ordered **for**?

How much...?

Quanto costa un biglietto per lo spettacolo di stasera?	**How much** is a ticket for this evening's performance?
Quanto costa il programma?	**How much is it** for a programme?
Quanto costa l'ingresso?	**How much does it cost** to get in?

How long...?

Quanto dura l'opera?	**How long** is the opera?
Quanto restate in questo bar?	**How long** are <u>you</u> going to be in this bar?
Quanto ci si mette per arrivare allo stadio?	**How long** does it take to get to the stadium?

What...?

Che genere di musica fanno?	**What** kind of music do they play?
In **che** bar andate?	**What** bar are <u>you</u> going to?
Per **quale** spettacolo avete biglietti?	**Which** showing have You got tickets for?
Cosa danno al cinema?	**What**'s on at the cinema at the moment?

ASKING FOR THINGS

When you're asking for things, the easiest way to say what you want is to use **vorrei** (*I'd like*) or **vorremmo** (*we'd like*). **vorrei** and **vorremmo** are from the verb **volere** (*to want*). For more information on **volere**, see page 285.

I'd like...

Vorrei un Campari, per favore.	**I'd like** a Campari, please.
Vorrei due biglietti per lo spettacolo di stasera.	**I'd like** two tickets for tonight's show.
Vorrei un biglietto per la partita del Milan.	**I'd like** a ticket for the Milan match.
Vorrei un posto in galleria.	**I'd like** a seat in the upper circle.
Vorremmo il conto, per favore.	**We'd like** the bill, please.

I'll have...

Prendo un tè al latte, senza limone.	**I'll have** a cup of tea.
Prendo un gin tonic.	**I'll have** a G & T.
Prendiamo un'altra bottiglia di vino bianco della casa.	**We'll have** another bottle of house white.

To ask someone for something, use **Mi dà...?** (*Can I have...?*) or
Ci dà...? (*Can we have...?*).

Can I have...?

Mi dà una caraffa d'acqua?	**Can I have** a jug of water?
Mi dà un biglietto per lo spettacolo?	**Can I have** a ticket for the show?
Ci dà quattro posti in platea, per favore?	**Can we have** four seats in the stalls, please?

SAYING WHAT YOU LIKE, DISLIKE, PREFER

When you're out socializing you will probably want to say what
you like or dislike. To say what you like, you can use **mi piace** (*I
like*) with singular nouns or **mi piacciono** with plural nouns. If
you want to say that you don't like something, use **non mi piace**
or **non mi piacciono** (*I don't like*).

I like...

Mi piace la musica techno.	**I like** techno music.
Mi piace andare al cinema.	**I like** going to the cinema.
Mi piacciono i film dell'orrore.	**I like** horror films.
Adoro l'opera.	**I love** opera.

I don't like...

Non mi piace la birra alla spina.	**I don't like** draught beer.
Non mi piace andare a teatro.	**I don't like** going to the theatre.
Non mi piacciono le commedie musicali.	**I don't like** musicals.
Odio l'operetta.	**I can't stand** operetta.

To talk about what you prefer, use **preferisco** (*I prefer*).
preferisco comes from the verb **preferire**. For more information
on **–ire** verbs like **preferire**, see page 268.

I prefer...

Preferisco il cinema d'essai.	**I prefer** arthouse films.
Preferisco andarci un altro giorno.	**I'd prefer** to go another day.
Preferisco il vino **alla** birra.	**I prefer** wine **to** beer.
Preferisco vedere un film **piuttosto** che un concerto.	**I'd rather** see a film **than** go to a concert.
Preferisci il cinema italiano o quello americano?	**Which do you prefer**, Italian or American films?

If you want to ask other people what they like, use **Ti piace..?**
or **Ti piacciono...?** (*Do you like...?*) for someone you know well
or for someone young. Use **Le piace...?** or **Le piacciono...?**
for someone you do not know well and **Vi piace...?** or **Vi
piacciono...?** for more than one person.

Do you like...?

Ti piace il calcio?	**Do you like** football?
Le piacciono le commedie musicali?	**Do You like** musicals?
Vi piace andare al cinema?	**Do you like** going to the cinema?

If you want to say that you enjoyed a play, film and so on, you
can say **mi è piaciuto** (*I enjoyed*).

I enjoyed...

Mi è piaciuto il film.	**I enjoyed** the film.
Mi è piaciuto molto.	I really **enjoyed it**.
Non ci è piaciuto per niente.	**We didn't enjoy it** at all.
Ti è piaciuto?	**Did you enjoy it**?
Le è piaciuta l'opera?	**Did You enjoy** the opera?

EXPRESSING OPINIONS

If you want to express your opinion of something you've seen or of somewhere you've been, you can use **penso che** and **credo che** (*I think*) to say what you think. These are followed by the subjunctive or the future tense. For more information on the subjunctive and the future tense, see pages 273 and 271.

I think...

Penso che ti piacerà.	**I think** you'll like it.
Penso che sia una splendida attrice.	**I think** she is a fantastic actress.
Credo che vinceranno.	**I think** they'll win.
Credo sia un buon film.	**I think** it's a good film.
Non pensa che la commedia fosse un po' troppo lunga?	**Don't You think** the play was a bit long?

In my opinion...

Secondo me Spielberg è un regista formidabile.	**In my opinion**, Spielberg is a wonderful director.
Secondo me questa sala concerti non ha uguali.	**In my opinion**, this concert hall is second to none.
Secondo me la fine lasciava molto a desiderare.	**In my view**, the ending was very weak.

What do you think of...?

Cosa pensa dei suoi film?	**What do You think of** his films?
Cosa pensi del rap?	**What do you think of** rap music?
Che te ne pare di questo bar?	**What do you make of** this bar?

If you want to agree or disagree with someone, you can say
sono d'accordo (*I agree*) or **non sono d'accordo** (*I don't agree*).

I agree...

Sono d'accordo con te.	**I agree** with you.
Sono d'accordo con lei.	**I agree** with You.
Sono completamente **d'accordo** con quello che dice.	I totally **agree** with what You say.
No, **non sono d'accordo**.	No, **I don't agree**.
Non sono affatto **d'accordo**.	**I don't agree** at all.

ASKING FOR PERMISSION

When you're out, you may want to ask someone if it's okay for
you to do something. One useful way of asking for permission
is to use **Posso...?** (*Can I...?*) or **Possiamo...?** (*Can we...?*). **posso**
and **possiamo** are from the verb **potere** (*to be able*). For more
information on **potere**, see page 284.

Can I...?

Posso sedermi dove voglio?	**Can I** sit where I like?
Posso pagare con la carta?	**Can I** pay by card?
Posso prendere questa sedia?	**Can I** take this chair?
Possiamo sederci fuori?	**Can we** sit outside?
Possiamo fumare qui?	**Can we** smoke here?

Do you mind if...?

Le dispiace se ci sediamo qua?	**Do You mind if** we sit here?
Vi dispiace se mi metto qui con voi?	**Do <u>you</u> mind if** I join you?
Le dà fastidio se fumo?	**Do You mind if** I smoke?

LISTEN OUT FOR

Here are some key phrases which you are likely to hear when you're going out.

Dove vuole sedersi?	Where would You like to sit?
Per quante persone?	How many people?
Biglietto, per favore.	Can I see your ticket, please?
Vuole comprare un programma?	Would You like to buy a programme?
Le dispiace se ci scambiamo di posto?	Would You mind swapping places?
Sei libera domani?	Are you free tomorrow?
La settimana prossima ho da fare.	I'm busy next week.
Quando ti andrebbe bene?	When would be a good time for you?
Cosa prende?	What can I get You?
Ti offro da bere.	Let me get you a drink.
Offro io.	This is on me.
Ti sei divertito stasera?	Did you have a good time tonight?
Grazie dell'invito.	Thank you for inviting me.
Grazie, non c'era bisogno.	Thank you, you shouldn't have.

Lifestyle Tips

In a café or bar:
• If you want a quick coffee you can stand at the bar. You pay less than if you are served at a table. On their way to work many Italians call in for coffee, often accompanied by **una pasta** (*a cake*) or **un cornetto** or **un croissant** (*a croissant*).

• Sometimes you have to begin by paying for what you're going to have **alla cassa** (*at the cashdesk*) and then go to the bar with your **scontrino** (*receipt*). It's worth checking if this is what people are doing. Otherwise you may end up waiting at the bar, only to be sent off to **la cassa**.

• If you're going to sit down, the waiter will come to you. The waiter will just leave **lo scontrino** (*the bill*) on your table, and you pay when you're ready.

• If you ask for **un caffè**, you will be given an espresso. It is worth remembering that the coffee you get in Italy is not always the same as the one you might be used to at home. For example, **un cappuccino** in Italy is often smaller than the version usually served outside Italy.

• When you order **un tè** (*tea*), normally you will be asked **latte o limone?** (*with milk or black, with lemon*).

• If you order **un aperitivo** (*an aperitif*), you will usually be served some snacks to go with your drink.

• Italian people don't really buy rounds. Someone might offer to pay if it's two people or a group; otherwise everybody will chip in.

• Expressions for *Cheers!* in Italian include **Salute!** and **Cin Cin!** To one person you know well, say **Alla tua!**. If you want to make a toast, say **Facciamo un brindisi!**

• When you leave a restaurant don't forget to take your **ricevuta fiscale** (*receipt*). You are required by law to do this!

At somebody's house:
• You may be invited **a cena** (*to dinner*), **a pranzo** (*to lunch*), or sometimes just **per l'aperitivo** (*for a pre-dinner drink*). This is a handy way of inviting someone without making a night of it.

• When invited to someone's house for dinner, Italian people usually bring patisserie, chocolates, or flowers. If bringing wine, it's normal to bring dessert wine, champagne, spirits or some expensive special wine. If an Italian-speaking person brings you a gift, you can say **Grazie, non c'era bisogno** (*thank you, you shouldn't have*).

At the cinema:
• New films come out on a Friday (**venerdì**) in Italy. There are **cinema di prima visione** where new films are shown first. After that they go to the **cinema di seconda visione**.

Museums, monuments and much more

Buona giornata! – Have a nice day!

If you're planning to see the sights in an Italian city, the phrases in this unit will give you the confidence to ask where you can go, what you can do there and how much it will cost using natural Italian.

SAYING WHAT YOU WANT TO DO

You may need to be able to say what you'd like to do in Italian. To do this, you can use **vorrei** (*I'd like*). **vorrei** comes from the verb **volere** (*to want*). For more information on **volere**, see page 285.

I'd like to...

Vorrei salire sul campanile.	**I'd like to** go up the tower.
Vorrei fare delle foto di questo quadro, se si può.	**I'd like to** take some pictures of this painting, if that's ok.
Vorremmo andare alla cattedrale con l'*au*tobus.	**We'd like to** take the bus to the cathedral.
Vorremmo visitare la mostra d'arte.	**We'd like to** see the art exhibition.

You may also want to show your enthusiasm about doing something. To say *I'd love to*, you can use **mi piacerebbe tantissimo** followed by a verb in the infinitive.

I'd love to...

Mi piacerebbe tantissimo visitare le grotte.	**I'd love to** see the caves.
Mi piacerebbe tantissimo portare i bambini a G*a*rdaland.	**I'd love to** take the kids to Gardaland.
Mi piacerebbe tantissimo passare una serata al Lido.	**I'd love to** spend an evening at the Lido.
Le piacerebbe tantissimo visitare G*u*bbio.	**She'd love to** see Gubbio.

TALKING ABOUT YOUR PLANS

It is very likely that you will want to talk about what you are planning to do on your trip. In English we often say *I'm going to* to talk about the future. To say that you're going to do something in Italian, you can use the future tense. It is also quite common to use the present tense. For more information on the future and the present tenses, see page 271.

I'm going to...

Andrò a visitare il Castello Sforzesco.	**I'm going to visit** the Sforza Castle.
Telefonerò per informarmi se è aperto la domenica.	**I'm going to phone** to find out if it's open on Sundays.
Portiamo i bambini con noi.	**We're going to take** the kids with us.
Farai l'intera visita guidata?	**Are you going to do** the whole guided tour?

You can use **ho intenzione di** or **penso di** (*I intend to*) to talk about what you intend to do.

I intend to...

Ho intenzione di andarci con una guida alpina.	**I intend to** go with a mountain guide.
Ho intenzione di ritornare ai Musei Vaticani la prossima volta.	**I intend to** go back to the Vatican Museums next time.
Penso di fare l'escursione sul vulcano la settimana prossima.	**I intend to** go on the excursion to the volcano next week.
Pensate di passarci molto tempo?	**Do you intend to** spend much time there?
Cosa **pensate di** visitare prima di tutto?	What **do you plan to** visit first?

If you want to talk about the plans that have been made, you can use **dovrei** (meaning *I'm planning to*) followed by the infinitive. **dovrei** comes from the verb **dovere**. For more information on **dovere**, see page 281.

I'm planning to...

Dovrei visitare i giardini botanici nel pomeriggio.	**I'm planning to** visit the botanic gardens in the afternoon.
Dovrei raggiungere la comitiva alle quattro.	**I'm planning to** meet up with the group at four.
Dovremmo passare la notte in una baita e raggiungere la cima il giorno dopo.	**We're planning to** spend the night in a mountain hut and reach the summit the following day.
A che ora **dovremmo** arrivare?	What time **are we supposed to** get there?

> **BUONO A SAPERSI!**
> As well as using **dovrei** to talk about your plans, you can also use it to talk about what you should do or ought to do, as in **dovrei andarmene** (*I should go*).

MAKING SUGGESTIONS

You may wish to make a suggestion to your colleagues or friends about where you should go or what you should visit in Italian. One way of doing this is to use **propongo di** (*I suggest*) followed by the verb in the infinitive. **propongo** comes from the verb **proporre** (*to suggest*). For more information on verbs like **proporre**, see page 268.

I suggest...

Propongo di visitare il Museo del Mare.	**I suggest** we visit the Maritime Museum.
Propongo di rimandare la visita allo zoo a lunedì.	**I suggest** we postpone the trip to the zoo until Monday.
Propongo un picnic al parco.	**I suggest** we have a picnic in the park.
Cosa ci **propone di** fare?	What **do You suggest** we do?

You can make a suggestion using the phrase **Perché non...?** (*Why don't...?*) followed by the present tense.

Why don't...?

Perché non facciamo una passeggiata nella città vecchia?	**Why don't** we walk round the old town?
Perché non fai delle foto dalla torre?	**Why don't** you take some pictures from the tower?
Perché non facciamo un giro della città in carrozza?	**Why don't** we go round the town in a horse-drawn carriage?
Perché non prendi la metropolitana per andare in Piazza Duomo?	**Why don't** you take the underground to Piazza Duomo?

Another way of making suggestions is to say **dovremmo** (*we should*). **dovremmo** comes from the verb **dovere**. For more information on **dovere**, see page 281.

We should...

Dovremmo salire con la funivia.	**We should** take the cable car to the top.
Dovremmo tornare domani per vedere tutto il resto.	**We should** come back tomorrow to see all the rest.
Stasera **dovreste** andare a vedere lo spettacolo di luci e suoni.	**You should** go to the laser show tonight.
Dovrebbe noleggiare una bicicletta per fare il giro dell'isola.	**You should** hire a bike to cycle round the island.

ASKING FOR INFORMATION

If you need some information about the things you plan to see or do, you can use **È...?** to ask *Is it...?*.

Is it...?

È una visita guidata?	**Is it** a guided tour?
È una camminata impegnativa?	**Is it** a difficult walk?
È accessibile ai disabili?	**Is it** accessible to disabled people?

You often put the thing you're asking about (for example, *the castle* or *the museum*) at the end of the Italian question.

Is...?

È interessante il castello?	**Is** the castle interesting?
È gratuita l'entrata?	**Is** admission free?
È aperto il museo?	**Is** the museum open?

You may also need to ask if something is available in the place you're visiting. Use **C'è...?** or **Ci sono...?** to ask *Is there...?* and *Are there...?*.

Is there...?

C'è un caffè con wifi qui vicino?	**Is there** cafe with wi-fi nearby?
Ci sono cose da vedere nel paesino?	**Is there** anything to see in the village?
C'è uno sconto studenti?	**Is there** a student discount?
Ci sono mummie nel museo?	**Are there** any mummies in the museum?
Cosa **c'è** da vedere a Bergamo? Vale la pena visitarla?	What **is there** to see in Bergamo? Is it worth a visit?

In order to obtain more specific information, you can use **Che...?** or **Quale...?** (*What...?*), **A che ora...?** (*What time...?*) or **Quanto costa...?** (*How much is...?*).

What...?

Che genere di dipinto è?	**What** type of painting is it?
In **che** lingua è scritto il depliant?	**What** language is the leaflet written in?
Quale è la stazione più vicina al Campidoglio?	**What** is the nearest station to the Campidoglio?
Qual è l'orario di apertura?	**What** are the opening hours?

What time...?

A che ora ci si ritrova al pullman?	**What time** do we meet at the bus?
A che ora chiude il parco?	**What time** does the park close?
A che ora c'è la prossima visita guidata?	**What time** is the next guided tour?
A che ora è meglio andarci?	**What**'s the best time to go?

How much is...?

Quanto costa questa cartolina, per favore?	**How much is** this postcard, please?
Quanto costa un biglietto per studenti?	**How much is** a student ticket?
Quanto costa la traversata in traghetto?	**How much is** the ferry crossing?
Quanto costa fare una gita a Capri?	**How much is it** to take a trip to Capri?

To find out how long something lasts, or how long it takes to get somewhere, you can use **Quanto...?** (*How long...?*).

How long...?

Quanto dura la visita?	**How long** does the tour last?
Quanto dura la gita in barca?	**How long** is the boat trip?
Quanto ci si mette per arrivarci?	**How long** does it take to get there?

To ask how you do something, you can use **Come si...?** (*How do you...?*), followed by the verb in the 'he/she/it' form, or **Come si fa a...?** followed by the verb in the infinitive.

How do you...?

Come si arriva alla città vecchia?	**How do you** get to the old town?
Come si accede al secondo piano?	**How do you** get to the second floor?
Come si fa a scegliere la lingua per la visita registrata?	**How do you** select the language of the audio tour?
Come si fa a comprare i biglietti?	**How do you** get tickets?

When you're out and about in an Italian town, you will want to be able to ask for things in Italian. Use **Mi dà...?** (*Can I have...?*) which comes from the verb **dare**. For more information on **dare**, see page 280.

Can I have...?

Mi dà due biglietti d'ingresso per il museo, per favore?	**Can I have** two tickets for the museum, please?
Mi dà il programma per il concerto di stasera?	**Can I have** the programme for this evening's concert?
Mi dà le cuffie per la visita registrata?	**Could I have** headphones for the audio tour?
Mi dà una piantina del museo?	**Could I have** a map of the museum?

Very often you will want to say that you need something in particular. To do this use **ho bisogno di** or **avrei bisogno di** (*I need*). Remember that **avrei bisogno** sounds slightly more polite than **ho bisogno**.

I need...

Ho bisogno di altri due biglietti.	**I need** two more tickets.
Ho bisogno di una guida che parli inglese.	**I need** a guide who can speak English.
Ha bisogno delle cuffie.	**She needs** a pair of headphones.
Avrei bisogno di una piantina della città.	**I need** a street map of the city.
Avrei bisogno dell'indirizzo del museo.	**I need the** address of the museum.

If you want to find out if something is available, use **Ha...?** (*Do You have...?*) or **Avrebbe...?** (*Would You have...?*). **ha** and **avrebbe** are from the verb **avere** (*to have*). For more information on **avere**, see page 279.

Do you have...?

Ha degli opuscoli in inglese?	**Do You have** any brochures in English?
Ha guide registrate in altre lingue?	**Do You have** audio guides in other languages?
Ha un giornale locale, per favore?	**Have You got** a local newspaper, please?
Avrebbe informazioni su escursioni in questa zona?	**Would You have** any information on trips in this area?

When you want to ask if someone can do something for you, use **Può...?** (*Can You...?*) or **Potrebbe...?** (*Could You...?*), or **Puoi...?** or **Potresti...?** if you are addressing somebody younger. These come from the verb **potere** (*to be able*). For more information on **potere**, see page 284.

Can you...?

Può farci una foto?	**Can You** take a picture of us?
Mi **può** dire l'orario di apertura?	**Can You** tell me what the opening hours are?
Potrebbe farmi passare per la città vecchia?	**Could You** take me through the old town?
Mi **potresti** aiutare, per favore?	**Could you** help me, please?

There may be occasions where you want to ask for permission to do something. To do this, use **Posso...?** (*Can I...?*) or **Potrei...?** (*Could I...?*). **posso** and **potrei** come from the verb **potere** (*to be able*). For more information on **potere**, see page 284.

Can I...?

Posso fare foto?	**Can I** take pictures?
Posso entrare con la borsa?	**Can I** take my bag in?
Possiamo parcheggiare qui?	**Can we** park our car here?
Potrei prendere in prestito il tuo cellulare per un minuto?	**Could I** borrow your phone for a moment?

Another way of asking for permission is to use **Le dispiace se...?** (*Do You mind if...?*).

Do you mind if...?

Le dispiace se entro con la borsa?	**Do You mind if** I take my bag in with me?
Le dispiace se ci sediamo sull'erba?	**Do You mind if** we sit on the grass?
Le dispiace se lascio il passeggino qui?	**Do You mind if** I leave the pushchair here?

Is it a problem if...?

È un problema se fumo?	**Is it a problem if** I smoke?
Mi scusi, **è un problema se** faccio delle foto?	Excuse me, **is it a problem if** I take pictures?
È un problema per lei **se** pago con la carta?	**Is it a problem** for You **if** I pay by card?

SAYING WHAT YOU LIKE, DISLIKE, PREFER

If you want to talk about what you like, use **mi piace** (*I like*) for singular nouns or **mi piacciono** for plural nouns. To say what you don't like, use **non mi piace** or **non mi piacciono** (*I don't like*).

I like...

Mi piace visitare le gallerie d'arte moderna.	**I like** visiting modern art galleries.
Mi piacciono i fuochi d'artificio.	**I like** fireworks.
Questa scultura **mi piace molto**.	**I like** this sculpture **a lot**.
Mi piacciono tantissimo i paesini dell'Umbria.	**I love** the small villages in Umbria.
Ti piace questo genere di architettura?	**Do you like** this type of architecture?

I don't like...

Non mi piace l'arte greca.	**I don't like** Greek art.
Non mi piacciono le gite in pullman.	**I don't like** bus tours.
Non mi piacciono le montagne russe.	**I don't like** roller-coasters.
Non mi piace affatto dover fare la fila.	**I really don't like** having to queue.

If you want to say what you prefer, you can use **preferisco** (*I prefer*). If you want to say that something would suit you better, use **preferirei** (*I'd rather*).

I prefer...

Preferisco evitare quella zona.	**I prefer to** avoid that area.
Preferisco andare a piedi.	**I prefer to** walk.
Preferisco i musei **agli** edifici di interesse religioso.	**I prefer** museums **to** religious buildings.

I'd rather...

Preferirei passare tutta la settimana a Napoli.	**I'd rather** spend the whole week in Naples.
Preferirei prendere la funicolare.	**I'd rather** take the funicular railway.
Preferiremmo raggiungere la comitiva più tardi.	**We'd rather** meet up with the group later.
Preferiremmo andarci a piedi **piuttosto che** con l'autobus.	**We'd rather** walk **than** take the bus.

EXPRESSING OPINIONS

To say what you think of something, use **penso che** or **trovo che** (I think that). They are both followed by the subjunctive. For more information on the subjunctive, see page 273.

I think...

Penso che sia organizzato molto bene.	**I think** it's very well organized.
Penso che la guida non sia abbastanza chiara nello spiegare le cose.	**I don't think that** the guide explains things clearly enough.
Trovo che sia un po' caro per quello che è.	**I think** it's a bit expensive for what it is.
Non ho trovato il museo molto interessante.	**I didn't find** the museum very interesting.

One way of expressing your disappointment in something is to use **peccato che** (it's a shame that). The verb that follows is in the subjunctive.

It's a shame that...

Peccato che non ci sia niente per i bambini.	**It's a shame that** there's nothing for children.
Peccato che il depliant sia solo in italiano.	**It's a shame that** the leaflet is only in Italian.
Peccato che sia chiuso l'edificio principale.	**It's a shame** the main building isn't open.

Even in Italy, you may have to complain about something which you're disappointed or unhappy with.

I'm disappointed with...

Sono deluso del modo in cui ci hanno trattati.	**I'm disappointed with** the way we were treated.
La gita **mi ha** proprio **deluso**.	**I was** really **disappointed with** the trip.
I bambini **erano delusi di** non aver visto i pagliacci.	The children **were disappointed that** they didn't see the clowns.

I'm not happy with...

Non siamo rimasti soddisfatti della guida.	**We weren't happy with** our guide.
Il servizio qui **lascia proprio a desiderare**.	**I'm not happy** with the service here.
Non abbiamo mai visto un tale caos.	**We have never seen** such chaos.
Non solo era in ritardo, **ma** è stata **anche** sgarbata.	**Not only** was she late, she was **also** rude.

If you want to describe a situation, you can use **c'è** (*there is*) and **ci sono** (*there are*).

There's...

C'è un sacco di rumore nel museo.	**There's** a lot of noise in the museum.
Ci sono pochissime informazioni sulla storia di questo posto.	**There's** very little information about the history of this place.
Non ci sono strutture per i disabili.	**There are no** facilities for the disabled.

Here are some key phrases which you are likely to hear when you're sightseeing.

In quale lingua volete le informazioni?	What language would <u>you</u> like the information in?
Ecco un depliant in inglese.	Here's a leaflet in English.
Ha la tessera studentesca?	Do You have a student card?
Il museo è aperto dalle nove alle tre.	The museum's open from nine to three.
La galleria è chiusa la domenica.	The gallery's closed on Sundays.
La prossima visita guidata è alle dieci.	The next guided tour's at ten.
Quanti biglietti vuole?	How many tickets would You like?
Sono otto euro a testa.	It's eight euros each.
È vietato fotografare.	You're not allowed to take pictures.
Posso guardare nella sua borsa?	Can I search Your bag?
Per cortesia lasci borsa e cappotto nel guardaroba.	Please leave Your bag and coat in the cloakroom.
Le è piaciuto?	Did You enjoy it?

Lifestyle Tips

• The **Giornate Europee del Patrimonio** in the third week of September correspond to the *Doors Open* days in Britain. You can visit monuments and museums for free, and also get into many places that are not normally open to the public.

• In the high season there is often a lot going on; websites in Italian or English are a good way of keeping you informed about social and cultural events and telling you what there is to see in a given area. On Fridays most national newspapers publish **un inserto** (*insert*) in big cities with events listings for theatre, music, exhibitions, cinema etc.

• Many cities bring history to life in annual events such as Siena's famous **Palio** (*a horse race*), Arezzo's **Giostra del Saraceno** (*jousting*) and Firenze's **Calcio in Costume** (*football in medieval costume*). These events are not organized for the benefit of tourists – hundreds of local citizens participate, and thousands watch them.

• **Il carnevale** is another traditional event involving music and costume. It takes place in February, during the week before the start of Lent. The most famous one is in **Venezia**, but **carnevale** is celebrated all over Italy.

• The most famous Italian museums and galleries are so popular that you need to book in advance. You can do this online. Your ticket entitles you to spend a certain length of time there – often two hours. Remember that many museums are closed on Mondays.

Retail therapy

Prego, desidera ? – Can I help you?

Whether you're planning to shop for clothes or household items, get in your groceries or just pick up a postcard, the phrases in this unit will help give you the confidence to find the best bargains and shop till you drop using typical natural Italian.

ASKING FOR THINGS

When you're shopping in Italy, you may be asked **È servito?** or **È servita?** (*Are You being attended to?*). If you're just browsing, say **do solo un'occhiata** (*I'm just browsing*), or if someone else is already serving you, you can say **già servito, grazie** or **già servita, grazie** (*I'm already being served, thanks*). Alternatively, if you know what you want, use **vorrei** (*I'd like*). **vorrei** is from the verb **volere** (*to want*). For more information on **volere,** see page 285.

I'd like...

Vorrei due chili di patate, per favore.	**I'd like** two kilos of potatoes, please.
Vorrei una scheda memoria per la macchina fotografica digitale.	**I'd like** a memory card for my digital camera.
Vorrei un melone ben maturo, per favore.	**I'd like** a melon that's nice and ripe, please.
Vorrei provare il numero 38 di queste scarpe.	**I'd like** to try a 38 in these shoes.
Ne **voglio** ancora due, per favore.	**I want** two more of these, please.

At the market or in shops where an assistant is serving you, you can ask for something by saying **Mi dà...?** (*Could I have...?*) followed by what you want and **per favore**. This comes from the verb **dare** (*to give*). For more information on **dare**, see page 280.

Could I have...?

Mi dà un chilo di arance, per favore?	**Could I have** a kilo of oranges, please?
Mi dà 10 francobolli?	**Could I have** 10 stamps?
Mi dà una borsa, per favore?	**Could I have** a carrier bag, please?
Mi dà due etti di prosciutto crudo, per favore?	**Could I have** 200 grams of Parma ham, please?

You can also say what you are looking for by using **cerco** (*I'm looking for*). **cerco** comes from the verb **cercare** (*to look for*).

I'm looking for...

Cerco del coriandolo fresco.	**I'm looking for** fresh coriander.
Cerco del tofu.	**I'm looking for** tofu.
Cerco un paio di calzoncini per mio figlio di dieci anni.	**I'm looking for** shorts for my ten-year-old son.
Cerco un regalo per un bebè.	**I'm looking for** a present for a baby.

When you've chosen what you want to buy, you can say **prendo** (*I'll take*). If you haven't made up your mind, say **non ho ancora deciso** (*I haven't decided yet*).

I'll take...

Prendo queste due cartoline.	**I'll take** these two postcards.
Prendo quelli blu invece di quelli marroni.	**I'll take** the blue ones instead of the brown ones.
Prendo la prima borsa che mi ha fatto vedere.	**I'll take** the first bag You showed me.
Non prendo i jeans, sono piccoli.	**I won't take** the jeans, they're too small.

SAYING WHAT YOU HAVE TO DO

Shopping isn't always what you'd choose to do, is it? To say that you have to buy something or that you have to do something in Italian, you can use **devo** (*I have to*) and then the verb in the infinitive. **devo** comes from the verb **dovere** (*to have to*). For more information on the verb **dovere**, see page 281.

I have to...

Devo comprarmi delle scarpe nuove.	**I have to** buy some new shoes.
Devo passare in panetteria.	**I have to** stop at the baker's.
Se vuoi provare qualcosa **devi** chiedere alla commessa.	**You have to** ask the assistant if you want to try something on.
Dobbiamo comprare un nuovo aspirapolvere.	**We have to** buy a new vacuum cleaner.

I must...

Devo trovare un vestito per la festa di sabato.	**I must** find a dress for the party on Saturday.
Devo trovare un regalo di compleanno per mia sorella.	**I must** find a birthday present for my sister.
Devo comprare un completo per il colloquio.	**I must** buy a suit for the interview.

If you want to talk about things you need, use **ho bisogno di** (*I need*).

I need...

Ho bisogno di occhiali da sci.	**I need** some ski goggles.
Ho bisogno di due etti di funghi porcini. Ne avete ancora?	**I need** 200 grams of porcini mushrooms. Do you have any left?
Ho bisogno di pile per la sveglia.	**I need** some batteries for my alarm clock.
Di cosa **hai bisogno** per le vacanze?	What **do you need** for your holidays?

TALKING ABOUT YOUR PLANS

You may want to talk about what you're thinking of buying or where you're thinking of going. Italian uses the phrase **penso di** (*I'm thinking of*) followed by a verb in the infinitive.

I'm thinking of...

Penso di andare al mercato domani.	**I'm thinking of** going to the market tomorrow.
Penso di andare a fare shopping a Milano.	**I'm thinking of** going shopping in Milan.
Non pensiamo di andare in centro questo fine settimana.	**We don't think we**'ll go into town this weekend.
Pensi di passare al supermercato al rientro?	**Do you think you**'ll stop at the supermarket on your way home?

I hope to...

Spero di trovare qualcosa per meno di venti euro.	**I hope to** find something for under 20 euros.
Spero di trovare un divano in svendita a metà prezzo.	**I hope to** get a half-price sofa in the sales.
Speriamo di trovare un regalo per Carlo e Mariella.	**We hope to** find a present for Carlo and Mariella.

When talking about what you intend to do, you can use **ho intenzione di** (*I intend to*) followed by a verb in the infinitive.

I intend to...

Ho intenzione di andare a vedere le svendite questo fine settimana.	**I intend to** go to the sales this weekend.
Ho intenzione di comprarmi un nuovo costume da bagno.	**I'm going to** buy a new swimming costume.
Abbiamo intenzione di comprare un nuovo letto.	**We're going to** buy a new bed.

As you look at items for sale, you may well want to make comments to an Italian-speaking friend or to the shop assistant. To give your opinion, use **penso** (*I think*) or **trovo**. These come from the verbs **pensare** and **trovare**. For more information on **–are** verbs, see page 268. When **pensare** and **trovare** are used with **che**, the verb that follows is in the subjunctive. You can find out more about the subjunctive on page 273.

I think...

Penso che questo negozio sia esageratamente caro.	**I think** this shop is far too expensive.
Trovo questo tappeto veramente bello.	**I think** this rug is really lovely.
Non penso che questo maglione sia abbastanza caldo.	**I don't think** this jumper is warm enough.
Che ne pensi di questa camicia?	**What do you think of** this shirt?

In my opinion...

Secondo me questo vestito è troppo lungo.	**In my opinion,** this dress is too long.
Secondo me questo rossetto è un po' troppo scuro.	**In my opinion,** this lipstick is slightly too dark.
Secondo lei, tra questi cappelli, quale mi sta meglio?	**In your opinion**, which of these hats looks best on me?
Ho bisogno della **tua opinione** su questa macchina fotografica digitale.	I need **your opinion** on this digital camera.

You can use **direi che** (*I'd say that*) to give your opinion about something. **direi** comes from the verb **dire** (*to say*). Here, it is in the conditional, which can be used to say things in a less definite way. For more information on the conditional, see page 274.

I'd say...

Direi che mi è un po' stretto.	**I'd say** it's a bit tight for me.
Direi che è un affare.	**I'd say that** it's a bargain.
Che ne dici di questa lampada?	**What do you think of** this lamp?

If you want to ask for someone's opinion or advice, you can use **Mi consiglia di...?** (*Do You think I should...?*). This comes from the verb **consigliare**.

Do you think I should...?

Mi consiglia di prendere quello blu o quello rosso?	**Do You think I should** get the blue one or the red one?
Quale **mi consiglia di** prendere?	Which **do You think I should** get?
Cosa **mi consiglia**?	What **do You recommend**?

ASKING FOR INFORMATION

If you're in a strange town, you may want to ask for some information, for example if there is a particular shop in the area. Simple! Use **C'è...?** for *Is there...?* and **Ci sono...?** for *Are there...?*.

Is there...?

C'è un supermercato qui vicino?	**Is there** a supermarket near here?
C'è un parcheggio vicino al mercato?	**Is there** a car park near the market?
C'è un reparto di prodotti biologici?	**Is there** an organic food section?
C'è una garanzia?	**Does it have** a guarantee?
Ci sono carrelli?	**Are there** any trolleys?

Is this...?

È questo l'unico modello che avete in negozio?	**Is this** the only model <u>you</u> stock?
È questa la taglia più grande che avete?	**Is this** the biggest size <u>you</u> have?
Sono gli unici colori che avete?	**Are these** the only colours <u>you</u> have?
Questo è il prezzo al pezzo o al chilo?	**Is this** the price for one or per kilo?

To find out if something's available, you'll need to use the question **Avete...?** (*Do you have...?*) or **Avreste...?** (*Would you have...?*). **avete** and **avreste** are from the verb **avere** (*to have*). For more information on **avere**, see page 279.

Do you have...?

Avete prodotti del commercio equo e solidale?	**Do you have** Fairtrade products?
Ce l'**avete** in una taglia più piccola?	**Do you have** it in a smaller size?
Avete abbigliamento per bambini?	**Do you do** children's clothes?
Lo **avreste** in un altro colore?	**Would you have** it in another colour?

In order to obtain specific information, for example, where something is, which item you should buy or when something will happen, you may want to ask **Dove...?** (*Where...?*), **Che...?** or **Quale...?** (*Which...?*), or **Quando...?** (*When...?*).

Where...?

Dov'è il Bancomat più vicino, per favore?	**Where**'s the nearest cash point, please?
Dov'è la cassa, per favore?	**Where**'s the cash desk, please?
Mi può dire **dov'è** il servizio clienti, per favore?	Can You tell me **where** customer services are, please?
Dove trovo gli occhiali da sole?	**Where** can I find sunglasses?

Which...?

Che marca mi consiglia?	**Which** make do You recommend?
Che batterie devo comprare per la mia macchina fotografica?	**Which** batteries do I need to buy for my camera?
A che piano si trova l'abbigliamento per uomo?	**Which** floor is the menswear department **on**?
Che giorno c'è il mercato?	**What** day is market day?
Quali prendi?	**Which ones** are you going to get?
Quale di queste due è la meno cara?	**Which** of these two is the cheaper?

When...?

Quando chiudete per pranzo?	**When** do you close for lunch?
Quando cominciano le svendite?	**When** do the sales start?

What time...?

A che ora aprite al mattino?	**What time** do you open in the morning?
A che ora arriva al mercato?	**What time** do You get to the market?

To be able to ask the price of something, you can use either **Quanto costa...?**, **Quant'è...?** or **Quanto viene...?** (*How much is...?*). If you're asking about more than one thing, use **Quanto costano...?**, **Quanto sono...?** or **Quanto vengono...?** (*How much are...?*).

How much is...?

Quanto costa questa lampada?	**How much is** this lamp?
Quant'è una bottiglia di aranciata?	**How much is** a bottle of fizzy orange?
Quanto viene quel braccialetto?	**How much is** that bracelet?
Quanto vengono i fichi, per favore?	**How much are** the figs, please?
Quanto costano al chilo le ciliegie?	**How much are** the cherries a kilo?
Quanto sono le scarpe?	**How much are** the shoes?
Quanto le devo?	**How much** do I owe You?

If you want to ask whether you can do something while you are out shopping, use **Posso...?** (*Can I...?*).

Can I...?

Posso pagare con la carta di credito?	**Can I** pay by credit card?
Posso avere la ricevuta, per favore?	**Can I** have a receipt, please?
Mi può fare un pacchetto regalo?	**Can I** have it giftwrapped?
Mi **può** fare uno sconto?	**Can You** give me a discount?

BUONO A SAPERSI!!
To say *keep the change* in Italian, use the expression **tenga il resto**. If you are talking to somebody young you would address with *tu*, use **tieni il resto**.

To say that you like something, you can say **mi piace** (literally, *this pleases me*). You use **mi piace** with singular words and **mi piacciono** with plural ones. To say that you don't like something, you can use **non mi piace** or **non mi piacciono**.

I like...

Mi piace questo negozio.	**I like** this shop.
Mi piacciono molto queste scarpe.	**I like** these shoes very much.
Mi piacciono i negozi di antiquariato.	**I like** antique shops.
Compralo, se **ti piace**.	Buy it if **you like it**.
Mi piace un sacco andare a fare shopping con un'amica.	**I love** going shopping with a friend.

I don't like...

Non mi piace questo stile.	**I don't like** this style.
Non mi piacciono i grandi magazzini.	**I don't like** big stores.
Questi guanti **mi piacciono meno**.	**I don't like** these gloves **as much**.
Non ci piace fare la fila.	**We don't like** queuing.

Of course you might not just want to say what you like and what you don't like when out shopping, you may also want to talk about what you prefer. To say that you prefer A to B, use **preferisco A a B**. For more information on **a** followed by articles (**il, la** and so on) see page 255.

I prefer...

Preferisco quello verde.	**I prefer** the green one.
Preferisco i negozi piccoli **ai** supermercati.	**I prefer** small shops **to** supermarkets.
Preferiamo i prodotti freschi **a** quelli surgelati.	**We prefer** fresh produce **to** frozen.
Preferisco comprare su Internet **piuttosto che** andare per negozi.	**I prefer** to buy online **rather than** go to the shops.

I'd rather...

Preferirei qualcosa di più classico.	**I'd rather** go for something more classic.
Preferirei dei prodotti biologici.	**I'd rather** have organic products.
Preferirei provarlo prima di comprarlo.	**I'd rather** try it before buying it.
Preferiremmo comprare solo prodotti locali.	**We'd rather** buy only local produce.

MAKING SUGGESTIONS

On shopping expeditions you may well want to make suggestions about what to choose or what to do next. You can do this by putting **E se...?** (*How about...?*) at the beginning of a sentence. The verb that follows is in the imperfect subjunctive. You can find out more about the subjunctive on page 273.

How about...?

E se andassimo a fare shopping un'altra volta?	**How about** we go shopping another time?
E se provassimo quella nuova libreria?	**How about** trying that new bookshop?
E se lo comprassimo su Internet?	**How about** we buy it online?

To suggest what you and your friends could do, you can use **potremmo** (*we could*).

We could...

Potremmo andare a vedere in un altro negozio.	**We could** go and look in another shop.
Potremmo chiedere se ce lo ordinano.	**We could** ask them to order it for us.
Potresti chiedergli di farti uno sconto.	**You could** ask him to knock something off the price.

Another simple way of making suggestions is to raise the tone of your voice at the end of a normal sentence.

Shall I...?

Prendo del pane?	**Shall I** get some bread?
Compro un dolce per stasera?	**Shall I get** a cake for tonight?
Compriamo del gelato?	**Shall we buy** some ice cream?
Andiamo al supermercato?	**Shall we go** to the supermarket?

When offering to do something, you can say **lasci che** or, more informally or to somebody younger, **lascia che** (*let me*). These are from the verb **lasciare**. The verb that follows is in the subjunctive. You can find out more about the subjunctive on page 273.

Let me...

Lascia che paghi **io**.	**Let me** pay for this.
Lasci che l'aiuti.	**Let me** help You.
Lasciami portare la spesa.	**Let me** carry the shopping.

ASKING FOR PERMISSION

To ask if you can do something, such as try on an item of clothing, use **Posso...?** (*Can I...?*) or **Potrei...?** (*Could I...?*). These come from the verb **potere** (*to be able*). For more information on **potere**, see page 284.

Can I...?

Posso provarmi questa gonna?	**Can I** try on this skirt?
Posso tenere l'appendino?	**Can I** keep the hanger?
Me li **posso** provare?	**Can I** try them on?
Ci **potrei** pensare ancora per qualche minuto?	**Could I** think about it for another few minutes?

I'll... if you don't mind

Se non le dispiace mi provo di nuovo gli altri pantaloni.	**I'll try** the other trousers on again, **if You don't mind**.
Se non le dispiace do un'occhiata in giro.	**I'll have a look round**, if You don't mind.
Se non le dispiace ripasso sabato.	**I'll come back** on Saturday, **if You don't mind**.

To ask for permission in a polite and slightly formal way, use **Permette che...** (*May I...?*) followed by the verb in the subjunctive. You can find out more about the subjunctive on page 273.

May I...?

Permette che lo guardi più da vicino?	**May I** have a closer look?
Permette che assaggi l'uva?	**May I** try one of the grapes?
Permette che tiriamo la sveglia fuori dalla scatola?	**May we** take the alarm clock out of its box?
Permette che mia figlia si provi la giacca che è in vetrina?	**Could my daughter** try on the jacket that's in the window?

Here are some key phrases which you may hear when out shopping.

È servito?	Are You being served?
Prego?	Can I help you?
Che taglia porta?	What size are You?
Ha bisogno di una taglia più piccola?	Do You need a smaller size?
Le cerco una taglia più grande?	Shall I look for a larger size for You?
In che colore le piacerebbe?	What colour would You like it in?
Quanto pensava di spendere?	How much were You thinking of spending?
Al momento non l'abbiamo in magazzino.	We don't have any in stock at the moment.
Altro?	Anything else?
È un regalo?	Is it a present for someone?
Le faccio un pacchetto regalo?	Shall I giftwrap it for You?
Purtroppo accettiamo solo contanti.	It's cash only, I'm afraid.
Carta o Bancomat?	Credit or debit card?
Mi spiace, ma non accettiamo carte di credito.	I'm afraid we don't take credit cards.
Una firma, per favore.	Your signature, please.
Deve digitare il codice.	You have to key in your PIN.

Lifestyle Tips

• When entering a shop in Italy you usually greet the shopkeeper or sales assistant by saying **buongiorno** or **buonasera**, depending on the time of day. You say **arrivederci** (*goodbye*) when you leave. It is also customary to greet the checkout operator in a supermarket.

• Be cautious about helping yourself in small shops such as greengrocers or at fruit and vegetable stalls at markets. You'll normally see a sign saying **vietato toccare la merce** (*do not touch the goods*), and you will either be served by the shopkeeper or stallholder or can use **guanti usa e getta** (*disposable gloves*).

• You will have to take a ticket to get a place in the queue at the meat or cheese counters in most supermarkets or bakeries. If you can't see where to get your ticket from, try asking **Dove prendo il numerino?** (*Where do I get a ticket?*).

• The price of some foods, particularly cheese and delicatessen items may be given per **etto** (*one hundred grams*). When buying such things you can ask for **un etto**, or **due etti** etc.

• The first thing a shop assistant, or market stallholder says to a customer is often **Dica!** (*What can I do for you?*), which literally means *Speak!* Stallholders may offer you a taste of their wares, saying **Vuole assaggiare?** and suggest an item which is on special offer – **in offerta** – or offer you **uno sconto** (*a special price*).

Service
with a smile

Un servizio impeccabile! – Excellent service!

The phrases in this unit will help you make sure that, when you're in Italy, you can communicate your needs in natural Italian. You could be at the bank or police station, the hairdresser's, looking for insurance or seeking advice on any other kind of service – the language you need is covered here.

GREETINGS

It is crucial if you want to sound natural in Italian that you greet people correctly. Say **buongiorno** or, later in the day, **buonasera**, to someone you've never met. You can also use **salve**, which is more informal. Say **ciao** to somebody younger and with whom you feel comfortable using the *tu* form.

Good...

Buongiorno!	**Good morning**!
Buonasera!	**Good afternoon**!
Buonasera!	**Good evening**!
Salve, Luigi!	**Hello**, Luigi!
Ciao bella!	**Hello** darling!

BUONO A SAPERSI!
When entering public places or shops, especially in smaller towns and villages, it's usual to greet the shopkeeper and other customers by saying **buongiorno** or **buonasera** and to say **arrivederci** (*goodbye*) when leaving.

When you want to say *goodbye*, use **arrivederci** . To say *See you!*, use **Ci vediamo!** .

See you...!

OK, ti chiamo la settimana prossima. **Ci vediamo**!	OK, I'll give you a ring next week. **See you**!
Ci vediamo tra due settimane!	**See you** in two weeks!
A domani!	**See you tomorrow**!
A questa sera!	**See you tonight**!
A lunedì!	**See you on Monday!**
Ci vediamo alle cinque, allora. **A più tardi**!	5 o'clock then. **See you later**!

BUONO A SAPERSI!

In Italian, if you use **a più tardi** for *see you later*, you expect to see the person later on that day, not just some time in the future. If you mean *see you sometime*, use **ci vediamo** .

Have a good...!

Buona giornata!	**Have a good** day!
Buon fine settimana!	**Have a good** weekend!
Buon divertimento!	**Have a good** time!

TALKING ABOUT YOURSELF

Very often you will need to give someone some personal details and some information about where you're staying and so on. To say what your name is, use **mi chiamo** (*my name is*) and then your name.

My name is...

Mi chiamo Richard Davidson.	**My name is** Richard Davidson.
Mi chiamo Mary Rogers.	**My name is** Mary Rogers.
Mio marito si chiama Peter Brown.	**My husband's name is** Peter Brown.

I'm staying...

Sto in un albergo.	**I'm staying** at a hotel.
Sto in un appartamento qui vicino.	**I'm staying** at an apartment nearby.
Sono ospite di una famiglia.	**I'm staying** with a host family.
Abbiamo affittato una casa.	**We're staying** in a rented house.

My address is...

Abito in Italia. **Il mio indirizzo è** via Mazzini 3, 34100 Trieste.	I live in Italy. **My address is** via Mazzini 3, 34100 Trieste.
Il mio indirizzo permanente **è** 29 Kelvin Close, L3 0QT Liverpool.	**My** permanent **address is** 29 Kelvin Close, L3 0QT Liverpool.
L'indirizzo dell'albergo **è** Hotel Milano, via Segantini 4.	**The address of** my hotel **is** Hotel Milano, via Segantini 4.

To say where you're from and how long you're staying, you can use **sono**. **sono** comes from the verb **essere** (*to be*). For more information on **essere**, see page 282.

I am...

Sono in vacanza.	**I'm** on holiday.
Sono inglese.	**I'm** English.
Sono di Aberdeen, in Scozia.	**I'm from** Aberdeen in Scotland.
Siamo qui per tre settimane.	**We're** here for three weeks.

SAYING WHAT YOU HAVE TO DO

When you're dealing with one kind of service or another, you may want to say that you have to do something in Italian. To do this, you use **devo** (*I have to*) followed by the verb in the infinitive. **devo** comes from the verb **dovere** (*to have to*). For more information on **dovere**, see page 281.

I have to...

Devo prima passare in lavanderia.	**I have to** call in at the dry-cleaner's first.
Devo prendere nota dei particolari del prodotto.	**I have to** take down the details of this product.
Dovrò ricaricare il mio cellulare.	**I'm going to have to** charge my phone.

devo can also be used to say *I must*.

I must...

Devo far stampare le foto.	**I must** get the photos printed.
Devo portare a riparare la macchina fotografica.	**I must** get my camera repaired.
Dobbiamo passare all'agenzia immobiliare per restituire le chiavi.	**We must** call at the estate agent's to return the keys.
Non devo dimenticarmi di prendere appuntamento dall'estetista.	**I mustn't forget to** make an appointment at the beautician's.

I need...

Ho bisogno di un consiglio.	**I need** some advice.
Ho bisogno di ritirare del contante prima di martedì.	**I need to** take out some cash before Tuesday.
Ho bisogno di fare delle fotocopie a colori.	**I need** to make some colour photocopies.
Abbiamo bisogno di parlargli.	**We need** to speak to him.

To say *I don't have to*, you can use **non occorre che** followed by the subjunctive, or **non sono obbligato a** followed by the infinitive. For more information on the use of the subjunctive and the infinitive, see pages 273 and 267.

I don't have to...

Non occorre che vada in banca oggi.	**I don't have to** go to the bank today.
Non occorre che vada in ufficio oggi.	**I don't have to** go to the office today.
Non sono obbligato ad aprire un altro conto immediatamente.	**I don't have to** open another account straightaway.

SAYING WHAT YOU WANT TO DO

To say what you would like to do in Italian, use **vorrei** (*I'd like*). **vorrei** comes from **volere** (*to want*). For more information on **volere**, see page 285.

I'd like...

Vorrei comprare una macchina fotografica digitale.	**I'd like** to buy a digital camera.
Vorrei segnalare un problema.	**I'd like** to report a problem.
Vorrei fissare un appuntamento per tagliarmi i capelli.	**I'd like** to make an appointment to get my hair cut.
Vorrei sapere il tasso di cambio.	**I'd like** to know what the exchange rate is.

desidero or **desidererei** (*I wish*) are polite ways of saying what you want to do. They come from the verb **desiderare** (*to wish*). For more information on –**are** verbs like **desiderare**, see page 268.

I wish...

Desidero fare un versamento.	**I wish** to make a payment.
Desidero cambiare delle sterline in euro.	**I wish** to change pounds into euros.
Desidererei parlare al direttore della banca.	**I wish** to speak to the bank manager.

If you want something to be done for you, you say **voglio far** with the infinitive. For more information on the infinitive, see page 267.

I want to have...

Voglio far trasferire questa somma sul mio conto inglese.	**I want to have** this amount transferred to my British account.
Voglio far reparere la macchina fotografica.	**I want to have** my camera repaired.
Voglio far stampare le mie foto digitali.	**I want to have** my digital photos printed.
Devo far autenticare la firma da un notaio.	**I need to have** the signature authenticated by a notary.

ASKING FOR INFORMATION

When you're asking for information about particular services, you can ask someone if they know something by asking **Sa...?** (*Do You know...?*) or **Saprebbe...?** (*Would You know...?*) followed by **dove** (*where*), **quando** (*when*), **come** (*how*) and so on. **sa** and **saprebbe** come from **sapere** (*to know*).

Do you know...?

Sa dove posso farmi fare un doppione della chiave?	**Do You know** where I can have a second key cut?
Sa quando le arriverà il pezzo di ricambio?	**Do You know** when you'll get the spare part?
Saprebbe dove posso prendere una ricarica per il cellulare?	**Would You happen to know** where I can top up my phone?

You can use **C'è...?** or **Ci sono...?** to ask *Is there...?* and *Are there...?*.

Is there...?

C'è un caffè con wifi in questa zona?	**Is there** café with wi-fi in this area?
C'è un buon parrucchiere in città?	**Is there** a good hairdresser in town?
Ci sono dei computer in biblioteca?	**Are there** computers in the library?

A couple of key questions you'll want to ask when finding out about services are to do with prices, and how long things will take. Use **quanto** to ask these questions.

How much is it...?

Quanto costa un taglio e colpi di sole?	**How much is it** for a cut and highlights?
Quanto costa far sbloccare il mio cellulare?	**How much is it** to have my phone unlocked?
Quanto verrebbe far pulire questa giacca?	**How much would it be** to have this jacket dry-cleaned?

How long does it take...?

Quanto ci mettono ad arrivare i soldi?	**How long does it take** for the money to come through?
Quanto ci mettete a rifare la stanza?	**How long will it take <u>you</u>** to get the room ready?
Quanto tempo ci vuole per aprire un conto in banca?	**How long does it take** to open a bank account?

Use **Come si...?** (*How do you...?*) followed by the present tense to ask how you do something. You can also use **Come si fa a...?** followed by the infinitive. For more information on the infinitive, see page 267.

How do you...?

Come si scrive?	**How do you** spell that?
Come si accende?	**How do you** switch this on?
Come si fa a ingrandire un documento?	**How do you** enlarge a document?
Come si fa ad aprire un conto in banca?	**How do you** open a bank account?
Come si fa a mandare dei soldi in Gran Bretagna?	**How do you** send money to the UK?

If you want to ask when something will be ready or available, use **Quando...?** (*When...?*).

When...?

Quando saranno pronti i documenti?	**When** will the documents be ready?
Quando posso ritirare i biglietti?	**When** can I pick up the tickets?
Quando chiudete?	**When** do you close?
Quando ci può ricevere?	**When** are You free to see us?

To get something done the way you like it, you'll need to say what you'd like and how you want it done. To say what you'd like, you can use **vorrei** (*I'd like*) which come from the verb **volere** (*to want*). For more information on **volere**, see page 285.

I'd like...

Vorrei un modulo per la domanda, per favore.	**I'd like** an application form, please.
Vorrei trasferire dei soldi.	**I'd like to** transfer some money.
Vorrei fissare un appuntamento per lunedì pomeriggio, per favore.	**I'd like to** make an appointment for Monday afternoon, please.
Vorrei dei colpi di sole.	**I'd like** highlights, please.

When asking someone to do something for you, you can use **Può...?** (*Can You...?*). Questions beginning with **Potrebbe...?** (*Could You...?*) sound more polite than ones beginning with **Può...?**, so you may prefer to use this form instead. Both are followed by the verb in the infinitive. **potrebbe** and **può** come from the verb **potere** (*to be able*). For more information on **potere**, see page 284.

Can you...?

Può darmi una ricevuta, per favore?	**Can You** give me a receipt, please?
Mi **può** telefonare quando è riparato?	**Can You** phone me when it's fixed?
Mi **può** fare un preventivo?	**Can You** give me an estimate?
Potrebbe dare un'occhiata alla mia macchina fotografica?	**Could You** have a look at my camera?
Mi **potrebbe** dire se si può riparare, per favore?	**Could You** tell me if it can be repaired, please?

Would you mind...?

Le dispiacerebbe aspettare prima di incassare l'assegno?	**Would You mind** waiting before cashing the cheque?
Le dispiacerebbe darmi una fotocopia del contratto?	**Would You mind** giving me a photocopy of the contract?
Le dispiacerebbe spedirmelo via email?	**Would You mind** sending it to me by email?

Could you possibly...?

Le sarebbe forse possibile ricevermi oggi pomeriggio?	**Could You possibly** see me this afternoon?
Le sarebbe forse possibile trasferire queste foto su un CD?	**Could You possibly** put these photos onto a CD?
Potrebbe forse estendere la garanzia?	**Could You possibly** extend the guarantee?

When you want to find out if something is available, use **Ha...?** or **Avrebbe...?** (*Have You got...?*) to ask someone if they have something. **ha** and **avrebbe** come from the verb **avere** (*to have*). For more information on **avere**, see page 279.

Have you got...?

Ha della documentazione riguardo le vostre polizze di assicurazione?	**Have You got** any documentation about your insurance policies?
Ha il wifi?	**Have You got** wi-fi?
Ha qualcosa per togliere questa macchia?	**Do You have** something to remove this stain?
Avrebbe delle pile AA?	**Do You have** any AA batteries?

Do you sell...?

Vendete pellicole in bianco e nero?	**Do you sell** black and white film?
Vendete prodotti biologici?	**Do you sell** organic products?
Avete lenti a contatto usa e getta?	**Do you have** disposable contact lenses?

You may want to ask for advice or a recommendation. To ask for suggestions, use **Mi consiglia di…?** (*Do You think I should…?*). **consiglia** comes from the verb **consigliare** (*to advise*).

Do you think I should…?

Mi consiglia di cambiare i soldi in banca o in un cambiavalute?	**Do You think I should** change money at a bank or a bureau de change?
Mi consiglia di aprire un conto di risparmio?	**Do You think I should** open a savings account?
Ci consiglia di cambiare le serrature?	**Do You think we should** change the locks?
Cosa **mi consiglia di** fare?	What **do You think I should** do?

Would you recommend…?

Ci **consiglia** questo modello?	**Would You recommend** we get this model?
Ci **consiglia** questo prodotto?	**Would You recommend** this product?
Ci **consiglierebbe di** farci una assicurazione kasko?	**Would you recommend that** we take out comprehensive insurance?

You can use **Dovrei…?** (*Should I…?*) with the infinitive to ask whether you should do something. For more information on the infinitive, see page 267.

Should I…?

Dovrei chiamare l'idraulico?	**Should I** call the plumber?
Dovrei informare la mia banca?	**Should I** inform my bank?
Dovrei chiedere un preventivo?	**Had I better** ask for an estimate?
Cosa **dovrei** fare?	What **should I** do?

MAKING SUGGESTIONS

Occasionally you might want to make a suggestion with regard to a particular service. To do this you can use **potrei** (*I could*). **potrei** comes from the verb **potere** (*to be able*). For more information on **potere**, see page 284.

I could...

Potrei contattare la mia banca in Gran Bretagna.	**I could** contact my bank in the UK.
Potrei spostare l'appuntamento a venerdì.	**I could** change the appointment to Friday.
Potremmo tornare più tardi.	**We could** come back later.

Can we agree on...?

Possiamo accordarci su un prezzo?	**Can we agree on** a price?
Possiamo accordarci su una data?	**Can we agree on** a date?
Ci mettiamo d'accordo su che ora incontrarci?	**Can we agree on** a time to meet up?

MAKING ARRANGEMENTS

To obtain services, you'll need to make arrangements with people. A simple way of asking someone what suits them, is to use **Le va bene se...?** (*Is it okay with You if...?*). **va** comes from the verb **andare**. For more information on **andare**, see page 278.

Is it okay with you if...?

Le va bene se torno alle cinque?	**Is it okay with You if** I come back at five?
Le va bene se passo nel suo ufficio domani?	**Is it okay with You if** I call in at Your office tomorrow?
Le va bene se invio il documento via email?	**Is it okay with You if** I send the document by email?

To discuss what the best arrangement is, you can use **È meglio se...?** (*Would it be best if...?*) or **Sarebbe meglio per lei se...?** (*Would it be better for You if...?*) followed by the verb in the subjunctive. For more information on the subjunctive see page 273.

Would it be best if...?

È meglio se vengo di mattina?	**Would it be best if** I came in the morning?
È meglio se consulto un avvocato?	**Would it be best if** I checked with a laywer?

Would it be better for you if...?

Sarebbe meglio per lei se aspettassimo un po'?	**Would it be better for You if** we waited a little?
Sarebbe meglio per lei se avessimo un accordo scritto?	**Would it be better for You if** we had a written agreement?
Sarebbe meglio per lei se le dessimo un acconto?	**Would it be better for You if** we gave You a deposit?
Sarebbe meglio telefonare nel pomeriggio?	**Would it be better** to phone in the afternoon?

...would be best for me

Per me sarebbe meglio di tutto vederci alle dieci nel suo ufficio.	Ten o'clock in Your office **would be best for me**.
La consegna a domicilio **sarebbe meglio di tutto per me**.	Home delivery **would be best for me**.
Per me andrebbe meglio di tutto un appuntamento nel pomeriggio.	An afternoon appointment **would be best for me**.

TALKING ABOUT YOUR PLANS

In English, we often say *I'm going to* to talk about the future. In Italian, you can use the future tense or the present tense. To learn more about these tenses, see page 271.

I'm going to...

Comprerò una nuova SIM card.	**I'm going to buy** a new SIM card.
Mi informerò presso la mia banca in Gran Bretagna.	**I'm going to ask** my bank in Britain.
La **pagheremo** con un assegno.	**We're going to pay** You by cheque.
Vedo il direttore della mia banca oggi pomeriggio.	**I'm going to see** my bank manager this afternoon.
Vediamo un appartamento questa settimana.	**We're looking at** a flat this week.

Italian speakers often use **ho intenzione di** to say *I intend to*. **ho** comes from the verb **avere** (*to have*). For more information on **avere**, see page 279.

I intend to...

Ho intenzione di trasferirmi qui in modo definitivo.	**I intend to** move here permanently.
Ho intenzione di aprire un nuovo conto.	**I intend to** open a new account.
Ho intenzione di comprare una macchina fotografica più sofisticata.	**I intend to** buy a more sophisticated camera.

I'm hoping to...

Spero di ricevere i documenti la settimana prossima.	**I'm hoping to** receive the documents next week.
Spero di finire i lavori entro dicembre.	**I'm hoping to** get the work finished by December.
Speriamo di poter traslocare prima possibile.	**We're hoping to** move in as soon as possible.

You can use **Ha intenzione di...?** (*Do You intend to...?*) to ask people if they're going to do something. **ha** comes from the verb **avere** (*to have*). For more information on **avere**, see page 279.

Do you intend to...?

Ha intenzione di cambiare la lente?	**Do You intend to** change the lens?
Ha intenzione di mettere in conto la manodopera?	**Do You intend to** charge for labour?
Ha intenzione di lasciare gli attrezzi qua?	**Are You planning to** leave your tools here?

To ask what someone is going to do, use **Cosa ha intenzione di...?** Or **Cosa intende...?** (*What are You going to...?*) followed by the infinitive. For questions asking when or how somebody is going to do something, just replace **cosa** with **quando** (*when*), **come** (*how*) and so on.

What are you going to...?

Cosa ha intenzione di dire all'assicurazione?	**What are You going to** tell the insurance company?
Cosa intende fare?	**What are You going to** do?
Quando ha intenzione di finire i lavori?	**When are You going to** finish the work?
Come intende risarcirmi?	**How are You going to** compensate me?

SAYING WHAT YOU LIKE, DISLIKE, PREFER

To say what you like, use **mi piace** (I like) with singular nouns and **mi piacciono** for plural nouns. To say what you don't like, use **non mi piace** or **non mi piacciono** (I don't like).

I like...

Mi piace avere le foto su un CD.	I **like** my photos on CD.
Mi piace tenere i capelli corti.	I **like** to keep my hair short.
Mi piace molto andare dalla manicure.	I really **like** getting my nails done.
Mi piacciono i colpi di sole.	I **like** highlights.

I don't like...

Non mi piace avere addosso troppi contanti.	I **don't like** having too much cash on me.
Veramente **non mi piace** lasciare la macchina in officina.	I **don't** really **like** leaving my car at the garage.
Non mi piacciono i lettini solari.	I **don't like** sunbeds.
Non sopporto questa suoneria.	I **can't stand** this ringtone.

If you want to say what you prefer, use **preferisco** (I prefer). To say that you prefer A to B, use **preferisco A a B** or **preferisco A piuttosto che B**. **preferisco** comes from the verb **preferire**. For more information on **-ire** verbs like **preferire**, see page 268.

I prefer...

Preferisco un contratto scritto.	I **prefer** a written contract.
Preferisco pagare a rate.	I **prefer** to pay in instalments.
Preferiamo non firmare nulla per ora.	**We prefer not** to sign anything for now.
Preferisco le foto in bianco e nero **a** quelle a colori.	I **prefer** black and white photos **to** colour ones.
Preferisco avere un contratto **piuttosto che** usare una scheda.	I **prefer** to have a contract **rather than** using top-up cards.

Use **preferirei che** (*I'd rather*) followed by the verb in the subjunctive to say that you'd rather someone did something. For more information on the subjunctive, see page 273.

I'd rather...

Preferirei che mi rimborsasse.	**I'd rather** You gave me my money back.
Preferirei che mi spedisse la pratica per posta.	**I'd rather** You sent me the file by post.
Preferirei che ci telefonasse prima di venire.	**I'd rather** You phoned before dropping in.

LISTEN OUT FOR

Here are some key phrases which you are likely to hear when obtaining services.

Prego, desidera?	Can I help You?
Sarà pronto domani.	It'll be ready tomorrow.
Non è ancora pronto.	It's not ready yet.
Ha lo scontrino?	Do You have your receipt?
Ha bisogno di una ricevuta?	Do You need a receipt?
Ha un documento d'identità?	Have You got some identification?
A che ora le andrebbe meglio?	What time would suit You best?
Ha un appuntamento?	Have You got an appointment?
Richiami domani, per favore.	Please ring back tomorrow.
Come vuole pagare?	How would You like to pay?
A chi tocca?	Who's next?
Mi dispiace, siamo chiusi il lunedì.	Sorry, we are closed on Mondays.
Deve andare all'altro sportello.	You need to go to the other counter.
Magari telefoni prima di venire di persona.	It may be best to phone before coming in person.

Lifestyle Tips

• When getting things done, you'll need to to know about **l'orario di apertura** (*opening times*). Opening times vary throughout Italy but shops and businesses such as hairdresser's, dry cleaner's and so on usually open at around nine in the morning and close at seven in the evening. Many public offices close at lunchtime, around one, with one day of **orario continuato** (*all-day opening*). Banks often close at one thirty and reopen for one hour in afternoon.

• In the past it was common to take a very long lunch break (with people working proportionately later in the evening) but increasingly people work **l'orario continuato** (*all-day opening*), with just a short break for lunch.

• Except in bigger towns, most businesses close on Sundays, and many close on Mondays too, so that employees can have a two-day break.

• When you walk along shopping streets in August you'll see many shops and restaurants with a sign saying **chiuso per ferie** (*closed for the holidays*). The middle of August is the peak time for people to take holidays, and businesses are often closed then for two weeks.

• Italians use a debit card called **la carta Bancomat** more than credit cards – but credit cards are now much more widely accepted than in the past. When you hand over your credit card you may be asked **Carta o Bancomat?** to which you should reply **Carta** (*credit card*). The next thing you hear may be **Può digitare il codice?** (*Type in your PIN!*).

• In Italy banks have security doors. To get in, you press a button marked **Premere per entrare** (*Press to enter*), and the outer door opens, letting you into a glass cabin, where you wait for the inner door to open.

• If you want to make an appointment at the hairdresser's and so forth, the word for an *appointment* is **appuntamento**. For instance, you could say **vorrei fissare un appuntamento per giovedì mattina** (*I'd like to make an appointment for Thursday morning*).

• By law in Italy **lo scontrino** (a *receipt*) has to be given to a customer who has paid for goods or services, and receipts have to be accepted. This is why, if you are leaving a counter without picking up your receipt, you will always be reminded to do so.

Ouch!

Tanti auguri di pronta guarigione! – Get well soon!

If you happen to be taken ill, have an accident, get toothache or need some kind of medical advice while in Italy, the phrases in this section will give you the confidence to talk to a doctor, dentist or pharmacist to help you get what you need.

DESCRIBING THE PROBLEM

You may find yourself in a situation where you have to describe what the problem is. To do this, you can generally use **ho**. This comes from the verb **avere** (*to have*). For more information on **avere**, see page 279.

I've got a...

Ho febbre.	**I've got** a temperature.
Ho il raffreddore.	**I've got** a cold.
Ho la pressione alta.	**I have** high blood pressure.
Ho tachicardia.	**I've been having** palpitations.
Non so **cos'ho**.	I don't know **what's wrong with me**.
Mio figlio **soffre di** mal di cuore.	My son **has** a heart condition.

I've got a ...ache

Ho mal di testa.	**I've got a** head**ache**.
Ho mal di stomaco.	**I've got** stomach**ache**.
Ha mal di denti.	**She's got** tooth**ache**.
Ho mal di schiena.	**My** back **is sore**.
Mi fa male qui.	**It hurts** here.

I feel...

Mi sento sempre stanco.	**I feel** tired all the time.
Mi sento malissimo.	**I feel** awful.
Adesso **mi sento** meglio.	**I'm feeling** better now.
Ieri **mi sentivo** bene.	**I felt** fine yesterday.

SAYING WHAT HAPPENED

If you've had some kind of accident, you will probably need to explain what happened. You can use **ho** or **sono** followed by the past participle. **Ho** and **sono** come from the verbs **avere** (*to have*) and **essere** (*to be*). For more information on these verbs and on the past tense, see pages 279, 282 and 269.

I've...

Ho avuto un incidente.	**I've had** an accident.
Ho sbattuto la testa.	**I've bumped** my head.
Sono caduto dalle scale.	**I fell down** the stairs.
Mi è saltata un'otturazione.	**I've lost** a filling.
Si è scottata sulla stufa.	**She burnt herself** on the heater.

I've never...

Non ho mai avuto un mal di testa così forte.	**I've never had** such a bad headache.
Non ha mai avuto un attacco.	**He's never had** a fit before.
Non sono mai stata così male.	**I've never felt** so ill.
Non mi era mai successo.	**It's never happened to me before**.

You may be unlucky enough to have had a more serious accident. To say that you have broken something, use **mi sono rotto...** or, if you are a woman, **mi sono rotta...** (*I've broken...*).

I've broken...

Mi sono rotto la clavicola l'anno scorso.	**I broke** my collarbone last year.
Si è rotto una gamba.	**He's broken** his leg.
Si è rotta un dente.	**She's broken** a tooth.
Credo di **essermi rotta** il braccio.	I think **I've broken** my arm.
Mi sono slogato la caviglia.	**I've sprained** my ankle.

BUONO A SAPERSI!
Italian speakers say *I've broken a leg* or *the ankle* and so on instead of *I have broken my leg* or *my ankle* and so on.

ASKING FOR INFORMATION

When you need information you may have to get someone's attention in order to ask them a question. To do this you can use either **scusi** or **mi scusi**. You can use **C'è...?** or **Ci sono...?** to ask *Is there...?* or *Are there...?*.

Is there...?

Scusi, **c'è** un ospedale qui vicino?	Excuse me, **is there** a hospital near here?
Ci sono farmacie di turno qui vicino?	**Are there** any pharmacies open near here?
Sa se **c'è** un dentista in questa zona?	Do You know if **there's** a dentist in this area?
Scusi, **dove posso trovare** un medico?	Excuse me, **where can I find** a doctor?
Mi scusi, **dove posso trovare** un pronto soccorso?	Excuse me please, **where can I find** an A&E department?

When you need an explanation of what something is exactly, or what it's for, use **Cos'è...?** (*What is...?*) or **Cosa sono...?** (*What are...?*). For other questions asking for information, use **Che...?** (*What...?*) or **Quale...?** (*Which...?*).

What is...?

Cos'è questa medicina?	**What is** this medicine?
Cosa sono queste compresse?	**What are** these tablets?
Per cosa sono queste compresse?	**What are** these tablets **for**?
Che numero si fa per chiamare un'ambulanza?	**What's** the number to call for an ambulance?
Qual è l'indirizzo dell'ospedale?	**What's** the address of the hospital?

Which...?

In **quale** via si trova la clinica?	**Which** street is the clinic in?
Mi può dire in **quale** reparto è?	Can you tell me **which** ward she's in?
Con **quale** dottore posso prendere appuntamento?	**Which** doctor can I get an appointment with?
Quale è meglio per le punture d'insetti?	**Which** is best for insect bites?

In order to get more specific information, you may need to ask questions such as **Come...?** (*How...?*) or **Quando...?** (*When...?*).

How...?

Come si fa a prendere appuntamento con il dentista?	**How** do you make an appointment with the dentist?
Come va presa questa medicina?	**How** do you take this medicine?
Come si fa per iscriversi al Servizio Sanitario Nazionale?	**How** do we register with Social Security?

When...?

Quando devo fare l'iniezione?	**When** do I have to have the injection?
Quando viene il medico?	**When** is the doctor coming?
Quando comincia l'orario delle visite?	**When** does visiting time start?
Quando devo prendere le pasticche?	**When** do I have to take the tablets?
A che ora apre l'ambulatorio?	**What time** does the doctor's surgery open?

If you want to ask *Is it...?*, you can start questions just with **È...?**
(*Is it...?*).

Is it...?

È grave?	**Is it** serious?
È contagioso?	**Is it** infectious?

Is the...?

È lontano l'ospedale?	**Is the** hospital far?
È aperto di pomeriggio il poliambulatorio?	**Is the** health centre open in the afternoon?

BUONO A SAPERSI!
When you want to ask *Is the...?* in Italian you put the thing
you're asking about (for example, hospital, health centre) last.

ASKING FOR THINGS

When you want to find out if something is available, for
example, medication or medical help, use **Ha...?** (*Have You got...?*) or
Avete...? (*Have you got...?*). They both come from the verb
avere (*to have*). For more information on **avere**, see page 279.

Have you got...?

Ha qualcosa per il mal di testa?	**Have You got** anything for a headache?
Ha qualcosa per la febbre da fieno?	**Have You got** anything for hay fever?
Avete un numero di telefono per le emergenze?	**Do you have** an emergency telephone number?
Avete tachipirina per bambini?	**Do you have** infant paracetamol?

If you want to ask for something in Italian, use **Mi dà...?** (*Can I have...?*). **dà** comes from the verb **dare** (*to give*). For more information on **dare**, see page 280.

Can I have...?

Mi dà un appuntamento per domani, per favore?	**Can I have** an appointment for tomorrow, please?
Mi dà una confezione di aspirina, per favore?	**Can I have** a packet of aspirins, please?
Mi dà una fascia di ricambio?	**Can I have** a spare bandage?

Can I...?

Posso vedere il dentista stamattina?	**Can I** see the dentist this morning?
Posso parlare con un pediatra adesso?	**Can I** talk to a paediatrician right away?
Posso bere alcolici con questa medicina?	**Can I** drink alcohol with this medicine?
Quando **possiamo** passare a prendere i risultati?	When **can we** get the results?

If you are asking someone whether they can do something for you, you should use **Può...?** (*Can You...?*) or **Potrebbe...?** (*Could You...?*). **può** and **potrebbe** come from the verb **potere** (*to be able*). For more information on **potere**, see page 284.

Can you...?

Mi **può** prescrivere qualcosa per il mal d'orecchi, per favore?	**Can You** prescribe something for earache, please?
Può mandare un'ambulanza immediatamente?	**Can You** send an ambulance immediately?
Può chiamare un medico, per favore?	**Can You** call a doctor, please?
Può darmi qualche cosa per il bambino che sta mettendo i denti?	**Can You give me** something for my baby as he's teething?

Could you...?

Ci **potrebbe** portare all'ospedale più vicino?	**Could You** take us to the nearest hospital?
Potrebbe controllarmi la pressione?	**Could You** check my blood pressure?
Mi potrebbe dare un appuntamento per una visita di controllo?	**Would You mind** giving me an appointment for a checkup?
Le dispiacerebbe trovarmi un'infermiera che parli inglese?	**Would You mind** finding me an English-speaking nurse?

SAYING WHAT YOU WANT TO DO

If you want to say what you'd like to do in Italian, use **vorrei** (*I'd like*). **vorrei** comes from the verb **volere** (*to want*). For more information on **volere**, see page 285.

I'd like to...

Vorrei prendere appuntamento con il medico.	**I'd like** to make an appointment with the doctor.
Vorrei vedere un dentista subito.	**I'd like** to see a dentist straightaway.
Vorrei comprare qualcosa per la tosse.	**I'd like** to buy something for a cough.
Vorrei farmi fare un'otturazione.	**I'd like** to have a tooth filled.

I'd rather...

Preferirei andare in una clinica privata.	**I'd rather** go to a private hospital.
Preferirei vedere una dottoressa **piuttosto che** un dottore.	**I'd rather** see a female doctor **than** a male one.
Preferirei prendere delle pasticche **piuttosto che** fare un'iniezione.	**I'd rather** take tablets **than** have an injection.
Preferiamo i rimedi naturali.	**We prefer** natural remedies.

In Italian you can tell somebody what you need by using **ho bisogno di** (*I need*).

I need...

Ho bisogno della pillola del giorno dopo.	**I need** the morning-after pill.
Ho bisogno della ricetta?	**Do I need** a prescription?
Abbiamo bisogno di un medico che possa venire qui.	**We need** a doctor who can come here.
Dobbiamo chiamare urgentemente un'ambulanza.	**We** urgently **need** to call an ambulance.

MAKING SUGGESTIONS

You may wish to make a suggestion in Italian. One way of doing this is to use **potremmo** (*we could*). This comes from the verb **potere** (*to be able*). For more information on **potere**, see page 284.

We could...

Potremmo chiedere in farmacia.	**We could** ask in the chemist's.
Potremmo prendere degli antidolorifici in farmacia.	**We could** get some painkillers at the chemist's.
Potremmo telefonare alla famiglia.	**We could** phone his family.

Another way of making suggestions in Italian is to ask **Perché non...?** (*Why don't...?*).

Why don't...?

Perché non chiamiamo un medico?	**Why don't** we call a doctor?
Perché non chiediamo un appuntamento col cardiologo?	**Why don't** we ask for an appointment with the heart specialist?
Perché non chiediamo come vanno presi gli antibiotici?	**Why don't** we ask how the antibiotics should be taken?
Perché non spiega il problema al medico?	**Why don't** You explain the problem to the doctor?

Here are some key phrases which you are likely to hear at the doctor's or the hospital.

Come sta?	How are You?
Cosa succede?	What seems to be the problem?
Ha febbre?	Have You got a temperature?
Da quanto si sente così?	How long have You been feeling like this?
Soffre di altre malattie?	Do You have any existing medical conditions?
Prende altri farmaci?	Are You on any other medication?
Soffre di nausea?	Do You feel sick?
Le gira la testa?	Do You feel dizzy?
Dove le fa male?	Where does it hurt?
Se vuole togliersi la camicia.	Would You mind taking off your shirt?
Può rivestirsi.	You can get dressed.
Non beva alcolici insieme a questo farmaco.	Don't drink alcohol while you're taking this medicine.
Riempia questo modulo, per favore.	Please fill in this form.
Mi dà gli estremi della sua assicurazione medica?	Can I have your medical insurance details?
I risultati sono buoni.	The results are fine.
Mi faccia sapere se i sintomi persistono.	Let me know if the symptoms don't go away.

Lifestyle Tips

• If you think you need a doctor, you can go to **il Pronto Soccorso** – the A&E department of a hospital.

• If you visit a doctor or dentist, you may be given **una ricetta** (*a prescription*) to take to **la farmacia** (*the chemist's*). The prescription charge is called **il ticket**. Not everyone has to pay a prescription charge – pensioners, people on low incomes and the unemployed, for instance, are exempt.

• When going to a health professional in Italy, you will be asked for your **tessera europea d'assicurazione malattia** – your *European Health Insurance Card* – which now replaces the E111 form. Like its predecessor, this card aims to make access to healthcare in any EU country hassle-free for all citizens of EU member states. It also enables you to reclaim medical costs.

• In Italy, **le farmacie** (*chemist's*) are easily recognizable from a distance thanks to the **croce verde** (*green cross*) sign displayed outside them. You can ask pharmacists about minor health problems – they are qualified to give advice and can dispense some medicines without a doctor's prescription. They can also refer you to a local doctor.

• There is always a **farmacia di turno** (*duty chemist's*) open when other chemists are shut. Its address will be prominently displayed outside all the other local pharmacies as well as in local newspapers.

• In an emergency phone 118 and ask for **ambulanza**.

• As in most other European countries, tough anti-smoking legislation has banned smoking in the workplace, and in bars and restaurants.

• In Italy when someone sneezes, you can say **Salute!** (*Bless you!* or literally *To your health!*).

Help!

Niente paura! – Don't worry!

If you find yourself in a situation in Italy in which you need help, for example if you break down, are involved in an accident or are robbed, or even if you simply can't get the heating to come on, the phrases in this unit will give the language to help you cope with confidence.

DESCRIBING THE PROBLEM

If you are asking somebody for help of some kind, you will need to be able to describe what the problem is. Use **c'è** and **ci sono** to say *there is* and *there are*, and **non c'è** and **non ci sono** to say *there isn't any* or *there aren't any*.

There is...

C'è odore di gas nella mia stanza.	**There's** a smell of gas in my room.
Ci sono scarafaggi nell'appartamento.	**There are** cockroaches in the apartment.
Non c'è sapone in bagno.	**There isn't any** soap in the bathroom.
Non ci sono asciugamani nella stanza.	**There aren't any** towels in my room.
C'è stato un incidente.	**There's been** an accident.

You may need to explain exactly what the problem is – you can often use **ho** (*I've got*) or **non ho** (*I haven't got*). **ho** comes from the verb **avere** (*to have*). For more information on **avere**, see page 279.

I've got...

Ho un problema.	**I've got** a problem.
Ho una ruota a terra.	**I've got** a flat tyre.
Non ho una pompa.	**I haven't got** a pump.
Siamo stati derubati e **non abbiamo** abbastanza soldi per tornare a casa.	We've been robbed and **we haven't got** enough money to get back home.

The problem you are having may be because you are not able to do something. In Italian you can use **non riesco a** to say what you can't do.

I can't...

Non riesco a far partire la macchina.	**I can't** get the car to start.
Non riesco a far funzionare boiler – è rotto.	**I can't** get the boiler to work – it's broken.
Non riusciamo ad aprire la porta della camera da letto.	**We can't** open the door to the bedroom.

It may be, however, that you do not know how to do something. In Italian you would use **non so** to talk about what you don't know how to do.

I can't...

Non so cambiare una gomma.	**I can't** change a tyre.
Non so guidare.	**I can't** drive.
Non so parlare italiano molto bene.	**I can't** speak Italian very well.

If you want to say that you don't understand something, use **non capisco**.

I don't understand...

Non capisco cosa intende.	**I don't understand** what You mean.
Mi dispiace, ma **non capisco** le istruzioni.	I'm sorry but **I don't understand** the instructions.
Non capiamo perché non funziona.	**We can't understand** why it's not working.

SAYING WHAT HAPPENED

You will probably need to explain to somebody what happened. You can use **ho** followed by the past participle. **ho** and **sono** come from the verbs **avere** (*to have*) and **essere** (*to be*). For more information on forming the past tense, see page 269.

I have...

Ho perso il passaporto.	**I've** lost my passport.
Ho avuto un incidente.	**I've** had an accident.
La mia valigia **non è** arrivata.	My suitcase **hasn't** arrived.
Ci **siamo** chiusi fuori dall'appartamento.	**We've** locked ourselves out of the apartment.
Siamo in panne.	**We've** broken down.
Abbiamo finito la benzina.	**We've** run out of petrol.

I've been...

Mi hanno aggredita.	**I've been** mugged.
Mi hanno svaligiato la casa.	**I've been** burgled.
Hanno forzato la serratura della mia macchina.	My car**'s been** broken into.
Mi **hanno** scippato.	My bag**'s been** snatched.
Ci hanno fatto pagare troppo.	**We've been** overcharged.

DESCRIBING PEOPLE AND THINGS

If you have some kind of problem in Italy you may need to be able to give a description of someone or something. To do this you can simply use **è** (*it is*) or **sono** (*they are*) followed by an adjective. **è** and **sono** come from the verb **essere** (*to be*). For more information on **essere**, see page 282.

It is...

È una macchina nera sportiva.	**It's** a black sports car.
È uno smartphone.	**It's** a smartphone.
Sono documenti molto importanti.	**They're** very important documents.
La borsa **è** rossa.	The bag**'s** red.
La valigia **è** verde ed ha le ruote.	The suitcase **is** green and has wheels.
Il mio portafoglio **è** di pelle.	My wallet**'s made of** leather.

You may also be asked to give more details about yourself or somebody else, for example, age, hair colour and so on. To do this, you can use the verb **avere** (*to have*) or, sometimes, **essere** (*to be*). For more information on **avere** and **essere**, see pages 279 and 282.

He's got...

Ha i capelli biondi corti.	**He's got** short blond hair.
Ha i capelli castani.	**She's got** brown hair.
Ha gli occhi verdi.	**She's got** green eyes.
Entrambi **hanno** gli occhi marroni.	**They** both **have** brown eyes.

BUONO A SAPERSI!

Remember that in Italian you use the article before the part of the body you are talking about, for example, **Ho i capelli corti** (*I have short hair*), **Ha le gambe lunghe** (*She has long legs*).

He's...

Ha cinque anni.	**He's** five.
Ha otto anni.	**She's** eight.
Ho trent'anni.	**I'm** thirty.
È alto e di aspetto piuttosto giovanile.	**He's** tall and quite young-looking.
È piuttosto magra.	**She's** rather thin.

She's wearing...

Indossa jeans e una maglietta verde.	**She's wearing** jeans and a green T-shirt.
Ha un vestito arancione.	**She's wearing** an orange dress.
Indossava pantaloni neri.	**He was wearing** black trousers.

ASKING FOR INFORMATION

When you need information you may have to get someone's attention in order to ask them a question. To do this you can use either **scusi** or **mi scusi**. If you are asking somebody younger, use **scusa** or **scusami**.

Excuse me...?

Scusi, c'è un'officina nei paraggi?	**Excuse me**, is there a garage around here?
Mi scusi, ci sono alberghi qui vicino?	**Excuse me**, are there any hotels near here?
Scusa, c'è un elettricista in questa zona?	**Excuse me**, is there an electrician in this area?
Scusami, hai l'ora?	**Excuse me**, do you have the time?

In order to obtain specific information, for example what to choose, how to do something, when something will happen or how much it will cost, you may want to ask **Quale...?** or **Che...?** (*Which...?*), **Come...?** (*How...?*), **Quando...?** (*When...?*) or **Quanto...?** (*How much...?*).

Which...?

Quale idraulico mi consiglia?	**Which** plumber do You recommend?
Quali documenti devo presentare?	**Which** documents do I need to show?
Scusi, **che** numero si fa per chiamare la polizia?	Excuse me, **what** number do I dial for the police?

How...?

Come facciamo a denunciare un furto?	**How** do we report a theft?
Come si fa a prendere la linea esterna?	**How** do I get an outside line?
Scusi, **come** si arriva all'officina?	Excuse me, **how** do we get to the garage?
Mi può dire **come** facciamo a recuperare la valigia?	Can You tell me **how** we can get the suitcase back?

When...?

Quando viene a riparare il condizionatore d'aria?	**When** will You come to fix the air conditioning?
Quando recapitate la valigia?	**When** will <u>you</u> deliver the suitcase?
Quando posso portare la macchina in officina?	**When** can I bring the car in?
Sa **quando** potremo vedere l'avvocato?	Do You know **when** we'll be able to see the lawyer?

How much...?

Quanto costerà far riparare la moto?	**How much** will it cost to repair the motorbike?
Mi può dire **quanto** mi costa ripararlo?	Can You tell me **how much** You will charge to fix this?
Quanto costa l'iscrizione?	**How much** are the registration fees?

ASKING FOR THINGS

If you want to ask for something in Italian, use **Mi dà...?** or **Mi può dare...?** (*Can I have...?*). Use **mi dai** or **mi puoi dare** with people you call *tu*. **dà** and **dai** come from the verb **dare** (*to give*). For more information on **dare**, see page 280.

Can I have...?

Mi dà un'altra coperta, per favore?	**Can I have** another blanket, please?
Mi può dare un altro modulo?	**Can I have** another form?
Mi dai il tuo numero di telefono?	**Can I have** your phone number?
Mi puoi dare il cellulare per una chiamata urgente?	**Can I borrow** your mobile to make an urgent call?

If you want to find out if something is available, use **Ha...?** or, more informally, **Hai...?** (*Do you have...?*). They both come from the verb **avere** (*to have*). For more information on **avere**, see page 279.

Do you have...?

Mi scusi, **ha** questo documento in inglese?	Excuse me, **do You have** this document in English?
Scusi, **ha** un opuscolo con informazioni su questa zona?	Excuse me, **do You have** a brochure about this area?
Hai dei cavi per la batteria?	**Do you have** jump leads?

If you are asking someone whether they can do something for you, you should use **Può...?** (*Can You...?*) or **Potrebbe...?** (*Could You...?*). Use **puoi** or **potresti** with people you call *tu*. They all come from the verb **potere** (*to be able*). For more information on **potere**, see page 284.

Can you...?

Può chiamare la polizia?	**Can You** call the police?
Potrebbe mostrarmi come funziona la doccia?	**Could You** show me how the shower works?
Mi potrebbe fare un preventivo, per favore?	**Could You** give me an estimate, please?
Mi **puoi** aiutare, per favore?	**Can you** help me, please?
Potresti consigliarmi un elettricista?	**Could you** recommend an electrician?

SAYING WHAT YOU WANT TO DO

You may need to be able to say what you want or what you'd like to do in Italian. To do this, you can use either **voglio** (*I want*) or **vorrei** (*I'd like*). They both come from the verb **volere** (*to want*). For more information on **volere**, see page 285.

I want to...

Voglio denunciare un furto.	**I want to** report a theft.
Voglio parlare con un avvocato.	**I want to** speak to a lawyer.
Vorrei telefonare.	**I'd like to** make a call.

I don't want to...

Non voglio restare in questa stanza.	**I don't want to** stay in this room.
Non voglio lasciare qua la macchina.	**I don't want to** leave my car here.
Non vogliamo andare in albergo senza i bagagli.	**We don't want to** go to the hotel without our luggage.

If you want to say what your preference is, use **preferirei** (*I'd rather*), from the verb **preferire**. For more information on **-ire** verbs like **preferire**, see page 268.

I'd rather...

Preferirei prendere un avvocato che parli l'inglese.	**I'd rather** use a lawyer who can speak English.
Preferirei stare al piano terra **piuttosto che** al primo piano.	**I'd rather** be on the ground floor **than** on the first floor.
Preferiremmo leggere i documenti in inglese, se possibile.	**We'd rather** read the documents in English, if possible.

SAYING WHAT YOU HAVE TO DO

You may want to say what you have to do in Italian. Use **devo** (*I have to*) followed by the verb in the infinitive. **devo** comes from the verb **dovere** (*to have to*). For more information on **dovere** and the infinitive, see pages 281 and 267.

I have to...

Devo andare all'ambasciata britannica.	**I have to** go to the British embassy.
Devo ricaricare il cellulare.	**I have to** charge my phone.
Devo parlare con un avvocato.	**I must** speak to a lawyer.

You can also use **ho bisogno di** (*I need*) with the verb in the infinitive.

I need...

Ho bisogno di un nuovo pneumatico.	**I need** a new tyre.
Ho bisogno di fare una telefonata.	**I need** to make a call.
Ho bisogno di chiamare un elettricista.	**I need** to call an electrician.

MAKING SUGGESTIONS

You may wish to make a suggestion to your Italian-speaking acquaintances. One way of doing this is to use **potremmo** (*we could*). **potremmo** comes from the verb **potere** (*to be able*). For more information on **potere**, see page 284.

We could...

Potremmo chiamare un fabbro.	**We could** call a locksmith.
Potremmo chiedere a qualcuno il numero di un idraulico.	**We could** ask someone for the number of a plumber.
Potremmo sempre andare all'ufficio oggetti smarriti.	**We could** always go to the lost property office.

To suggest doing something, you can also use **E se...?** (*How about...?*) followed by a verb in the imperfect subjunctive. For more information on the subjunctive, see page 273.

How about...?

E se parlassimo con un avvocato?	**How about** talking to a lawyer?
E se chiamassimo il suo consolato?	**How about** calling Your consulate?
E se segnalassimo il guasto alla portineria?	**How about** reporting the fault to reception?

Another way of making suggestions is to ask **Perché non...?** (*Why don't...?*).

Why don't...?

Perché non chiediamo aiuto ai vicini?	**Why don't** we ask the neighbours for help?
Perché non chiamiamo la portineria?	**Why don't** we call reception?
Perché non va in commissariato a denunciare il furto?	**Why don't** You go to the police station to report the theft?

TALKING ABOUT YOUR PLANS

In English we often say *I'm going to* to talk about the future. To say that you're going to do something in Italian you can use the future tense or often simply the present tense.

I'm going to...

Chiamerò l'officina.	**I'm going to phone** the garage.
Chiamo soccorso col cellulare.	**I'm going to call** for help on my mobile.
Chiameremo un elettricista per riparare l'impianto elettrico.	**We're going to phone** an electrician to fix the wiring.
Ci chiamate quando è pronta?	Will **you** call us when it's ready?

You can also express your intentions by saying **Ho intenzione di...** (*I intend to...*) followed by the infinitive.

I intend to...

Ho intenzione di denunciare il furto alla polizia.	**I intend to** report the theft to the police.
Ho intenzione di parlare con un avvocato.	**I intend to** talk to a lawyer.
Ha intenzione di rimorchiare la nostra macchina?	Are **You going to** tow our car away?
Avete intenzione di venire oggi?	Are **you** going to come out today?

LISTEN OUT FOR

Here are some key phrases which you are likely to hear when you have some kind of problem.

Qual è il problema?	What's the problem?
Che è successo?	What happened?
Mi dà gli estremi dell'assicurazione?	Can I have Your insurance details?
Cosa hanno rubato?	What's been stolen?
Mi date il vostro indirizzo, per favore?	Can I have your address, please?
Di dove siete?	Where are you from?
Dove alloggia?	Where are You staying?
Favorisca la patente, prego.	Can I have Your driving licence?
C'erano testimoni?	Were there any witnesses?
Compili questo modulo, per cortesia.	Please fill in this form.
È previsto un addebito per l'intervento.	There'll be a call-out charge.

Lifestyle Tips

• If you lose your passport or if you have to report a crime such as a car theft or mugging to the police in Italy, you'll need to go to the **commissariato di polizia** or the **questura** (*police station*) where you'll have to **fare una denuncia** (*file a report*).

• In Italy there are two police forces: the **polizia di stato**, and the **carabinieri**, who are soldiers and have a military-style uniform. The functions of the two forces are complementary, and you can seek help from either.

• The **vigili urbani** are similar to traffic wardens – they direct traffic and hand out parking fines. The traffic police are the **polizia stradale**.

• The general emergency phone number in Italy is 113: it gets you through to the **polizia**. There are other emergency numbers for specific services: dial 112 for the **carabinieri**, 115 for the **vigili del fuoco** (*fire brigade*), 116 for **soccorso stradale** (*roadside assistance*) and 118 for an **ambulanza** (*ambulance*). On motorways there are emergency phones every 2km. One has a green spanner symbol for breakdowns, and the other has a red cross for a medical emergency.

• As in the UK, if you're driving around Italy, you'll need to be careful where you park if you want to avoid paying **una contravvenzione** or **multa** (*a fine*) or having your car clamped or towed away by the **carro attrezzi** (*tow truck*) and then having to get it back at great expense from the **depositeria** (*pound*). Make sure you look at any signs and ask **Cosa vuol dire quel cartello?** (*What does this sign mean?*) if you don't understand them.

Getting in touch

Pronto, chi parla? – Who's calling please?

Talking on the phone is one of the hardest things to do in a foreign language, because you can't see the person you're speaking to, and therefore you can't rely on body language and facial expressions to help you understand and communicate. This unit gives you the language to overcome this and to help you to sound natural and confident when speaking on the phone in Italian. It also covers other means of communication, whether it's email, texting, social media or the good old post.

MAKING A TELEPHONE CALL

The Italian expressions for calling someone are **telefonare a qualcuno** (*to phone somebody*) and **dare un colpo di telefono a qualcuno** (*to give somebody a ring*). The second one is less formal, just as it is in English. If you want to tell someone that you need to make a phone call, use **devo** (*I need to*). **devo** comes from the verb **dovere** (*to have to*). For more information on **dovere**, see page 281.

I need to...

Devo fare una telefonata.	**I need to** make a call.
Devo telefonare a mia moglie.	**I need to** phone my wife.
Devo dare un colpo di telefono al mio amico.	**I need to** give my friend a ring.
Non scordarti che **devi** richiamare la mamma stasera.	Don't forget **you need to** call your mum back tonight.
Dobbiamo chiamare l'Inghilterra.	**We need** to call England.

If you want to ask if someone has something, for example a telephone number, use **Ha...?** (*Do You have...?*), **Hai...?** (*Do you have...?*) or **Avete...?** (*Do you have...?*).

Do you have...?

Ha il numero di casa della signora Kay, per favore?	**Do You have** Mrs Kay's home number, please?
Hai un numero di cellulare?	**Do you have** a mobile number?
Avete un indirizzo email?	**Do you have** an email address?

You can ask for something such as a telephone number in Italian by using **Che...?** or **Quale...?** (*What...?*), or **Qual è...?** (*What's...?*).

What...?

Quale linea posso usare per telefonare?	**What** line can I use to make a call?
Che numero faccio per prendere la linea esterna?	**What** number do I dial to get an outside line?

What's...?

Qual è il suo numero di telefono?	**What's** her phone number?
Qual è il numero del pronto soccorso?	**What's** the number for A&E?
Qual è il prefisso per l'Irlanda?	**What's** the dialling code for Ireland?

Once you've made the call and someone answers, you will need to say *hello* and tell them who's calling. To do this use **Pronto?** (literally meaning *ready*), which is always the same whether it's a man or a woman who's speaking on the phone. Always make sure you introduce yourself to the person who picks up the phone using **sono...** or **parla...** (*this is...*).

Hello, this is...

Pronto, **sono** la signora Bancroft.	**Hello**, **this is** Mrs Bancroft.
Pronto, **sono** Giulia, ti disturbo?	**Hi**, **this is** Giulia, is this a bad time?
Pronto signor Franceschini, **parla** Michelle.	**Hello** Mr Franceschini, **this is** Michelle **speaking**.
Buonasera signora Paoletti, **sono** la signora Marsh.	**Good evening** Mrs Paoletti, **this is** Mrs Marsh **speaking**.
Buongiorno, c'è Stefania? **Sono** Marie.	**Hello**, is Stefania in? **This is** Marie.
Ciao Tarik, **sono** Julia.	**Hi** Tarik, Julia **here**.

I'm...

Sono una collega di Nicola.	**I'm** a colleague of Nicola's.
Sono un amico di Stefano.	**I'm** a friend of Stefano's.
Sono la figlia del signor Nichol.	**I'm** Mr Nichol's daughter.
Pronto, **sono** l'inquilina di via Bramante 6.	Hello, **I'm** the tenant in via Bramante 6.

If you want to ask for somebody in particular, use **C'è...?** (*Is... there?*) or **Ci sono...?** (*Are... there?*).

Is... there?

C'è Martina, per favore?	**Is** Martina **there**, please?
Mi può dire se **c'è** la signora Paoletti?	Could you tell me if Mrs Paoletti **is in**?
Ci sono Martina e Roberto, per favore?	**Are** Martina and Roberto **there**, please?
Sono in casa i tuoi genitori?	**Are** your parents **in**?

If the person you want to speak to isn't there, the answer you may hear is **mi dispiace, non c'è** which means *sorry, he's (or she's) not here*.

Is that...?

Parlo con Mario?	**Is that** Mario?
Parlo col commissariato di polizia?	**Is that** the police station?
Parlo con lo 08 13 76 89 98?	**Is this** 08 13 76 89 98?
Questo è il numero del municipio, **vero**?	**This is** the number for the town hall, **isn't it**?

Remember to use the article in Italian when you are talking about a telephone number, as in **Mi passa il 37 45 96?**. Use **lo** instead of **il** when the number starts with zero: **Mi passa lo 040 39 78 55?**. For more on how to read out Italian numbers, see pages 180–181.

There are several ways of asking whether you may do something. You can start your question with **posso** (*Can I...?*) or **potrei** (*Could I...?*). They both come from the verb **potere** (*to be able*). For more information on **potere**, see page 284.

May I...?

Potrei parlare con il direttore, per favore?	**Could I** speak to the manager, please?
Posso parlare con Sabrina, per favore?	**Can I** speak to Sabrina, please?
Potrei avere il numero dell'Hotel Europa?	**Could I** have the number of the Europa hotel?

STARTING A CONVERSATION

One of the first things you might want to ask when you speak to someone is how they are. To do this you can use **Come sta?** (*How are You?*) or less formally, **Come stai?**. **Come va?** can also be used.

How are you?

Come sta, signora Prandi?	**How are you**, Mrs Prandi?
Come stai, Mario?	**How are you**, Mario?
Buongiorno Signora, **come va**?	Good morning, **how are You**?
Ciao Silvia, **come va**?	Hello Silvia, **how's it going**?
Come va la vita?	**How's life**?

BUONO A SAPERSI!

If you use **Come va?** you don't have to change it according to who you're speaking to.

In response to being asked how you are, you can use several different phrases.

Fine, thanks.

Bene, grazie, e lei?	**I'm fine, thanks**, how about You?
Bene, grazie, e tu?	**Fine, thanks**, and you?
Non c'è male, e tu?	**Not bad**. And yourself?
Non tanto bene, ultimamente.	**I haven't been too good** lately.

SAYING WHY YOU'RE CALLING

In the course of the telephone call you will often want to explain to someone why you are calling or where you're calling from. To do this, you can use the verb **chiamare** (*to call*). For more information on **-are** verbs like **chiamare**, see page 268.

I'm phoning about...

Chiamo per parlare con Maria.	**I'm phoning to** talk to Maria.
Chiamo per avere ulteriori informazioni sulle vostre tariffe.	**I'm phoning to** get further details on your rates.
Chiamo a proposito di domani sera.	**I'm phoning about** tomorrow night.
Chiamo a proposito del vostro annuncio sul giornale.	**I'm phoning about** <u>your</u> ad in the paper.

I'm calling from...

Chiamo da una cabina.	**I'm calling from** a public phone.
Chiamo dal cellulare.	**I'm calling from** my mobile.
La **chiamo dall'**ufficio.	**I'm calling** You **from** work.
Sono in treno.	I'm on the train.

If you want to ask whether you can do something, use **Posso...?** (*Can I...?*).

Can I...?

Posso lasciare un messaggio?	**Can I** leave a message?
Posso richiamare?	**Can I** call back later?
Le **posso** lasciare il mio numero?	**Can I** leave my number with You, please?

If you are asking someone whether they can do something for you, you should use **Può...?** (Can You...?) or **Potrebbe...?** (Could You...?). These come from the verb **potere** (to be able). For more information on **potere**, see page 284.

Can you...?

Gli **può** dire che ha chiamato Paul, per favore?	**Can You** tell him Paul rang, please?
Mi **può** passare Giovanna, per favore?	**Can You** put me through to Giovanna, please?
Gli **può** dare un messaggio da parte mia, per favore?	**Can You** give him message from me, please?
Le **potrebbe** dare un messaggio?	**Could You** give her a message?
Le **potrebbe** chiedere di richiamarmi, per favore?	**Could You** ask her to call me, please?

GIVING INFORMATION

When you make a phone call in Italian, you may well be asked to give certain pieces of information. To give your phone number or address, use **il mio numero è** (my number is) and **il mio indirizzo è** (my address is).

My number is...

Il mio numero di casa è...	**My** home **phone number is**...
... e **il mio numero** di cellulare è...	... and **my** mobile **number is**...
Il **numero di telefono** dell'albergo è...	**My** hotel **phone number is**...
Il mio numero di telefono fisso è...	**My** landline **is**...

My address is...

Il mio indirizzo a Genova è...	**My address** in Genoa **is**...
Il mio indirizzo in Inghilterra è...	**My address** in England **is**...
Abito al numero 6 di Maryhill Drive a Cork.	**My home address is** 6, Maryhill Drive, Cork.
Alloggio all'Hotel Mediterraneo.	**I'm staying** at the Mediterraneo Hotel.

To give details of where you can be contacted, you can use **mi può contattare...** (*You can contact me...*).

You can contact me...

Mi può contattare al mio numero fisso.	**You can contact me** on my landline.
Mi può contattare allo 09 98 02 46 23.	**You can contact me** on 09 98 02 46 23.
Mi puoi contattare sul mio cellulare.	**You can contact me** on my mobile.
La può trovare tra mezzogiorno e le due.	**You can get her** between twelve and two.
Mi puoi lasciare un messaggio sulla segreteria.	**You can** leave me a message on my answer phone.

ANSWERING THE TELEPHONE

You always answer the telephone with the Italian expression **Pronto?**. You use the same word **Pronto** to say hello when answering the phone as you do when making a phone call.

Hello?

Pronto?	**Hello**?
Pronto, chi parla?	**Hello**, who's calling, please?
Sì, pronto?	**Hello**?

If the person on the other end of the line asks for you, you answer **sì, sono io** (*speaking*).

Speaking.

Sì, sono io.	**Speaking**.
Sì, sono io, desidera?	**Speaking**, how can I help You?
Sì, sono io, chi parla?	**Yes, speaking**, who's calling, please?

When you answer the telephone you often need to ask whether the caller would like to leave a message, call back later and so on. Use **Vuole...?** to someone you don't know well, and **Vuoi...?** (*Would you like to...?*) to someone you know well. **vuole** and **vuoi** both come from the verb **volere** (*to want*). For more information on **volere**, see page 285.

Would you like to...?

Vuole lasciare un messaggio?	**Would You like to** leave a message?
Vuole richiamare più tardi?	**Would You like to** call back later?
Vuoi che ti richiami?	**Would you like** him **to** call you back?

Would you mind...?

Le dispiacerebbe parlare più lentamente, per favore?	**Would You mind** speaking more slowly, please?
Le dispiacerebbe ripetere, per favore? La sento male.	**Would You mind** saying that again, please? I can't hear You very well.
Le dispiacerebbe dirmi come si scrive, per favore?	**Would You mind** spelling that, please?
Ti dispiacerebbe richiamarmi domani?	**Would you mind** calling me back tomorrow?

ENDING A TELEPHONE CALL

When you end a telephone call in Italian, you can say goodbye as you normally would face to face. Use **arrivederci** to say goodbye to people you don't know well or to somebody older, and just **ciao** to a friend or to somebody young.

Goodbye!

Arrivederci, signor Franceschi!	**Goodbye**, Mr Franceschi!
Ciao, Maria!	**Goodbye** Maria!
Allora **ciao**, Emma. Ci sentiamo!	Right, **bye** Emma! Talk to you later!

Have a nice...!

Buona serata!	**Have a nice** evening!
Buona giornata!	**Have a nice** day!
Buon weekend!	**Have a nice** weekend!

To say *See you...!*, use **a** followed by **domani** (*tomorrow*), **più tardi** (*later*), **stasera** (*tonight*) and so on.

See you...!

A domani, Luigi!	**See you** tomorrow, Luigi!
A più tardi!	**See you** later!
A più tardi, signora!	**See You** later!
A stasera!	**See you** tonight!
A presto!	**See you** soon!

BUONO A SAPERSI!

Only use **a più tardi** if you expect to see someone later that day. Use **ci vediamo** if you'll be seeing them sometime in the future, but you don't know when.

As part of saying your goodbyes, you may want to send greetings or best wishes to other people. To do this, use **mi saluti** or, more informally, **salutami** (*say hello to*).

Say hello to...

Mi saluti sua moglie.	**Say hello to** Your wife **for me**.
Salutami la tua famiglia.	**Say hello from me to** your family.
Salutami tua sorella.	**Say hi to** your sister **from me**.
Tanti cari saluti a suo padre.	**Give** Your father **my best wishes**.

BUONO A SAPERSI!

You may be interested to know that the Italian for *to hang up on someone* is **chiudere il telefono in faccia a qualcuno** which literally means *to shut the phone in somebody's face*.

Occasionally you may have to finish a call quickly, especially on a mobile phone.

I've got hardly any... left

Ho il cellulare **quasi scarico**.	**I've got hardly any** battery **left**.
Ho quasi finito la scheda.	**I've got hardly any** credit **left**.

BUONO A SAPERSI!

Of course, the main reason for mobile calls ending suddenly is that the network coverage isn't adequate. To say that in Italian use **non c'è campo**. To tell someone that they're breaking up, use **non ti sento, la linea è disturbata** (*I can't hear you, it's a bad line*).

LISTEN OUT FOR

Here are some key phrases which you may hear when using the telephone.

Chi parla?	Who's calling, please?
Chi lo desidera?	Who shall I say is calling, please?
Attenda in linea.	Hold the line, please.
Un momento, ora lo chiamo.	Hang on a minute, I'll get him.
Mi dispiace, al momento non c'è.	I'm afraid she's not here.
Vuole lasciare un messaggio?	Would you like to leave a message?
Magari la richiama quando rientra.	He could call You back when he returns.
Ha sbagliato numero.	You've got the wrong number.
Ha il numero dell'interno?	Do You have the extension number?
Le passo l'interno.	I'll put You through.
Il numero da lei selezionato è inesistente.	The number You have dialled has not been recognized.
Il numero da lei selezionato è occupato.	The number You called is busy.
Questo è lo 09 73 47 60 21.	You've reached 09 73 47 60 21.
Lasciate un messaggio dopo il segnale acustico.	Please leave a message after the tone.
Per questa chiamata è previsto un addebito di 1 euro al minuto.	This call will be charged at 1 euro per minute.
I nostri operatori sono tutti impegnati, siete pregati di richiamare.	All our operators are busy, please call back later.
La vostra chiamata è stata inoltrata al servizio di segreteria.	Your call is being forwarded to the mobile messaging service.
Ti sento male.	I can't hear you.
Grazie della chiamata.	Thanks for calling.

WRITING EMAILS AND LETTERS

There will be times when you need to send an email or write a letter in Italian. Here are some useful phrases which you can use to do this. You can also have a look at examples of letters and emails in Italian.

Starting a personal email or letter

Cara Francesca,...	Dear Francesca,...
Cara zia,...	My dear aunt,...
Ciao Marco!	Hi Marco!
Carissimo Giorgio,...	Dear Giorgio,...
Carissimi Franca e Dario,...	Dear Franca and Dario,...
Mia cara Daniela,...	Dear Daniela,...

Ending a personal email or letter

Tanti cari saluti,...	Yours,...
Con affetto, Giorgia.	Love, Giorgia.
Un abbraccio, Luca.	Love, Luca.
A presto,	See you soon,
Tanti cari saluti a Fabrizio.	Send my best wishes to Fabrizio.
Bacioni, Carla.	Love, Carla.

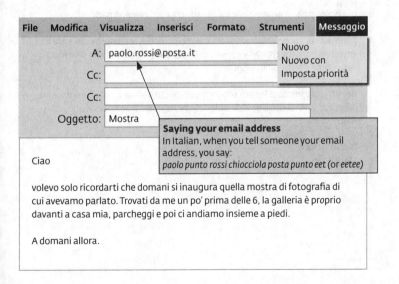

File   Modifica   Visualizza   Inserisci   Formato   Strumenti   Messaggio

Nuovo
Nuovo con
Imposta priorità

A: paolo.rossi@ posta.it

Cc:

Cc:

Oggetto: Mostra

Saying your email address
In Italian, when you tell someone your email address, you say:
paolo punto rossi chiocciola posta punto eet (or eetee)

Ciao

volevo solo ricordarti che domani si inaugura quella mostra di fotografia di cui avevamo parlato. Trovati da me un po' prima delle 6, la galleria è proprio davanti a casa mia, parcheggi e poi ci andiamo insieme a piedi.

A domani allora.

Starting a formal email or letter

Caro Dott. Franceschini,...	Dear Dr. Franceschini,...
Gent.ma Sig.ra Marullo,...	Dear Ms Marullo,...
Gent. Sig.na Rossi,...	Dear Miss Rossi,...
Egregio Prof. Gambini,...	Dear Prof. Gambini,...
Spett. Ditta,...	Dear Sirs,...

Ending a formal email or letter

Distinti saluti,	Yours faithfully/sincerely
Cordiali saluti,	Yours faithfully/sincerely
Le porgo i miei più distinti saluti,	Yours faithfully/sincerely

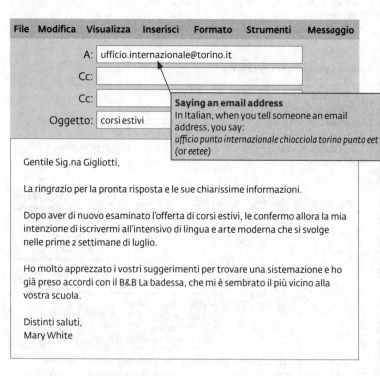

File   Modifica   Visualizza   Inserisci   Formato   Strumenti   Messaggio

A: ufficio.internazionale@torino.it

Cc:

Cc:

Oggetto: corsi estivi

Saying an email address
In Italian, when you tell someone an email address, you say:
ufficio punto internazionale chiocciola torino punto eet (or *eetee*)

Gentile Sig.na Gigliotti,

La ringrazio per la pronta risposta e le sue chiarissime informazioni.

Dopo aver di nuovo esaminato l'offerta di corsi estivi, le confermo allora la mia intenzione di iscrivermi all'intensivo di lingua e arte moderna che si svolge nelle prime 2 settimane di luglio.

Ho molto apprezzato i vostri suggerimenti per trovare una sistemazione e ho già preso accordi con il B&B La badessa, che mi è sembrato il più vicino alla vostra scuola.

Distinti saluti,
Mary White

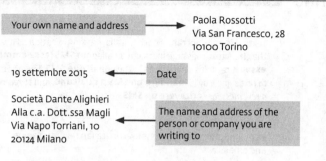

Your own name and address →

Paola Rossotti
Via San Francesco, 28
10100 Torino

19 settembre 2015 ← Date

Società Dante Alighieri
Alla c.a. Dott.ssa Magli
Via Napo Torriani, 10 ←
20124 Milano

The name and address of the person or company you are writing to

Gentile Dott.ssa Magli,

sono una studentessa al terzo anno di un corso di laurea in Informatica in Italia con il programma Erasmus e vorrei completare la mia esperienza di formazione partecipando ad una attività di volontariato.

In particolare, credo di poter contribuire con le mie competenze informatiche, al miglioramento della vostra pagina web.

Ho sempre conciliato l'impegno universitario con un lavoro nel sociale ed ora vorrei poter utilizzare le mie competenze e la mia capacità organizzativa per collaborare attivamente a uno dei vostri progetti di sviluppo.

Accludo il mio CV e in attesa di un cordiale riscontro Le porgo distinti saluti.

Paola Rossotti

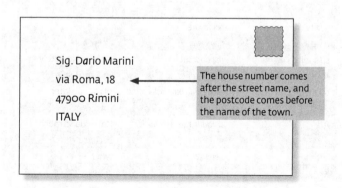

Sig. Dario Marini
via Roma, 18 ←
47900 Rimini
ITALY

The house number comes after the street name, and the postcode comes before the name of the town.

Texting is as important a part of Italian communication as it is in the UK. A text message in Italian is called **un SMS (esse emme esse)**. It remains unchanged in the plural: **due SMS**. The phrase *to text somebody* is **mandare un SMS a qualcuno**, and *to receive a text message* is **ricevere un SMS**.

Here are some abbreviations used in Italian text messaging and emails.

Abbreviation	Italian	English
2nite	stanotte	tonight
a	ha	he/she has
ai	hai	you have
ap	a presto	see you soon
asap	prima possibile	asap
bgg	buongiorno	hello
bn	bene	fine, good
c6?	ci sei?	are you there?
cvd	ci vediamo dopo	see you later
dom	domani	tomorrow
e	è	it's
hagn, bntt	buonanotte	good night
INK	incazzato/a	pissed off, annoyed
ke	che	what
ki	chi	who
lol	lol	LOL
mi di	mi dispiace	sorry
o	ho	I have
pls, x fv	per favore	please
pome	pomeriggio	afternoon
risp subito	rispondi subito	reply immediately
tat	ti amo tanto	love you loads
t tel + trd	ti telefono più tardi	I'll call you later
tu6	tu sei	you are
tvtb	ti voglio tanto bene	I love you so much
xké, xk	perché	because
xké?, xk?	perché?	why?
XXX	tanti baci	kisses

SOCIAL MEDIA

With social media an everyday means of communication, below are some useful phrases and terms to help you.

Italian	English
un amico, un'amica	a friend
aggiungere alla lista di amici	to friend
un blog	a blog
un account	an account
creare/aprire un account	to create/open an account
un filo di discussione	a (discussion) thread
un forum	a forum
un hashtag	a hashtag
lasciare un commento su	to comment on
un messaggio privato, un MP	a DM (direct message)
un aggiornamento di stato/status	a status update
un muro	a wall
scrivere sul muro di qualcuno	to write on somebody's wall
postare qualcosa sul muro di qualcuno	to post something on somebody's wall
un newsfeed	a news feed
una foto di un profilo	a profile picture
un profilo	a profile
un/una fan; un abbonato/un'abbonata	a follower
un tema di tendenza, un trend topic	a trending topic
seguire	to follow
taggare qualcuno in una foto	to tag somebody in a photo
un twit	a tweet
twittare (con)	to tweet about
retwittare	to retweet

Lifestyle Tips

• It is best to avoid loud ringtones (**suonerie**) and mobile-phone conversations in public places in Italy, especially on public transport and in restaurants.

• If you have to send a text message or to make a phone call while in company, you may want to apologize and explain: **scusi, devo fare una telefonata** (*sorry, I need to make a phone call*) or **devo mandare un SMS** (*I need to send a text message*).

• In Italy, you may come across **numero verde®** phone numbers with the prefix 0800. They are free from a landline.

• As in Britain, the use of a **telefono cellulare** (*mobile phone*) is forbidden while driving. The use of hands-free kits is however allowed.

• If you want to use **un Internet point** (*internet café*) to check your email, you won't have to look far. To ask how much it costs you can say **Quanto si paga?** (*How much does it cost?*).

• Remember to take your passport with you when you go to an **Internet point**, as ID is often required for registration. Anti-terrorism legislation requires internet cafes to keep records of the names of users, and periodically to inform the police of what websites they have visited.

Time, numbers, date

Tre, due, uno... via! – One, two, three... Go!

I NUMERI – NUMBERS

When communicating in Italian you'll often need to say and understand numbers, so here's a list to help you.

0	zero
1	uno
2	due
3	tre
4	quattro
5	cinque
6	sei
7	sette
8	otto
9	nove
10	dieci
11	undici
12	dodici
13	tredici
14	quattordici
15	quindici
16	sedici
17	diciassette
18	diciotto
19	diciannove
20	venti

BUONO A SAPERSI!

Italian speakers never use the letter O to refer to **zero** (zero), as we do in English. Also, remember to say **lo zero** and **uno zero**. With all other numbers use **il** and **un**: **il tre**, **il cinque** and **un tre**, **un cinque** and so on. Use **l'** with numbers starting with a vowel: **l'otto**, **l'ottocento**, **l'undici** and so on. You can use **il cinque** to say *number five*, or *the number five*.

In Italian, the word **uno** (*one*) can change its ending. The masculine form **uno** is used before words beginning with the letter Z, with S + a consonant (ST, SP, SC, SR and so on) and PN and PS, for example, **uno zaino** (*one rucksack*), **uno scolaro** (*one pupil*) and so on. In all other cases use **un** (or **una** with feminine nouns). **una** becomes **un'** before words beginning with a vowel.

one

Quanti DVD hai comprato? – Solo **uno**.	How many DVDs did you buy? – Only **one**.
Ho **un** fratello.	I've got **one** brother.
Mi è rimasta solo **una** caramella.	I've only got **one** sweet left.
Quante pagine hai scritto? – **Una**.	How many pages have you written? – **Una**.

21	ventuno
22	ventidue
23	ventitré
24	ventiquattro
25	venticinque
26	ventisei
27	ventisette
28	ventotto
29	ventinove
30	trenta
31	trentuno
40	quaranta
41	quarantuno
42	quarantadue
50	cinquanta
51	cinquantuno
53	cinquantatré
60	sessanta
64	sessantaquattro
70	settanta
71	settantuno
75	settantacinque
80	ottanta
81	ottantuno
90	novanta
91	novantuno
99	novantanove

In Italian, except for **uno/una**, numbers are invariable, that is, they remain unchanged whether they are followed by a feminine, a masculine or a plural noun.

There are...

Ci sono trentatré studenti nell'aula.	**There are thirty-three** students in the classroom.
Ci sono ventuno donne in questo reparto.	**There are twenty-one** women in this department.
Ci sono trentun giorni in gennaio.	**There are thirty-one** days in January.
Ci saranno cinquantuno persone nel gruppo.	**There'll be fifty-one** people in the group.
C'erano ventun bambini alla festa.	**There were twenty-one** children at the party.

You may hear people say **-un**, instead of **-uno** at the end of a number, but you can always use **-uno**.

Ho meno di **ventun anni**.	I'm under **twenty-one**.

BUONO A SAPERSI!
In Italian you say **ho... anni** (*I'm... years old*) to say how old you are.

A few numbers can drop the final vowel and take an apostrophe ('), when followed by the word **anni**, as in **novant'anni** (*90 years*).

I'm... years old

Ho diciott'anni.	**I'm eighteen years old**.
Avrà settant'anni.	**He must be around seventy**.
Compie trent'anni in maggio.	**He'll be thirty** in May.
Quanti **anni hai**? – **Ventuno**.	How **old are you**? – **Twenty-one**.

BUONO A SAPERSI!
Just as in English, you can name a year from the last century by the last two digits, but you add the word for *the*, **il novantotto** (*'98*), **nel novantotto** (*in '98*). It doesn't apply to the noughties and beyond, however, so for *'06* you would say **duemilasei** (*two thousand and six*).

100	cento
101	centouno
150	centocinquanta
200	duecento
300	trecento
400	quattrocento
500	cinquecento
600	seicento
700	settecento
800	ottocento
900	novecento

Like **uno**, **cento** (*one hundred*) can drop the final **–o** before **anni**, for example, **cent'anni**.

hundred

Ci sono **cento** centesimi in un euro.	There are **one hundred** cents in a euro.
Avete *La carica dei **centouno*** su DVD?	Do you have *One Hundred and One Dalmatians* on DVD?
Hai letto ***Cent'anni** di solitudine*?	Have you read *One Hundred* Years of Solitude?
Costa **centocinquanta** euro.	It costs **one hundred and fifty** euros.
Ci devono essere state più di **duecento** persone.	There must have been over **two hundred** people.
C'erano circa **cinquecentocinquanta** dipendenti nel palazzo.	There were around **five hundred and fifty** employees in the building.

In Italian, you can say **centouno**, **centodue**, **centoventi** for *one hundred and one*, *one hundred and two*, *one hundred and twenty* and so on. However, you can also separate the two numbers with an **e** (*and*), as in **cento e uno** (*one hundred and one*), **cento e due** (*one hundred and two*) and so on. **uno** will take the gender of the word that follows it: **cento e una pagina** (*one hundred and one pages*).

...hundred and...

Costa **cento e ottanta** euro.	It costs **one hundred and eighty** euros.
Ci sono **cento e una** pagina.	There are **one hundred and one** pages.

1.000	mille
1.001	mille e uno
1.020	mille e venti
1.150	millecentocinquanta
2.000	duemila
2.500	duemilacinquecento
3.400	tremilaquattrocento
100.000	centomila

BUONO A SAPERSI!
In Italian a full stop rather than a comma is used to separate thousands and millions.

mille means *one thousand*, or *a thousand*. You do not translate the *one*, or *a* in Italian. **mille** changes to **mila** in the plural, and joins onto other words, for example, **duemila** (*two thousand*), **duecentomila** (*two hundred thousand*).

one thousand to one hundred thousand

Questa città esiste da più di **mille** anni.	This city has been here for over **a thousand** years.
Quanto sono **centomila** euro in sterline?	How much is **100,000** euros in pounds?
La casa nuova gli costa **duecentocinquantamila** sterline.	He's paying **£250,000** for his new house.
Si sono sposati nel **duemiladieci**.	They got married in **2010**.
È tornato a Londra nel **duemiladodici**.	He went back to London in **2012**.

1.000.000	un milione
1.000.000.000	un miliardo
1.000.000.000.000	mille miliardi

To talk about a million or a billion things, you use **un milione di** and **un miliardo di**.

one million to one billion

Ha vinto **un milione di** sterline alla lotteria.	He won **a million** pounds in the lottery.
Il governo ha già speso **due miliardi di** sterline per questo progetto.	The government has already spent **two billion** pounds on this project.

If you want to say *about ten*, *about twenty*, *about a thousand* and so on in Italian, you can use the expressions below.

about...

una decina	**about ten**
una ventina	**about twenty**
una quarantina	**about thirty**
un centinaio	**about a hundred**
un migliaio	**about a thousand**
una dozzina	**a dozen or so**
C'erano **una settantina di** persone.	There were **about seventy** people.
Avrà **una sessantina d**'anni.	He must be **about sixty**.
Hanno **un'ottantina di** ospiti d'estate.	They have **about 80** guests during the summer.

In Italian, a decimal **virgola** (*comma*) is used rather than a decimal point.

... point ...

zero **virgola** cinque (0,5)	nought **point** five (0.5)
novantanove **virgola** nove (99,9)	ninety-nine **point** nine (99.9)
sei **virgola** ottantanove (6,89)	six **point** eight nine (6.89)
Hanno aumentato il tasso di interesse al quattro **virgola** cinque per cento (4,5%).	They've put interest rates up to four **point** five per cent (4.5%).

To read prices that include both euros and cents, put **euro** in the middle between the euro and the cent figures. The word **centesimi** is optional.

euros and cents

Sono **diciotto euro e novantanove**.	That'll be **18.99 €**.
Mi è costato **sessantacinque euro e venti centesimi**.	It cost me **65.20 €**.

BUONO A SAPERSI!
Remember that while in English you talk about *one euro* and *three euros*, in Italian **euro** is not made plural: **un euro** (*one euro*), **tre euro** (*three euros*), **quattro euro** (*four euros*) and so on.

kilos and grams

Vorrei **un chilo di** patate.	I'd like **a kilo of** potatoes.
Mi dà **due chili di** mele?	Can I have **two kilos of** apples?
Mi dà **mezzo chilo di** pomodori?	Can I have **half a kilo of** tomatoes?
Un chilo e mezzo di pesche, per favore.	Can I have **one and half kilos of** peaches, please?

The word **etto** is used to mean *a hundred grams*. You can also say **mezzo etto** (50 *grams*).

one hundred grams

Un etto di ricotta, per favore.	**One hundred grams of** ricotta, please.
Vorrei **due etti di** carne macinata.	I'd like **two hundred grams of** mince.
Mi dà **un etto e mezzo di** prosciutto, per favore?	I'd like **one hundred and fifty grams of** ham, please.

litres

Un **litro di** vino bianco, per favore.	A **litre of** white wine, please.
Quant'è la benzina al **litro?**	How much is a **litre** of petrol?
Bastano due **litri di** acqua minerale?	Will two **litres of** mineral water be enough?
Occorre **mezzo litro di** latte per questa ricetta.	You need **half a litre of** milk for this recipe.

kilometres, metres and centimetres

Andava a **centoquaranta chilometri all'ora**.	He was doing **140km an hour**.
Siamo a **trenta chilometri da** Siena.	We're **30km from** Siena.
Sono alta **un metro e sessantasei**.	I'm **one metre sixty-six centimetres** tall.
È **lungo venti centimetri e largo dieci**.	It's **twenty centimetres long by ten wide**.

percentages

L'inflazione è al **due virgola cinque per cento** (2,5%).	The inflation rate is **two point five per cent** (2.5%).
Il cinquantacinque per cento ha votato no al referendum.	**55%** voted no in the referendum.

temperature

La temperatura oscillerà tra **i dodici** e **i quindici gradi**.	Temperatures will range between **twelve** and **fifteen degrees**.
Sono **trenta gradi**.	It's **thirty degrees**.

The word for *half* in Italian is **mezzo**.

half

Ne è rimasto solo **mezzo**.	There's only **half** left.
Basta una bottiglia da **mezzo**.	A **half-litre** bottle will do.
Siamo dovuti tornare a casa **nel bel mezzo** della vacanza.	We had to go back home **halfway through** the holiday.

... and a half

Restiamo in Toscana un mese **e mezzo**.	We'll be spending a month **and a half** in Tuscany.
Ha nove anni **e mezzo**.	He's nine **and a half**.
Era alto un metro **e mezzo**.	He was one-**and-a-half** metres tall.
Ci ho messo due ore **e mezza**.	It took me two **and a half** hours.

There are times when you'll need to use numbers to show the order of things. As in English, in Italian there's another set of numbers you use for this. All these numbers change their ending depending on whether they are masculine, feminine or plural.

first	primo
second	secondo
third	terzo
fourth	quarto
fifth	quinto
sixth	sesto
seventh	settimo
eighth	ottavo
ninth	nono
tenth	decimo
eleventh	undicesimo
twelfth	dodicesimo
thirteenth	tredicesimo
twentieth	ventesimo
thirtieth	trentesimo
hundredth	centesimo
two hundredth	duecentesimo
thousandth	millesimo

Unlike in English, they are never used in dates, except for **primo**, e.g. **il primo maggio** (*May 1st*).

first, second, third

Oggi festeggiano il **primo** anniversario di matrimonio.	They're celebrating their **first** wedding anniversary today.
È la **prima** volta che viene.	This is the **first** time he's come.
È il mio **secondo** soggiorno in Toscana.	This is my **second** trip to Tuscany.
È arrivata **terza** nella gara.	She came **third** in the race.
I ragazzi sono arrivati **quarti**.	The boys came **fourth**.
Le ragazze si sono classificate **seconde**.	The girls got **second** place.

In English you can write these numbers as abbreviations (1st, 5th and so on). In Italian you can as well, by adding a small °or ª ($1°$, $5ª$ and so on) to the number, depending on the gender of the noun they refer to.

1st, 2nd, 3rd

Lavora sulla **5ª** Strada. (= *quinta*)	He works on **5th** Avenue.
È al **20°** piano. (= *ventesimo*)	It's on the **20th** floor.
È il **1°** aprile. (= *primo*)	It's April **1st**.

If you want to know what time it is in Italian, you can say **Che ora è?** or **Che ore sono?** (*What's the time?*). You can also ask **Scusi, ha l'ora?** (*Excuse me, do You have the time?*). Remember to use the article when telling the time in Italian. Use **Sono le...** (*It's... o'clock*) in all cases, except for **È l'una.** (*It's one o'clock.*), **È mezzanotte.** (*It's midnight.*) and **È mezzogiorno.** (*It's midday.*).

It's...o'clock.

Sono le sei.	**It's** six **o'clock**.
Sono le tre del mattino.	**It's** three in the morning.
Erano le quattro del pomeriggio.	**It was** four **o'clock** in the afternoon.
È l'una.	**It's** one **o'clock**.
È mezzanotte.	**It's** midnight.
Era mezzogiorno.	**It was** midday.
Devono essere più o meno le undici.	**It must be** about eleven.

BUONO A SAPERSI!
To say *it's three in the morning*, in Italian you can say **sono le tre di mattina** (or **del mattino**), as well as **sono le tre di notte** (*it's three o'clock in the night*).

To say the time in Italian, put the hour first, followed by **e** and the minutes, as in **le nove e dieci** (*ten past nine*).

It's...past...

È l'una **e** venticinque.	**It's** twenty-five **past** one.
Sono le sei **e** cinque.	**It's** five **past** six.
È l'una **e** un quarto.	**It's** quarter **past** one.
Sono le cinque **e** mezza.	**It's** half **past** five.

BUONO A SAPERSI!
When you're saying the time, **mezza** stands for **mezz'ora** (half an hour), so **le cinque e mezza** is literally *five hours and half an hour*.

To say *quarter to* in Italian say the hour followed by **meno un quarto**, as in **sono le sette meno un quarto** (*it's quarter to seven*). Do the same for *five to, ten to, twenty to* and so on: **sono le sette meno cinque** (*it's five to seven*).

It's...to...

È l'una **meno** un quarto.	**It's** quarter **to** one.
È l'una **meno** venti.	**It's** twenty **to** one.
Sono le otto **meno** dieci.	**It's** ten **to** eight.
Sono le tre **meno** cinque.	**It's** five **to** three.

When you're in Italy, to find out what time something is happening, you can say **A che ora...?** (*What time...?*).

What time...?

A che ora c'è il prossimo treno per Sassari?	**What time**'s the next train for Sassari?
A che ora comincia?	**What time** does it start?
A che ora ci troviamo?	**What time** shall we meet?
A che ora è finito il film?	**What time** did the film end?

To say what time something is happening at, use **a**. Remember that **a** combines with the article, as in the following examples: **all'una** (*at one o'clock*), **alle due** (*at two o'clock*), **alle tre e mezza** (*at half past three*) and so on. For more information on **a** with the article, see page 255.

at...

Comincia **alle** sette.	It starts **at** seven o'clock.
Il treno parte **alle** sette e mezza.	The train leaves **at** seven thirty.
Ci vediamo **alle** tre e mezza.	I'll see you **at** half past three.
Ci possiamo trovare **alle** cinque e un quarto.	We can meet up **at** quarter past five.
Ci vediamo **alla** mezza.	See you **at** half past twelve.

BUONO A SAPERSI!
In Italian, a possible time to have lunch is **la mezza**, which means the same as **mezzogiorno e mezzo** (*half past twelve*).

To say when something is happening by, use **entro**: **entro l'una**
(*by one o'clock*), **entro le due** (*by two o'clock*), **entro le tre e mezza**
(*by half past three*) and so on.

by...

Puoi arrivare **entro** le tre?	Can you be there **by** three o'clock?
Dobbiamo finire **entro** l'una meno un quarto.	We must be finished **by** quarter to one.

del mattino or **di mattina** (*in the morning*) are used in Italian
where in English we'd say *am*. **del pomeriggio** and **di sera** (*in the
afternoon, in the evening*) are used where we'd say *pm*. It is also
quite common to use the 24-hour clock in Italian.

at... am/pm

Il treno parte **alle otto del mattino**.	The train leaves **at eight am**.
Si deve alzare **alle cinque di mattina**.	She has to get up **at five am**.
Torno a casa **alle quattro del pomeriggio**.	I get home **at four pm**.
Il traghetto è **alle undici di sera**.	The ferry is **at eleven pm**.
Vediamoci **a mezzogiorno in punto**.	Let's meet **at 12 noon sharp**.
Comincia **alle venti e trenta**.	It starts **at 8.30pm**.

BUONO A SAPERSI!

The word **questa** (*this*) drops its first three letters and joins with
the words **mattina** and **sera**, to make **stamattina** (*this morning*)
and **stasera** (*this evening*). The same thing happens with **notte**,
but **stanotte** means *last night*.

LISTEN OUT FOR

Here are some key phrases to do with numbers and the time.

È a pagina ventidue.	It's on page 22.
Secondo piano, interno quindici.	Second floor, room 15.
Sono quasi due etti.	It's almost 200 grams.
Eri qua nel novantanove?	Were you here in '99?
Le va bene stasera alle sette?	Is 7pm this evening okay with You?
Il treno per Roma parte alle tredici e cinquantacinque.	The train for Rome leaves at 13:55.
Il treno delle quattordici e quindici per Palermo partirà dal binario due.	The 14:15 train to Palermo will depart from platform two.
La partenza del volo tre zero sette con destinazione Londra è prevista alle ore venti e quarantacinque.	Flight number 307 for London is due to take off at 20:45.
Il volo nove zero nove proveniente da Manchester viaggia in orario.	Flight 909 from Manchester is on time.
Il pullman arriva a Brindisi alle diciannove e dieci.	The coach gets to Brindisi at 19:10.

DURATA – SAYING HOW LONG

When you say *in an hour, in five minutes* and so on you use **in** in Italian.

in...

Ha completato l'esercizio **in** soli tre minuti.	He completed the exercise **in** only three minutes.
È riuscito a fare il lavoro **in** un'ora.	He was able to do the job **in** an hour.

When *in an hour* or *in five minutes* means *in an hour's time* or *in five minutes' time*, you use **fra** or **tra** instead of **in**.

Sarò di ritorno **tra** venti minuti.	I'll be back **in** twenty minutes.
Sarà qua **fra** una settimana.	She'll be here **in** a week's time.

To ask how long something is, or how long it takes, use **Quanto dura…?** or **Quanto tempo dura…?**. **dura** comes from the verb **durare**.

How long…?

Quanto dura il film?	**How long**'s the film?
Quanto dura la visita?	**How long** will the tour take?
Quanto è durata l'opera?	**How long** was the opera?
Quanto tempo ci vuole per raggiungere la costa?	**How long will it take to** get to the coast?
Quanto ci vuole per arrivare in centro?	**How long does it take to** get to the centre of town?

If you want to say how long something takes, you can use **ci vuole** or **ci vogliono** (*it takes*). **vuole** and **vogliono** come from the verb **volere**. For more information on **volere**, see page 285.

It takes…

Ci vuole un'ora di macchina.	**It takes** an hour by car.
Mi ci vogliono due ore per andare a piedi fino in paese.	**It takes me** two hours to walk to the village.
Ci vogliono meno di venti minuti per raggiungere il centro a piedi.	**It takes** less than twenty minutes to walk to the town centre.
Ci è voluta mezz'ora per convincerla.	**It took** half an hour to persuade her.
Si fa in cinque minuti.	**It takes** five minutes **to make**.

When referring to people, use the verb **mettere** (*to take*), with **ci** in front of it, as in the following examples:

It'll take you…

Ci metterai almeno un'ora con questo traffico.	**It'll take you** at least an hour in this traffic.
Quanto ci metti?	**How long will you be**?
Non ci metto molto a raggiungerti.	**It won't take me long** to join you.
Quanto tempo ci metterà a dipingere la stanza?	**How long will it take You** to paint the room?
Ci mettono un sacco di tempo a servirti qui.	**They take** ages to serve you here.

LE STAGIONE – THE SEASONS

These are the four seasons in Italian.

la primavera	spring
l'estate	summer
l'autunno	autumn
l'inverno	winter

When you talk about the seasons in Italian, you must use the article, even if you don't use it in English.

Non mi piace affatto **l'inverno**.	I don't like **winter** at all.
Mi piace più di tutto **la primavera**.	I like **the spring** best.

To say *in autumn, in winter, in summer* and *in spring*, use **in autunno**, **in inverno**, **in estate** and **in primavera**. However, you can also say **d'estate** and **d'inverno**.

in...

Il tempo migliore qui è **in primavera**.	We get the best weather here **in spring**.
In inverno qui nevica sempre.	It always snows here **in the winter**.
Non andiamo in campeggio **d'inverno**.	We don't go camping **in winter**.
D'estate vanno sempre al mare.	They always go to the seaside **in the summer**.

Use **questo** (or **quest'** before a vowel), to say *this summer, this winter* and so on.

this...

Quest'estate andiamo in Calabria.	We're going to Calabria **this summer**.
Vado a Cortina **quest'inverno**.	I'm going to Cortina **this winter**.

Use **scorso** to talk about *last* winter and so on, and **prossimo** to talk about *next* winter and so forth.

last.../next...

Ha fatto bel tempo **l'inverno scorso**.	The weather was good **last winter**.
L'estate scorsa abbiamo passato un mese in Sicilia.	**Last summer** we spent a month in Sicily.
Il prossimo inverno andiamo tutti a sciare.	**Next winter** we're all going skiing.
Avrà il bambino **la primavera prossima**.	She's expecting the baby **next spring**.

BUONO A SAPERSI!
Remember to use the article in Italian before **scorso** (*last*) and **prossimo** (*next*).

I MESI DELL'ANNO – THE MONTHS OF THE YEAR

The months of the year are always written with a small letter in Italian.

gennaio	January
febbraio	February
marzo	March
aprile	April
maggio	May
giugno	June
luglio	July
agosto	August
settembre	September
ottobre	October
novembre	November
dicembre	December

Just like in English, to say *in January*, *in February* and so on in Italian you say: **in gennaio**, **in febbraio**, and so forth. You can also say **a gennaio**, **a febbraio** and so on.

in...

Il mio compleanno è **in agosto**.	My birthday is **in August**.
Sono andato a trovare degli amici a Como **in settembre**.	I visited some friends in Como **in September**.
Andremo in vacanza in montagna **in agosto**.	We're going to go to the mountains for our holidays **this August**.
Probabilmente andremo in vacanza **a maggio**.	We'll probably go on holiday **in May**.

Use **scorso** to talk about *last* June and so on, and **prossimo** to talk about *next* June and so forth.

last.../next...

Dove sei andato in vacanza **lo scorso giugno**?	Where did you go on holiday **last June**?
Vado a Glasgow **il prossimo maggio**.	I'm going to Glasgow **next May**.
Spero di andare in Corsica **il prossimo luglio**.	I'm hoping to go to Corsica **next July**.

BUONO A SAPERSI!
Remember to use the article in Italian before **scorso** (*last*) and **prossimo** (*next*).

If you want to say that something is happening *at the beginning of* a month, you can use the expression **all'inizio di**. If you want to say that something is happening *at the end of* a month, you can use the expression **alla fine di**. Alternatively, you can say **a fine marzo**, **a fine giugno** and so on.

at the beginning/end of...

Comincia l'università **all'inizio di** ottobre.	She starts university **at the beginning of** October.
Morì **alla fine di** febbraio.	He died **at the end of** February.
Le vacanze estive cominciano **a fine** giugno.	The summer holidays start **at the end of** June.
Traslocano **a metà** marzo.	They're moving house **in the middle of** March.

LE DATE – DATES

To ask what the date is, you can use **Che data è oggi?** (*What's the date today?*). When talking about dates, Italian speakers use **due** (*two*), **tre** (*three*), **quattro** (*four*) and so on rather than **secondo** (*second*), **terzo** (*third*), and so on. For the *first* of the month, however, **primo** (*first*) is used.

It's the...of...

È il primo luglio.	**It's the first of** July.
Oggi **è il ventotto** dicembre.	**It's** December **28th** today.
Domani **è il dieci** gennaio.	Tomorrow**'s the tenth of** January.
Ieri **era il venti** novembre.	**It was 20th** November yesterday.
È giovedì **due** marzo.	**It's** Thursday, **2nd** March.

BUONO A SAPERSI!
When writing a letter, write the date in the form **lunedì, 27 agosto 2015**.

To say what date something is happening or happened on, use **il** before the number.

on the... of...

È nato **il quattordici febbraio** 1990.	He was born **on the fourteenth of February**, 1990.
Morì **il ventitré aprile** 1616.	He died **on April the twenty-third**, 1616.
Avevano in programma di sposarsi **il diciotto ottobre** 2016.	They were planning to get married **on October 18th** 2016.
Dove pensi che sarai **il venti ottobre**?	Where do you think you'll be **on the twentieth of October**?

I GIORNI DELLA SETTIMANA – THE DAYS OF THE WEEK

The days of the week are always written with a small letter in Italian.

lunedì	Monday
martedì	Tuesday
mercoledì	Wednesday
giovedì	Thursday
venerdì	Friday
sabato	Saturday
domenica	Sunday

To say what day it is, just say **è giovedì** (*it's Thursday*), **è sabato** (*it's Saturday*). You can also say **oggi è giovedì** (*today's Thursday*) and so on.

It's...

Che giorno è oggi? – **È** giovedì.	What day is it today? – **It's** Thursday.
Oggi **è** lunedì, no?	**It's** Monday today, isn't it?
Che bello! Oggi **è** sabato.	Great! **It's** Saturday today.

When making arrangements or saying when something happened you may want to specify the day. In Italian it's easy: just use the day in question **lunedì**, **venerdì** to mean *on Monday*, *on Friday* and so on.

on...

Vado a Dublino **lunedì**.	I'm going to Dublin **on Monday**.
Martedì è il mio compleanno.	It's my birthday **on Tuesday**.
Li vediamo **mercoledì**.	We'll see them **on Wednesday**.
Parto per le vacanze **martedì**.	I'm going on holiday **this Tuesday**.

To say that something regularly happens on a particular day, use either **il** or **di** and the day in question. So **il lunedì** and **di lunedì** both mean *on Mondays*.

Usciamo sempre **il venerdì**.	We always go out **on Fridays**.
Arriva sempre tardi **il lunedì**.	He's always late in **on Mondays**.
Di sabato andiamo in palestra.	We go to the gym **on Saturdays**.

If you want to specify the time of day, add **mattina** (*morning*), **pomeriggio** (*afternoon*) or **sera** (*evening, night*) after the day.

on... morning/afternoon/evening/night

Vado in officina **martedì mattina**.	I'm going to the garage **on Tuesday morning**.
Ci vediamo **venerdì pomeriggio**.	I'll see you **on Friday afternoon**.
C'era un bel film in tivù **domenica sera**.	There was a good film on television **on Sunday evening**.
Cosa fa **sabato sera**?	What are You doing **on Saturday night**?

You may want to say *every Monday*, *every Sunday* and so on. In Italian, you can say either **tutti i lunedì**, **tutte le domeniche** or **ogni giovedì**, **ogni domenica** and so on.

every...

Le telefoniamo **tutti i giovedì**.	We ring her **every Thursday**.
Gioca a golf **tutti i sabati**.	He plays golf **every Saturday**.
Una volta li vedevo **tutti i venerdì**.	I used to see them **every Friday**.
Facciamo le pulizie **tutte le domeniche mattina**.	We do the cleaning **every Sunday morning**.
Va a messa **ogni domenica**.	She goes to mass **every Sunday**.
Ogni sabato pomeriggio andava a trovare la nonna.	He used to visit his grandmother **every Saturday afternoon**.

You may want to say that you do something every other day, week and so on. To say *every other* use **uno... su due** (*one out of two...*), or **ogni secondo...** (*every second...*).

every other...

Ha i bambini **una domenica su due**.	He has the children **ever other Sunday**.
Giochiamo a pallone **un sabato su due**.	We play football **every other Saturday**.
Torna a casa **ogni secondo venerdì**.	He goes home **every other Friday**.

You can use **questo** (*this*), **scorso** (*last*) and **prossimo** (*next*) if you want to specify a day in particular.

this/next/last...

Questo venerdì è il nostro anniversario di matrimonio.	It's our wedding anniversary **this Friday**.
Ti ho mandato le foto via e-mail **venerdì scorso**.	I emailed you the photos **last Friday**.
Le andrebbe bene **venerdì prossimo**?	Would **next Friday** suit You?
Venerdì della settimana prossima è il mio compleanno.	It's my birthday **on Friday week**.
Ci siamo dati appuntamento per **venerdì della settimana prossima**.	We've arranged to meet up **a week on Friday**.

If you want to ask what day something is happening, use **Che giorno...?** (*What day...?*).

What day...?

Che giorno è la riunione? – Martedì.	**What day**'s the meeting? – Tuesday.
Sai **che giorno** viene? – Viene mercoledì.	Do you know **what day** he's coming? – He's coming on Wednesday.
Che giorno ci sei andata? – Martedì, credo.	**Which day** did you go there? – Tuesday, I think.

If you want to talk about the past, the present or the future, some of these phrases will be useful.

yesterday

ieri	**yesterday**
ieri mattina	**yesterday morning**
ieri pomeriggio	**yesterday afternoon**
l'altro ieri	**the day before yesterday**
ieri sera	**yesterday evening**, **last night**
Ieri è venuto a trovarmi Michael.	Michael came to see me **yesterday**.
L'altro ieri ha chiamato Beatrice.	Beatrice rang up **the day before yesterday**.

BUONO A SAPERSI!
Remember that the English word *night* may be translated **sera** (*evening*) and **notte** (*night time*) in Italian depending on the time of day.

today

oggi	**today**
Oggi è martedì.	**Today**'s Tuesday.

tomorrow

domani	**tomorrow**
domani mattina	**tomorrow morning**
domain sera	**tomorrow evening**, **tomorrow night**
dopodomani	**the day after tomorrow**
Domani è mercoledì.	**Tomorrow** is Wednesday.
Devo alzarmi presto **domani mattina**.	I've got to get up early **tomorrow morning**.
Andiamo a una festa **domani sera**.	We're going to a party **tomorrow night**.

To say that something happened a certain length of time ago, use **fa** after stating the period of time in question.

... ago

Mi ha chiamato **una settimana fa**.	She phoned me **a week ago**.
È nato **tre anni fa**.	He was born **three years ago**.
Si sono trasferiti nella casa nuova **una decina di giorni fa**.	They moved into their house **about ten days ago**.

One way to talk about how long you've been doing something is to use the verb in the present tense followed by **da** and the length of time. For more information on the present tense, see page 271.

... for...

Viviamo qui **da** dieci mesi.	We've been living here **for** ten months.
Sono sposati **da** dieci anni.	They've been married **for** ten years.
Non la vedo **da** una settimana.	I haven't seen her **for** a week.
Sono tre settimane **che** non li vedo.	I haven't seen them **for** three weeks.
Sono ore **che** aspetto.	I've been waiting here **for** hours.

BUONO A SAPERSI!
You can also change the sentence round by putting the length of time first and using **che** (*that*).

L'ALFABETO – THE ALPHABET

When you're in Italy, you may well need to spell something out in Italian. Italian letters are pronounced approximately as shown in the list below.

A	ah
B	bee
C	tchee
D	dee
E	e (as in *tent*)
F	effay
G	jee
H	akka
I	ee
J	ee loongo
K	kappa
L	ellay
M	emmay
N	ennay
O	o (as in *orange*)
P	pee
Q	koo
R	erray
S	essay
T	tee
U	oo
V	vee
W	vee doppioh
X	eeks
Y	ee grayko
Z	zaytah

BUONO A SAPERSI!

All letters are feminine in Italian. So you would say, **si scrive con una P** (*it's spelt with a P*). Letters don't have plurals: **una emme**, **due emme** (one M, two Ms).

LISTEN OUT FOR

Here are some key phrases which you may hear when spelling words out.

Come si scrive?	How do you spell it?
Mi può dire come si scrive?	Can You spell that for me?
Si scrive tee-akka-o-emmay-ah-essay.	That's T-H-O-M-A-S.
Le dico come si scrive?	Shall I spell it for You?
Si scrive con la B.	It's spelt with a B.
B come Bologna.	B for Bologna.
Marini, con la emme maiuscola.	That's Marini with a capital M.
Si scrive con due effe.	It's spelt with a double F.
Con una elle o due?	Is that with one L or two?
Dovrebbe essere maiuscolo.	That should be in capitals.
Tutto minuscolo.	All in small letters.
Come si pronuncia il suo nome?	How do you say your name?
Me lo può ripetere?	Please can you repeat that?

Interesting days and dates

• June 2 is a national holiday in Italy. It celebrates the founding of the Italian republic in 1946.

• Boxing Day in Italy is called **Santo Stefano**, after St Stephen, whose day it is. New Year's Eve is called either **la vigilia di Capodanno** or **San Silvestro** (after the saint). New Year's Day is **Capodanno**.

• Italian children get presents on January 6, which is the feast of the Epiphany and a national holiday. The presents are brought by **la Befana**, an old woman who, legend has it, comes down the chimney in the night with gifts for children who have been good and lumps of coal for those who have not.

• Another of Italy's public holidays is April 25. This commemorates Italy's liberation from Nazi occupation on April 25, 1945.

• **Ferragosto** is on August 15, the date of the Assumption of the Virgin (the name means *the August holiday*). It comes in the middle of the main holiday period in Italy, when many shops and restaurants in big towns and cities take their annual break.

• All Italian cities have a patron saint, and on that saint's day there are often special celebrations. **San Giovanni** (*St John*), for example, is the patron saint of **Firenze** (*Florence*), and on his day, June 24, there is the famous **Calcio in Costume**, a kind of football match in medieval costume.

• Most Christian names are associated with a Saint's day in Italian. If it's your Saint's day, people will wish you **Buon onomastico!** (*Happy Saint's Day!*).

In summary...

Allora, recapitolando… – So, to sum up…

This unit gives you quick access to all the important Italian structures that you'll have learned in the individual units. They are grouped by function to help you find what you're looking for.

CONTENTS

There are several ways to say *sorry* in Italian. You can say **scusa** or **scusami** to someone you call **tu**, and **scusi** or **mi scusi** to someone you call **lei**. Alternatively, you can say **chiedo scusa**, especially if you want to get past someone or if you've bumped into them.

Mi scusi...

Mi scusi, non sapevo.	**Sorry**, I didn't know.
Scusi, ho sbagliato numero.	**Sorry**, I've dialled the wrong number.
Scusa, non ti avevo visto.	**Sorry**, I didn't see you.

Chiedo scusa

Chiedo scusa! Posso passare?	**Sorry**! Can I get past?
Chiedo scusa! Le ho fatto male?	**Sorry**! Did I hurt You?

Another way to say *I'm sorry* is to use **mi dispiace**. You can use **mi dispiace** not only when you're apologizing but also when you're sympathizing with someone.

Mi dispiace...

Mi dispiace molto.	**I'm** very **sorry**.
Mi dispiace di non averla richiamata prima.	**I'm sorry** I didn't call You back sooner.
Mi dispiace per quello che è successo.	**I'm sorry** about what happened.

ASKING FOR AND GIVING EXPLANATIONS

perché means both *why* and *because*, so use it both when asking for explanations, and when giving them.

perché

Perché ride?	**Why** are You laughing?
Perché non vuoi venire con noi?	**Why don't** you want to come with us?
Perché no?	**Why** not?
Sai **perché** si sia arrabbiato tanto?	Do you know **why** he got so angry?
Non te ne ho parlato **perché** non ti volevo preoccupare.	I didn't tell you **because** I didn't want to worry you.
Sono dovuta andare via presto **perché** avevo una riunione.	I had to leave early **because** I had a meeting.

ASKING FOR INFORMATION

When you're asking for information you will need to use question words, for example, **Cosa...?** (*What...?*), **Quale...?** (*Which...?*), **Che...?** (*Which...?*), **Dove...?** (*Where...?*), **Quando...?** (*When...?*) and so on.

Cosa...?

Cos'è?	**What** is it?
Cosa fai nella vita?	**What** do you do for a living?
Cosa ha detto?	**What** did he say?
Cosa danno al cinema in questi giorni?	**What**'s on at the cinema at the moment?

Quale...?

Quale mi consiglia?	**Which** do You recommend?
Qual è quello meno caro?	**Which** one is cheaper?
Quale preferisci?	**Which** one do you like best?

In summary...

Che...?

Che macchina guida?	**What** car does he drive?
Che numero ha l'agenzia immobiliare?	**What's** the number of the estate agent's?
Che ora **è**?	**What** time **is** it?

Dove...?

Dov'è il commissariato di polizia?	**Where**'s the police station?
Dove sono le toilette?	**Where** are the toilets?
Dove devo firmare?	**Where** do I have to sign?
Dov'è il municìpio?	**Where**'s the town hall?

Quando...?

Quando vieni a cena?	**When** are you coming to dinner?
Quando vi sposate?	**When** are _you_ getting married?
Quando è il prossimo volo per Londra?	**When** is the next flight to London?

To ask what time something is due to happen, use **A che ora...?** (_What time...?_).

A che ora...?

A che ora chiude il museo?	**What time** does the museum close?
A che ora comincia il film?	**What time** does the film start?
A che ora pensi di andare?	**What time** are you thinking of going?

You use **C'è...?** and **Ci sono...?** for _Is there...?_ and _Are there...?_.

C'è...?

C'è una panetteria in questa zona?	**Is there** a baker's in this area?
C'è carne nel sugo?	**Is there** meat in the sauce?
Ci sono altre edìcole qui vicino?	**Are there** other newsagents round here?

To ask how you do something or what something is like, use
Come...?.

Come...?

Come va?	**How** are you?
Come si fa a procurarsi biglietti?	**How** do you get tickets?
Com'è Livorno?	**What**'s Livorno **like**?
Come si chiama?	**What**'s Your name?

To ask *how much* use **quanto** or **quanta**, to ask *how many*, use
quanti or **quante**.

Quanto...?

Quanto costa un biglietto per Genova?	**How much** is a ticket to Genoa?
Quanta medicina è rimasta?	**How much** medicine is left?
Quante cipolle sono rimaste?	**How many** onions are there left?
Quanti chilometri sono fino a Pavia?	**How many** kilometres to Pavia?
Quante fermate mancano al Duomo?	**How many** stops to the Duomo?
Quanto ci si mette per arrivare a Portofino?	**How long** does it take to get to Portofino?

ASKING FOR PERMISSION

The simplest way to ask for permission to do something is by
using **Posso...?** (*Can I...?*) or **Potrei...?** (*Could I...?*), followed by
a verb in the infinitive. **posso** and **potrei** come from the verb
potere (*to be able*). For more information on **potere**, see page
284.

Posso...?

Posso usare il telefono?	**Can I** use the phone?
Posso pagarla in due rate?	**Can I** pay You in two instalments?

Potrei...?

Potrei restare ancora una settimana?	**Could I** stay for another week?
Potrei parcheggiare qua la macchina?	**Could I** park my car here?

Alternatively, you can use **Le dispiace se...?** (*Do You mind if...?*) or, more informally, **Ti dispiace se...**, followed by a verb in the present tense. If you are talking to more than one person, use **Vi dispiace se...?**. For more information on the present tense, see page 271.

Le dispiace se...?

Le dispiace se fumo?	**Do You mind if** I smoke?
Le dispiace se apro la finestra?	**Do You mind if** I open the window?
Ti dispiace se invito degli amici stasera?	**Do you mind if** I have a few friends over tonight?
Vi dispiace se non vengo con voi stasera?	**Do <u>you</u> mind if** I don't come with <u>you</u> tonight?

ASKING FOR THINGS

To ask for things in Italian you can simply name what you want and say **per favore** (*please*). As an alternative to **per favore**, use **per piacere** or **per cortesia**.

Un..., per favore.

Un biglietto di sola andata per Parma, **per favore**.	**A** single to Parma, **please**.
Una limonata, **per favore**.	**A** lemonade, **please**.
Una ciabatta, **per piacere**.	**One** ciabatta, **please**.
Due panini **e quattro** pizzette, **per favore**.	**Two** rolls **and four** small pizzas, **please**.

To say what you'd like or what you want, you can use **vorrei** (*I'd like*), which comes from the verb **volere** (*to want*). For more information on **volere**, see page 285.

Vorrei...

Vorrei dei francobolli, per favore.	**I'd like** some stamps, please.
Vorrei due biglietti per la mostra.	**I'd like** two tickets for the exhibition, please.
Vorremmo un appartamento con vista mare.	**We'd like** a flat with a sea view.

BUONO A SAPERSI!
Remember that in Italian you don't need to use **per favore** as often as you use *please* in English. Your tone of voice can convey politeness.

One way of asking whether something is available is to use **Ha...?** (*Do You have...?*). **ha** comes from the verb **avere** (*to have*). For more information on **avere**, see page 279.

Ha...?

Ha il giornale di oggi?	**Do You have** today's newspaper?
Ha un indirizzo di posta elettronica?	**Do You have** an email address?

To say what you're looking for you can use **cerco**, which comes from the verb **cercare** (*to look for*).

Cerco...

Cerco un posto per mettere la tenda.	**I'm looking for** somewhere to camp.
Cerco un ristorante vegetariano.	**I'm looking for** a vegetarian restaurant.
Cerchiamo un albergo in centro.	**We are looking for** a hotel in the town centre.

To ask someone if they can do something for you, use **Può...?** (*Can You..?*) or **Potrebbe...?** (*Could You..?*) and then the verb in the infinitive. **può** and **potrebbe** come from the verb **potere** (*to be able*). For more information on **potere**, see page 284.

Può...?

Può darmi una borsa, per piacere?	**Can You** give me a carrier bag, please?
Può darci una ricevuta?	**Can You** give us a receipt?
Mi **può** fare una fotocopia della cartina, per favore?	**Can You** photocopy the map for me, please?
Ci **può** portare la lista dei vini, per favore?	**Can You** bring us the wine list, please?

BUONO A SAPERSI!
Remember that in Italian you can say **Mi può dare...?** or **Può darmi...?** (*Can you give me...?*).

Potrebbe...?

Potrebbe spostare la macchina, per favore?	**Could You** move your car, please?
Le potrebbe dare un messaggio?	**Could You** give her a message?
Mi potrebbe contattare sul mio cellulare?	**Could You** contact me on my mobile?
Ci potrebbe dare una ricevuta?	**Could you** give us a receipt?

You can use **Mi dà...?** followed by **per favore** to mean *Can I have..., please?* especially when asking for something at a counter or when asking someone to pass you something. If you are talking to somebody you know well, or somebody younger, use **Mi dai...?**.

Mi dà...?

Mi dà una ciabatta, per favore?	**Can I have** a ciabatta, please?
Mi dà una limonata, per favore?	**Can I have** a lemonade, please?
Mi dai la penna, per piacere?	**Can I have** your pen, please?

COMPLAINING

If you need to complain, you may want to use **c'è** and **non c'è** to talk about what there is and what there isn't. If you are referring to more than one thing, use **ci sono** and **non ci sono**.

C'è...

C'è troppo rumore.	**There's** too much noise.
Ci sono scarafaggi nell'appartamento.	**There are** cockroaches in the flat.
Non c'è acqua calda.	**There isn't any** hot water.
Non ci sono asciugamani puliti in camera.	**There aren't any** clean towels in the room.

You can also use **non c'è abbastanza**, or **non ci sono abbastanza**, to say that there isn't enough of something.

Non c'è abbastanza...

Non c'è abbastanza luce.	**There's not enough** light.
Non ci sono abbastanza informazioni.	**There isn't enough** information.
Non c'erano abbastanza sedie.	**There weren't enough** chairs.

When something has run out, you can use **non c'è più** or **non ci sono più**.

Non c'è più...

Non c'è più carta igienica nella toilette delle signore.	**There isn't any** toilet paper **left** in the ladies.
Non ci sono più depliant.	**There aren't any** leaflets **left**.

In summary...

When you're describing people or things, use **è** (*he/she/it is*) followed by an adjective.

È...

È molto alto.	**He's** very tall.
È simpatica.	**She's** nice.
È bello.	**It's** beautiful.
È lontano.	**It's** a long way away.
È pesantissimo.	**It's** really heavy.

BUONO A SAPERSI!

In Italian personal pronouns like **io**, **tu**, **lui**, **lei** etc. (*I, you, he, she* etc), are used much less than in English. They tend to be used for emphasis, for example, **è lei che dovrebbe chiedere scusa** (*it's she who should apologize*), **non sono stato io** (*it wasn't me*).

avere (*to have*) is used to talk about the characteristics that people have. Remember that it's also used with **anni** (*years*) to talk about ages. For more information about **avere**, see page 279.

Ha...

Ha i capelli grigi.	**He's got** grey hair.
Ha gli occhi azzurri.	**She's got** blue eyes.
Ha la carnagione scura.	**He has** a dark complexion.
Ho ventidue **anni**.	**I'm** twenty two.

BUONO A SAPERSI!

Remember to use the article in Italian (**il**, **la**, **gli** etc.) before the part of the body or feature you are talking about, for example, **ha gli occhi azzurri** (*she has blue eyes*).

To explain what the problem is, use **c'è** and **ci sono** to say *there is* and *there are*. If you are talking about the past, use **c'è stato** or **ci sono stati**.

C'è...

C'è uno strano rumore.	**There's** a strange noise.
Non ci sono asciugamani nella stanza.	**There aren't** any towels in my room.
C'è stato un incidente.	**There's been** an accident.
Non ci sono state lamentele.	**There have been** no complaints.

BUONO A SAPERSI!
Remember to match **stato** and **stati** to the gender of the word that follows: **non c'è stato un volo prima di oggi** (*there wasn't a flight before today*) but **non c'è stata una grande affluenza di pubblico** (*not many people attended*).

To say what you can't do, use **non riesco a** (*I can't*) followed by the infinitive.

Non riesco a...

Non riesco a far partire la macchina.	**I can't** get the car to start.
Non riesco a contattare la mia famiglia.	**I can't** get in touch with my family.
Non riusciamo a far funzionare il riscaldamento.	**We can't** get the heating to work.

You use **non so...** for *I can't* when you mean *I don't know how to*.

Non so...

Non so cucinare.	**I can't** cook.
Non so parlare molto bene l'italiano.	**I can't** speak Italian very well.
Non sa guidare.	**He can't** drive.

Use **penso che**, **trovo che** or **credo che** to mean *I think*. These are all followed by the subjunctive, or the future tense if you are talking about the future. For more information on the subjunctive and the future, see pages 273 and 271.

Penso che...

Penso che dovrebbe prenotare in anticipo.	**I think** You should book in advance.
Penso che pioverà.	**I think** it's going to rain.
Non penso che sia una buona idea.	**I don't think** it's a good idea.
Non penso che sia già arrivato.	**I don't think** he's arrived yet.
Cosa ne pensi?	**What do you think**?

Trovo che...

Trovo che abbia ragione.	**I think** he's right.
Trovo che sia un po' caro.	**I think** it's a bit expensive.
Trovo che sia un po' infantile.	**I think** he's a bit childish.
Non trovo che sia un bel film.	**I don't think** it's a very good film.

Credo che...

Credo che ti preoccupi per niente.	**I think** you're worrying about nothing.
Crede che ne valga la pena?	**Do You think** it's worth it?
Non credo che ce la faremo.	**I don't think** we'll make it.

Use **sono d'accordo** to say that you agree and **non sono d'accordo** to say that you disagree.

Sono d'accordo...

Sono d'accordo con te.	**I agree with** you.
Siamo entrambi **d'accordo**.	**We** both **agree**.
Non sono affatto **d'accordo**.	**I** completely **disagree**.

Use **potremmo** (*we could*) if you want to suggest doing something with someone.

Potremmo...

Potremmo andare al cinema.	**We could** go to the cinema.
Potremmo sederci fuori.	**We could** sit outside.

Another way to suggest something is to turn a simple sentence into a suggestion by using a questioning tone of voice.

Prendiamo qualcosa da bere?	**Shall we have** something to drink?
Diamo un'occhiata al menù?	**Shall we have a look at** the menu?

Perché non...? can be used to mean *Why don't we...?*.

Perché non...?

Perché non chiediamo a una commessa?	**Why don't** we ask a shop assistant?
Perché non facciamo una tappa a Urbino strada facendo?	**Why don't** we stop in Urbino on the way?

You can also use **E se...?** (*How about...?*) followed by a verb in the imperfect subjunctive to suggest doing something. For more information on the subjunctive, see page 273.

E se...?

E se passassimo la notte qui?	**How about** spending the night here?
E se ci andassimo in traghetto?	**How about** going there by ferry?
E se chiedessimo al carabiniere?	**How about** asking the police officer?
E se noleggiassimo una macchina?	**How about** hiring a car?

You can ask someone if they'd like to do something using **Le andrebbe di...?** or, more informally, **Ti andrebbe di...?** (*Would you like...?*) with the infinitive. If you are talking to more than one person, use **Vi andrebbe di...?**. **andrebbe** comes from the verb **andare**. For more information on **andare**, see page 278.

Le andrebbe di...?

Le andrebbe di venire a bere qualcosa?	**Would You like** to come and have a drink?
Ti andrebbe di visitare la cattedrale?	**Would you like** to see the cathedral?
Vi andrebbe di cenare da noi?	**Would <u>you</u> like** to come to dinner with us?

To ask someone if they fancy something, you can use **Hai voglia di...?** (*Do you fancy...?*) or more formally **Ha voglia di...?**, followed by the infinitive. If you are talking to more than one person use **Avete voglia di...?**.

Hai voglia di...?

Hai voglia di mangiare un gelato?	**Do you fancy** an ice cream?
Ha voglia di prendere un caffè?	**Do You fancy** going for a coffee?
Avete voglia di andare a fare un giro in barca?	**Do <u>you</u> fancy** going sailing?

To offer to do something, you can use **lasci che** (or the **tu** form **lascia che**) to mean *let me*, followed by a verb in the subjunctive. For more information on the subjunctive, see page 273.

Lasci che...

Lasci che l'aiuti.	**Let me** help You.
Lascia che ti porti la valigia.	**Let me** carry your suitcase.

Use **Le dispiace se...?** or, more informally, **Ti dispiace se...?** to say *Is it okay with you if...?*. If you are talking to more than one person use **Vi dispiace se...?**.

Le dispiace se...?

Le dispiace se la chiamo a casa?	**Is it okay with You if** I call You at home?
Ti dispiace se ripasso domani?	**Is it okay with you if** I come back tomorrow?
Vi dispiace se io resto qua?	**Is it okay with <u>you</u> if** I stay here?

If you want to say what would suit you better, you can use **Mi andrebbe meglio...** (*It would be better for me...*).

Mi andrebbe meglio...

Mi andrebbe meglio venerdì.	Friday **would be better for me**.
Mi andrebbe meglio incontrarvi là.	**It would be better for me** if I met <u>you</u> there.

SAYING WHAT'S HAPPENED

To talk about what has happened, in Italian you use the past tense made with **avere** (*to have*) or **essere** (*to be*) and the past participle. You can find out more about the past tense on page 269.

Ho...

Ho avuto un incidente.	**I've had** an accident.
Abbiamo mangiato molto bene.	**We ate** very well.
Abbiamo assistito a uno scippo.	**We've witnessed** a mugging.

Sono...

Sono arrivato stamattina.	**I arrived** this morning.
Mi sono rotta la gamba.	**I've broken** my leg.
È caduto.	**He fell**.

SAYING WHAT YOU HAVE TO DO

To say what you have to do, use **devo** (*I need to*) followed by a verb in the infinitive. **devo** is from the verb **dovere** (*to have to*). For more information on **dovere**, see page 281.

Devo...

Devo fare il pieno.	**I need to** fill up the car.
Devo fare una telefonata.	**I need to** make a phone call.
Dobbiamo andarli a prendere all'aeroporto.	**We have to** pick them up from the airport.

You can also use **bisogna che** followed by a verb in the subjunctive. For more information on the subjunctive, see page 273.

Bisogna che...

Bisogna che gli parli subito.	**I must** talk to him straightaway.
Bisogna che li avvertiamo per tempo.	**We must** let them know in advance.
Bisogna che tu vada di persona.	**You must** go in person.

To talk about what you should do, use **dovrei** (*I should*) followed by the infinitive. **dovrei** is from the verb **dovere** (*to have to*). For more information on **dovere**, see page 281.

Dovrei...

Dovrei andare.	**I should** go.
Dovrei fare le pulizie.	**I should** clean up.
Dovreste venire a trovarci.	**You should** come and see us.

In summary...

SAYING WHAT YOU LIKE, DISLIKE, PREFER

To say what you like in Italian, use **mi piace** (*I like*) with singular nouns and **mi piacciono** with plural nouns. To say what you dislike, use **non mi piace** or **non mi piacciono** (*I don't like*). You can use the verb **amare** to say you really love something.

Mi piace...

Mi piace questo quadro.	**I like** this painting.
Mi piace molto la Calabria.	**I like** Calabria **a lot**.
Mi piacciono i paesini dell'Umbria.	**I like** the small villages in Umbria.
Ti è piaciuta la commedia?	**Did you like** the play?
Mi piace di più suo fratello.	**I think** his brother is more attractive.

Amo...

Amo la poesia.	**I love** poetry.
Amo i film in bianco e nero.	**I love** black and white movies.
Ama cucinare.	**He loves** cooking.

Non mi piace...

Non mi piace la musica jazz.	**I don't like** jazz.
Non mi piacciono gli espressionisti.	**I don't like** expressionist painting.

BUONO A SAPERSI!

If you want to tell somebody that you like them, use **Mi sei simpatico** or **simpatica** if they are just a friend. To say *I love you* in Italian, use **Ti voglio bene** (*I care about you*), if you are talking to a friend, a child and so on, and **Ti amo** to somebody with whom you are romantically involved.

To say what you prefer, use **preferisco** (*I prefer*). To say that you prefer A to B, use **preferisco A a B**. **preferisco** comes from the verb **preferire**. For more information on **-ire** verbs like **preferire**, see page 268.

Preferisco...

Preferisco la camicia grigia.	**I prefer** the grey shirt.
Preferisco il treno **al** pullman.	**I prefer** the train **to** the bus.
Preferisco la cucina italiana **alla** cucina francese.	**I prefer** Italian food **to** French food.

SAYING WHAT YOU WANT TO DO

To say what you'd like to do, you can use **vorrei** and **mi piacerebbe** (*I'd like*). These come from the verbs **volere** and **piacere**.

Vorrei...

Vorrei andare a San Marco.	**I'd like** to go to San Marco.
Vorrei guadagnare di più.	**I'd like** to earn more.
Vorrei controllare la mia posta elettronica.	**I'd like** to check my emails.

Mi piacerebbe...

Mi piacerebbe vedere l'Arena.	**I'd like** to see the Arena.
Ci piacerebbe fermarci qui un po' di più.	**We'd like** to stay here a little longer.

To talk about what you'd rather do, use **preferirei** from the verb **preferire** (*to prefer*). For more information on **–ire** verbs like **preferire**, see page 268.

In summary...

Preferirei...

Preferirei partire al mattino presto.	**I'd rather** leave early in the morning.
Preferirei prendere in affitto un appartamentino.	**I'd rather** rent a small flat.
Preferiremmo non lasciare il bagaglio in macchina.	**We'd rather not** leave the luggage in the car.

If you want to sound more assertive, you can use **voglio** (*I want*) from the verb **volere** (*to want*) or **esigo** (*I demand*) from the verb **esigere** (*to demand*).

Voglio...

Voglio parlare con il responsabile.	**I want to** speak to the manager.
Voglio sapere perché l'appartamento non è più disponibile.	**I want to** know why the flat is no longer available.
Non voglio pagare nessun supplemento.	**I don't want to** pay a supplement.

Esigo...

Esigo una spiegazione!	**I demand** an explanation!
Esigo di essere risarcito di tutte le spese!	**I demand to** be refunded in full!

To talk about your plans, you can use either **ho intenzione di** or **conto di**. They both mean *I'm planning to* and are followed by a verb in the infinitive.

Ho intenzione di...

Ho intenzione di passare due settimane in Maremma.	**I'm planning to** spend two weeks in Maremma.
Ho intenzione di far costruire una casa.	**I'm planning to** have a house built.
Abbiamo intenzione di trasferirci qui.	**We're planning to** move here.

Conto di...

Conto di stare da un amico.	**I'm planning to** stay with a friend.
Non conto di fermarmi qui a lungo.	**I'm not planning to** stay here very long.
Contavamo di fermarci a dormire a Firenze.	**We were planning to** spend the night in Florence.

If you want to say what you're thinking of doing, you can use **penso di** (*I'm thinking of*) or **pensavo di** (*I was thinking of*) followed by a verb in the infinitive.

Penso di...

Penso di comprarmi una macchina nuova.	**I'm thinking of** buying a new car.
Penso di arrivare verso le cinque.	**I'm thinking of** arriving around five.
Pensavo di invitare Anna a cena.	**I was thinking of** inviting Anna to dinner.

One easy way of talking about what you're going to do is to use the future tense. For more information on the future tense, see page 271.

Chiamerò Simone.	**I'm going to phone** Simone.
Manderò una cartolina ai miei.	**I'm going to send** a postcard to my parents.
Andremo a vedere un appartamento questa settimana.	**We're going to** look at a flat this week.

You can also use the present tense to talk about something that you're definitely going to do. For more information on the present tense, see page 271.

Parto domani alle undici.	**I'm leaving** tomorrow at eleven.
Ceno da Marina stasera.	**I'm having dinner** at Marina's tonight.
Andiamo a Napoli tra due settimane.	**We're going** to Naples in two weeks.
Arriva la settimana prossima.	**She's coming** next week.

To talk about what you hope to do, you can use **spero di** (*I'm hoping to*) followed by the verb in the infinitive.

Spero di...

Spero di ritornarci un giorno.	**I'm hoping to** go back there one day.
Spero di potervi raggiungere sabato.	**I'm hoping to** be able to join you on Saturday.
Speriamo di arrivare in tempo.	**We hope** we'll get there in time.

To say what you may do, you can use **forse** (*perhaps*) followed by a verb in the present or in the future tense.

Forse...

Forse faccio una festa.	**I may** have a party.
Forse stasera vado a bere qualcosa con Thomas.	**I may** go and have a drink with Thomas tonight.
Forse si trasferirà per sempre in Italia.	**She may** move to Italy permanently.

One-stop
phrase shop

Chiedo scusa? – I beg your pardon?

Every day we use a variety of ready-made phrases that just trip off the tongue in English, such as *take a seat*, *hurry up*, *congratulations*, *happy birthday*, *have a nice day*, *thanks* and *the same to you*. In this unit we'll give you all these phrases and more that you'll need in Italian, so that you can say the appropriate thing with confidence.

CONTENTS

One-stop phrase shop

HELLOS AND GOODBYES

Creating a good first impression is important, so you'll want to say *hello* to people properly. Just as in English, there are several ways of doing this in Italian. If you are addressing someone you don't know well, or if you are in a shop or office, you can use **buongiorno** throughout the day or **buonasera** (*good afternoon* or *good evening*) later. You can also use the more informal **salve** (*hello*). If you know the person well or they are young, you can use **ciao** (*hi*).

Hello

Buongiorno, signora.	Good morning (*or* afternoon).
Buonasera, professore.	Good evening, professor.
Salve, mi sa dire dov'*è* la banca?	Hello, can you tell me where the bank is, please?
Ciao, c'è la mamma?	Hi, is your mum in?

> **BUONO A SAPERSI!**
> **signora** is much less formal than *madam* in English. You can use it when greeting a woman politely, whether a stranger or someone you know.

Goodbye

Arrivederci, signora!	Goodbye!
Ciao!	Bye!
Buongiorno!	Goodbye!
Buonasera!	Good night!

> **BUONO A SAPERSI!**
> As you'll have noticed, **ciao** can be used both when arriving and when leaving. **buongiorno** and **buonasera** can also be used in both situations. Use **buonanotte** (*good night*) only at bedtime.

See you...!

A dopo!	**See you** later!
A più tardi!	**See you** later!
A domani!	**See you** tomorrow!
A lunedì!	**See you** on Monday!
Ci vediamo!	**See you** again!

When you're introduced to someone, you need to know how to reply. **piacere** is what people usually say.

How do you do?

Piacere. – Piacere.	Nice to meet you. – Nice to meet you too.
Piacere di conoscerla. – Il piacere è mio.	Pleased to meet You. – Pleased to meet You too.
Piacere di conoscerti. – Altrettanto.	Nice to meet you. – Nice to meet you too.

To welcome somebody in Italian, use **benvenuto** (or **benvenuta**), followed by **a** with the name of a town and **in** with the name of most countries or regions.

Welcome to...!

Benvenuto!	Welcome!
Benvenuto in Italia!	Welcome to Italy!
Benvenuta a Perugia!	Welcome to Perugia!
Benvenuti in Sicilia, signori!	Welcome to Sicily, ladies and gentlemen!
Benvenute a Trieste, signore!	Welcome to Trieste, ladies!

How lovely to see you!

Che piacere rivederti, Gianni!	How lovely to see you again, Gianni!
Che piacere rivederla, signora!	How lovely to see You again!
Sono secoli che non ci vediamo!	I haven't seen you for ages!

One-stop phrase shop

As in English, in Italian there are several ways you can ask someone how they are, and a variety of ways to reply.

How are you?

Come va? – Bene, e tu?	**How are you**? – Fine thanks, and you?
Come sta, signora? – Bene, grazie, e lei?	**How are you**? – Fine thanks, and You?
Salve! **Come te la passi**?	Hello! **How's it going**?
Come ti senti?	**How are you feeling**?

I'm...

Bene, grazie, e tu?	I'm fine thanks. And you?
Non male!	Not too bad!
Si tira avanti!	Surviving!
Non mi posso lamentare.	Mustn't grumble.
Molto meglio, grazie.	A lot better, thanks.

A knock at the door

C'è qualcuno?	Is there anyone here?
Chi è?	Who is it?
Un momento!	One moment!
Arrivo!	I'm coming!

Asking someone in

Avanti!	Come in!
Dopo di lei!	After You!
Si accomodi!	Do sit down!
Prego, ragazzi, sedetevi pure.	Do sit down, everybody.
Fai come se fossi a casa tua.	Make yourself at home.

When requesting something from someone, you can use **per favore** (*please*). **per piacere** and **per cortesia** are also used.

Please

Mi dà una birra piccola, **per favore**?	Can I have a half of lager, **please**?
Mi passi il telecomando, **per favore**?	Could you give me the remote control, **please**?
Due chili di arance, **per cortesia**.	Two kilos of oranges, **please**.
Mi direbbe l'ora, **per piacere**?	**Please** could You tell me the time?
Sì, **grazie**.	Yes, **please**.

BUONO A SAPERSI!
In Italian, **per favore** is used less often than *please* is in English. You can still be polite by using the right tone of voice.

Like *thank you* in English, in Italian **grazie** on its own can be used with people you call *tu*, *lei* or *voi*.

Thank you!

Grazie!	**Thank you**!
Grazie del regalo.	**Thank you** for the present.
Mille **grazie**.	**Thank you** very much.
Molte **grazie**, signora!	**Many thanks**!
La ringrazio, signore.	**Thank You**, sir.
Ti ringrazio.	**Thank you**.
Ti ringrazio tanto della lettera.	**Thank you** very much for your letter.

BUONO A SAPERSI!
When you're offered something, you can accept by saying **sì grazie**, or just **grazie**, for example, **Beve qualcosa?** – **Sì, grazie** (*Would You like a drink? – Yes, please*).

The commonest response to **grazie** is **prego** (*you're welcome*), or you can say **di niente** (*not at all*). For greater emphasis you can use **s'immagini** or **si figuri** in the **lei** form, and **figurati** in the **tu** form (*don't mention it*).

Not at all

Grazie! – Prego!	Thank you! – You're welcome!
Di niente!	Not at all!
Si figuri!	Don't mention it!
Grazie, Andrea – Di niente, figurati!	Thank you, Andrea. – Don't mention it!
Grazie. – Grazie a lei!	Thank You. – Thank *You*!
Grazie tante, signora. – S'immagini, è un piacere!	Thank You. – Don't mention it, it's a pleasure.

ATTRACTING SOMEONE'S ATTENTION

To attract someone's attention, you can use **scusi** or **mi scusi**. Use **scusa** or **scusami** with somebody you know well or somebody younger.

Excuse me!

Scusi!	**Excuse me**, please!
Mi scusi, signora!	**Excuse me**!
Scusa!	**Excuse me**!
Scusami!	**Excuse me**!

Sometimes you might have a problem understanding what's been said or may not know the right words to express what you want to say in Italian. Here are some useful phrases to help you when this happens.

I don't understand

Scusi, **non capisco**.	Sorry, **I don't understand**.
Potrebbe ripetere? **Non ho capito**.	Please could You repeat that? **I didn't understand**.
Mi scusi, **non ho capito** quello che ha detto.	Sorry, **I didn't understand** what You said.

How do you say...?

Come si dice 'driving licence' in italiano?	**How do you say** 'driving licence' in Italian?
Come si chiama in italiano?	**What's this called** in Italian?

Would you mind...?

Le dispiacerebbe parlare più lentamente?	**Would You mind** speaking more slowly?
Le dispiacerebbe ripetere?	**Would You mind** repeating that?

What...?

Scusi, **cosa** ha detto?	Sorry, **what** did You say?
Scusa, **come** hai detto?	Sorry, **what** did you say?
Mi scusi, **cosa vuol dire** 'vietato'?	Sorry, **what** does 'vietato' mean?

One-stop phrase shop

CHECKING FACTS

To check your facts, you can use **vero?** and **no?**. They are used at the end of statements in the same way as *isn't it?*, *haven't you?* and so on are used in English.

... isn't it?

Siete di Napoli, **vero**?	You're from Naples, **aren't you**?
È rumoroso, **vero**?	It's noisy, **isn't it**?
Voi siete arrivati ieri, **no**?	You arrived yesterday, **didn't you**?
Vieni **o no**?	Are you coming **or not**?
Tu gli hai detto che andava bene, **no**?	You told him it was okay, **didn't you**?
Hai i passaporti, **vero**?	You do have the passports, **don't you**?

To say *Don't you think?* In Italian, you can use **non trova** when addressing someone you don't know well, **non trovi** when addressing somebody you know well or somebody young, and **non trovate** when you are talking to several people.

Don't you think?

Fa freddo, **non trova**?	It's cold, **don't You think**?
Le sta bene, **non trovi**?	It suits her, **don't you think**?
È bello, **non trovate**?	It's beautiful, **don't you think**?

To say that you hope someone will have a good time, a nice weekend and so on, use **buon** before a masculine word, **buona** before a feminine one.

Have a nice...!

Buon fine settimana!	Have a nice weekend!
Buon vi*a*ggio!	Have a good trip!
Buon appetito!	Enjoy your meal!
Buona notte!	Sleep well!
Buone vacanze!	Have a nice holiday!
Buon divertimento!	Have fun!
Alla salute!	Cheers! (*when drinking*)
Salute!	Bless you! (*when somebody sneezes*)

You can also use **buon** and **buona** when wishing someone *Happy...!*.

Happy...!

Buon Natale!	**Happy** Christmas!
Buon Anno!	**Happy** New Year!
Buon compleanno!	**Happy** birthday!
Buon anniversario di matrimonio!	**Happy** wedding anniversary!
Buona Pasqua!	**Happy** Easter!

BUONO A SAPERSI!

Altrettanto! (*The same to you!*) is a useful word. Use it in reply to expressions such as **Buon Natale!** (*Happy Christmas!*) and **Buon appetito!** (*Enjoy your meal!*), if you want to wish the other person the same thing back.

Good luck!

Buona fortuna!	**Good luck**!
Buona fortuna col nuovo lavoro!	**Good luck** with your new job!
Auguri per l'esame!	**Good luck** for the exam!

BUONO A SAPERSI!

Sometimes it's actually considered 'unlucky' to wish somebody good luck! Instead, you are supposed to say **In bocca al lupo!** (literally *In the wolf's mouth!*). It's informal, and the expected answer is **Crepi il lupo!** (*May the wolf die!*).

APOLOGIZING

To say *I'm sorry*, you can use **mi dispiace**, **mi scuso** or **scusa**. More formally, especially if you've done something more serious, you can use **sono desolato**, or **sono desolata** if you're a woman.

I'm sorry...

Mi dispiace, non intendevo offenderla.	**I'm sorry**, I didn't mean to offend You.
Mi dispiace di non averla richiamata prima.	**I'm sorry** that I didn't call You back sooner.
Mi scuso del ritardo.	**I'm sorry** I'm late.
Scusa, è colpa mia.	**Sorry**, it's my fault.
Sono veramente **desolato**!	**I'm** really **sorry**!

BUONO A SAPERSI!

You can also say **chiedo scusa** (*sorry* or *excuse me*), especially if you need to get past someone, or if you bump into them.

I'm afraid...

Ho paura di sì.	**I'm afraid** so.
Temo di sì.	**I'm afraid** so.
Temo di no.	**I'm afraid** not.
Ho paura di no.	**I'm afraid** not.
Temo di averlo rotto.	**I'm afraid** I may have broken it.

One-stop phrase shop

REASSURING SOMEONE

If someone apologizes to you or tells you they've accidentally done something, you can reassure them by saying **non fa niente** or **non importa** (*it doesn't matter*). There are also a number of other expressions you can use.

It doesn't matter

Non fa niente.	It doesn't matter.
Non importa.	It doesn't matter.
Non si preoccupi, signora!	Don't worry, madam!
Non preoccuparti!	Don't worry!
Non preoccuparti, non ha importanza.	Don't worry about it! It doesn't matter.
Nessun problema.	Don't worry about it.

OPINIONS

To express your opinion in Italian, you can use **credo**, **penso** (*I think*), or **suppongo** (*I suppose*).

I think so

Credo di sì.	I think so.
Penso di sì.	I think so.
Suppongo di sì.	I suppose so.

I don't think so

Non credo.	I don't think so.
Penso di no.	I don't think so.
Suppongo di no.	I suppose not.

I hope so

Lo spero.	I hope so.
Lo spero proprio.	I really hope so.
Spero di sì.	I hope so.
Spero proprio di no.	I really hope not.

I'm not sure

Non sono sicuro.	I'm not sure.
Non so.	I don't know.
Sei sicuro?	Are you sure?

BUONO A SAPERSI!

Remember that if you're a woman, you would say **sicura** instead of **sicuro**.

I doubt it

Ne dubito.	I doubt it.
Ho i miei dubbi.	I have my doubts.

I don't mind

Mi è indifferente.	I don't mind.
Non importa.	I don't mind.
Per me fa lo stesso.	It's all the same to me.

AGREEING, DISAGREEING AND DECLINING

The word for *yes* in Italian is **sì**.

Yes

Sì.	**Yes**.
Sì, certo.	**Yes**, of course.

That's true

È **vero**.	**That's true**.
Non **è** proprio **vero**.	**That's** not really **true**.
È proprio **così**.	**It's** exactly **that**.

I agree...

Sono completamente **d'accordo**.	I totally **agree**.
Sono d'accordo con Paola.	**I agree** with Paola.
Anch'io la penso così.	I think that too.

If someone asks you to do something, particularly useful phrases are **D'accordo!** (*OK!*), **Certo!** (*Of course!*) or **Nessun problema!** (*No problem!*). **OK** is also commonly used in Italian.

OK!

D'accordo!	OK!
Allora d'accordo.	OK, then.
OK, va bene così.	OK, that's fine.
Ti dispiace? – No, nessun problema.	Do you mind? – No, no problem.

Of course

Ma certo!	**Of course**!
Sì, **certo**.	Yes, **of course**.
Mi aiuterai? – Ma **certo**!	Will you help me? – **Of course** I will!

To disagree with someone or refuse something, you can use **no** or one of several other common sentences expressing disagreement.

No

No.	No.
Certo che no.	Of course not.
Non è vero.	That's not true.
Be', ti sbagli.	Well, you're wrong.
Non sono affatto d'accordo.	I don't agree at all.
Ha torto marcio.	He's completely in the wrong.

There are several words you can use with **non posso** (*I can't*) to say you regret being unable to do something, for example **onestamente** (*honestly*), **sinceramente** (*truly*), **sfortunatamente** (*unfortunately*).

I can't

Vorrei ma sfortunatamente **non posso**.	I'd like to but unfortunately **I can't**.
No, onestamente proprio **non posso**.	No, honestly, **I** just **can't**.
Mi dispiace ma **non posso**.	I'm afraid **I can't**.
Mi dispiace veramente, ma **non mi sarà possibile** venire.	I'm truly sorry, but **I won't be able** to make it.

If you don't want to commit yourself, **forse** is the easiest way of saying *perhaps* in Italian. There are several other ways of expressing uncertainty.

Perhaps

Forse.	Perhaps.
È possibile.	Possibly.
Potresti aver ragione.	You may be right.
Può essere benissimo.	It could well be.
Dipende.	It depends.
Vedremo.	We'll see.
Chissà, magari funziona.	Who knows, it might work.
Magari ce la facciamo.	We might still make it.

CONGRATULATING SOMEONE

To congratulate someone on their success, you can use
Complimenti! or **Congratulazioni!** (*Congratulations!*). More
informally, you can say **bravo** (*or* **brava** etc).

Congratulations!

Congratulazioni!	**Congratulations**!
Congratulazioni per aver superato gli esami!	**Congratulations** on passing your exams!
Complimenti!	
Complimenti per la tua promozione!	**Well done**!
	Congratulations on your promotion!
Bravo, complimenti!	
Bravissimi!	**Well done**!
Le mie più sentite **congratulazioni** agli sposi.	**Well done**, all of <u>you</u>!
	My warmest **congratulations** to the bride and groom.

REACTING TO GOOD AND BAD NEWS

It's important to know how to respond when someone tells you
that they're well or that something good has happened to them.

Glad to hear it

Mi fa piacere.	Glad to hear it.
Sono proprio contenta per te!	I'm really pleased for you!
È una gran bella notizia.	That's very good news.
Che splendida notizia!	What wonderful news!
Splendido!	How wonderful!
Ottimo!	That's great!
Fantastico!	Fantastic!

To say you're sorry about something bad that's happened, you can use **mi dispiace** (*I'm sorry*).

I'm sorry!

Mi dispiace.	**I'm sorry**.
Mi dispiace tanto per tua zia.	**I'm** really **sorry** to hear about your aunt.
Ci dispiace moltissimo **per** quanto è successo.	**We're** very **sorry about** what happened.
Sentite condoglianze a lei e alla sua famiglia.	**My condolences** to You and Your family.

There are lots of useful expressions which mean *things could be worse* or *it's not that bad*, for example, **non è poi così grave** (*it's not as bad as all that*).

It's not as bad as all that

Non è poi così grave.	It's not as bad as all that.
Non è andata poi così male.	It didn't go too badly after all.
Coraggio! Poteva andar peggio.	Cheer up! It could have been worse.
Potrebbe esser peggio.	Things could be worse.

EXCLAMATIONS

In English we often use *What a...!* when saying how something affects us or how we feel about it. In Italian, you can use **che** before a noun.

What a...!

Che paura!	**What a** fright!
Che peccato!	**What a** shame!
Che sfortuna!	**What** bad luck!
Ma guarda **che** sorpresa!	**What a** surprise!
Che splendido edificio!	**What a** wonderful building!

BUONO A SAPERSI!
The English *a* is not translated into Italian in expressions like these.

In English you can use *How...!* in exclamations. In Italian you can use **Com'è...!** or **Che...!**.

How...!

Com'è bello!	**How** beautiful!
Che generoso da parte sua!	**How** generous of him!
Che sciocco!	**How** silly!
Che delusione!	**How** disappointing!
Interessante!	Interesting!

BUONO A SAPERSI!
Like in English, sometimes **che** (*how*) can be omitted.

SURPRISE

There are many ways you can express surprise in everyday Italian.

È incredibile!	That's incredible!
Ma che sorpresa!	What a surprise!
Da non crederci!	I can't believe it!
Non può essere!	That's impossible.
Ma tu guarda!	Well, what do you know!
Davvero?	Really?
Santo cielo! È tardissimo!	Oh dear! Is that the time?

One-stop phrase shop

ENCOURAGING SOMEONE

If you need to hurry someone up or get them to do something, you can say **Forza!** (*Come on!*).

Come on!

Forza, andiamo!	**Come on!** Let's go!
Forza! Siamo in ritardo.	**Come on!** We're late.
Coraggio che ce la fai!	**Come on!** You're going to make it!
Non mollare! Quasi ci sei!	**Keep it up!** You're nearly there!
Presto! Il treno sta per partire!	**Quick!** The train is about to go!
Sbrigati! Il film sta per cominciare!	**Hurry up!** The film's about to begin!

BUONO A SAPERSI!

You use **Sbrigati!** with a person you call **tu**, **Si sbrighi!** with someone you call **lei**, and **Sbrigatevi!** with more than one person.

HANDING SOMEONE SOMETHING

If you're handing someone something, you can say **ecco** to say *here you are*. You can also say **tieni** or, more formally, **tenga**, from the verb **tenere**.

Here you are

Ecco.	Here you are.
Tieni, sono i soldi per la corriera.	Here's the money for the bus.
Tenga, questa è la chiave della cassaforte.	Here You are, this is the key for Your safe.

DANGERS AND EMERGENCIES

Certain phrases are useful to know in the event of danger or emergencies. Here are some, though let's hope you don't have to make use of them.

Look out!

Attenzione!	Look out!
Stai attento!	Be careful!
Stia attenta, signora!	Be careful, madam!
Tenete d'occhio la borsa!	Watch your bags!
Aiuto!	Help!
Aiutatemi!	Help me!
Al ladro!	Stop thief!
Al fuoco!	Fire!

SPEAKING YOUR MIND

If you get into an argument, here are some very common phrases which may come in handy! Be sure to use plenty of body language too.

For goodness sake!

Ma per piacere!	For goodness sake!
Ma cosa fa?	What do You think You're doing?
Ma chi crede di essere?	Who do You think You are?
Mi prendi in giro, vero?	Are you joking?
Figuriamoci!	Honestly!
Incredibile.	I don't believe it.
Neanche per sogno.	It's out of the question.
Sciocchezze!	Nonsense!
Ma siamo matti?	This is crazy!

• In English translations, You = polite form, you = informal form, you = plural form

CONVERSATIONAL WORDS

Just as in English, there are lots of Italian words and expressions for linking different points together or for showing what your attitude towards something is. Here are the most useful of them. If you use them they will make you sound more fluent and natural.

a dire il vero

A dire il vero, non è solo colpa sua.	It's not just his fault, **to be honest**.

alla fine

Lo hai trovato, **alla fine**?	Did you manage to get hold of him **in the end**?

allora

Sono stanca. – E **allora** va a dormire.	I'm tired. – Go to bed, **then**.
E **allora**, che si fa?	What are we doing, **then**?
Ma **allora** aveva proprio ragione lui!	**So**, he was right after all!
E **allora**? – **Allora**, cosa?	**So**? – **So** what?

a proposito

A proposito, suoni ancora il sax?	Do you still play the sax, **by the way**?

comunque

Comunque è coperto dall'assicurazione.	It's covered by the insurance **anyway**.
È meglio andarci **comunque**.	It's best to go **anyway**.

davvero

Ho deciso di non invitarla. – **Davvero**?	I've decided not to invite her. – **Really**?
È **davvero** incredibile.	It's **totally** unbelievable.

One-stop phrase shop

dunque

| **Dunque**, cos'hai deciso? | What have you decided, **then**? |

e per finire

| **E per finire**, una bella fetta di torta al cioccolato! | **And to finish**, a nice slice of chocolate cake! |

e poi

| **E poi** che facciamo? | **Then** what shall we do? |

finalmente

| **Finalmente**! È più di un'ora che ti aspetto! | **At last**! I've been waiting for you for over an hour! |

> **BUONO A SAPERSI!**
> Remember that the Italian **finalmente** means *at last*, and is never translated by the English *finally*.

innanzitutto

| **Innanzitutto** dovremmo telefonare all'agenzia. | **First of all**, we should call the agency. |

in ogni caso

| **In ogni caso**, il problema è suo, non nostro. | **In any case**, it's his problem, not ours. |

inoltre

| Sono stanca, e **inoltre** non ho nessuna voglia di andarci. | I'm tired and **what's more** I just don't feel like going. |

insomma

| Ma **insomma**! Te l'ho appena detto! | **But** I've just told you! |

ma dai

Ma dai! Non è poi così complicato!	**Oh come on**! It's not that hard!

> **BUONO A SAPERSI!**
> In Italian **ma** is often used at the start of a sentence to make
> it more emphatic, for example **Ma no!** (*No!!*), **Ma certo!** (*But of
> course!*), **Ma dai!** (*Oh come on!*).

però

Però è strano, vero?	**Still**, it's strange, isn't it?

può darsi

Tornate l'anno prossimo? – Sì, **può darsi**.	Are <u>you</u> coming back next year? – Yes, **maybe**.
Può darsi che abbia preso un altro treno.	She **might** have caught a different train.

purtroppo

Purtroppo ha ragione lui.	**Unfortunately**, he's right.

va bene

Va bene, vado io.	**OK**, I'll go.
Rispondi tu? – **Va bene**.	Can you get that? – OK.

One-stop phrase shop

NOUNS

The gender of nouns

In Italian all nouns are either masculine or feminine:

• **il**, **lo**, **un** or **uno** before a noun tells you that it is masculine
• **la** or **una** before a noun tells you that it is feminine

Whenever you are using a noun, you need to know whether it is masculine or feminine as this affects the form of other words used with it, such as:

• adjectives that describe it, for example **Che <u>bella</u> città!** (*What a <u>nice</u> town!*)
• articles that go before it, for example **<u>Il</u> treno è in ritardo** (*<u>The</u> train is running late*)
• pronouns that replace it, for example **Te <u>lo</u> presento dopo** (*I'll introduce <u>him</u> to you later*)

Adjectives, articles and pronouns are also affected by whether a noun is singular or plural.

Nouns referring to people

Most nouns referring to men and boys are masculine.

un uomo	a man
un ragazzo	a boy

Most nouns referring to women and girls are feminine.

una ragazza	a girl
una siciliana	a woman from Sicily

Nouns referring to things

In English we call all things – for example, *table, car, book* – 'it'. In Italian, however, things are either masculine or feminine.

In most cases, it is possible to work out a noun's gender by its ending:

• words ending in –**a** are generally feminine, for example, **una pasticceria** (*a baker's*), **una banca** (*a bank*)
• words ending in –**o** are generally masculine, for example, **un panino** (*a sandwich*), **un gatto** (*a cat*)
• words ending with a consonant are often masculine, for example, **il film** (*the film*), **un autobus** (*a bus*).

• words ending in –à, –sione and –zione are often feminine, for example, **una città** (*a town*), **una pensione** (*a guesthouse*), **la stazione** (*the station*)

Note that words ending in –e are masculine in some cases and feminine in others, for example, **il pallone** (*the ball*), **la gente** (*people*).

Also, be aware that a handful of very common words ending in –a are masculine: **un problema** (*a problem*), **il programma** (*the programme*), **il clima** (*the climate*). And some nouns ending with a consonant can be feminine, for example **una jeep**.

Names of days of the week and months are masculine, for example, **il lunedì** (*on a Monday*), **il luglio scorso** (*last July*), as are the names of languages, for example, **il francese** (*French*), **il giapponese** (*Japanese*). Names of towns are feminine in Italian: **Parigi è bella** (*Paris is beautiful*).

ARTICLES

Translating *the*

In Italian, articles – the words for *the* and *a* – vary according to the gender of the noun they are used with. The definite article *the* in English can be translated as follows:

the	with masculine nouns	with feminine nouns
singular	**il** or **lo (l')**	**la (l')**
plural	**i** or **gli**	**le**

There are a number of rules to help you remember which form of the definite article to use:

• Use **il** and **i** with most masculine nouns starting with a consonant:
e.g. **il ragazzo** (*the boy*), **i bambini** (*the children*).
• Use **la** and **le** with most feminine nouns starting with a consonant:
e.g. **la ragazza** (*the girl*), **le sorelle** (*the sisters*).
• Use **lo** and **gli** with nouns starting with **z**, or **s**+ another consonant, **gn**, **pn**, **ps**, **x** or **y**:
e.g. **lo zio** (*the uncle*), **lo stagno** (*the pond*), **lo yogurt** (*the yoghurt*), **gli zaini** (*the rucksacks*).
• Use **gli** before masculine plural nouns starting with a vowel or with **h**:
e.g. **gli amici** (*the friends*), **gli hotel** (*the hotels*).
• Use **l'** with all singular nouns, feminine or masculine, starting with a vowel or with **h**: e.g. **l'amico** (*the friend*), **l'arancia** (*the orange*), **l'hotel** (*the hotel*).

When using the definite article (**il**, **lo**, **la**, **l'**, **i**, **gli**, **le**) with the prepositions **a**, **da**, **di**, **in** and **su** (*to, from, of, in* and *on*) the preposition and the article can combine to make a new form:

- **a** + article → **al/allo/alla/all'/ai/agli/alle**
- **da** + article → **dal/dallo/dalla/dall'/dai/dagli/dalle**
- **di** + article → **del/dello/della/dell'/dei/degli/delle**
- **in** + article → **nel/nello/nella/nell'/nei/negli/nelle**
- **su** + article → **sul/sullo/sulla/sull'/sui/sugli/sulle**

Translating *a, an, some, any*

The indefinite articles *a* and *an* can be translated as **un** or **una** depending on whether the word they are used with is masculine or feminine.

	with masculine nouns	with feminine nouns
singular	**un** or **uno**	**una** or **un'**
plural	**dei** or **degli**	**delle**

un bambino	**a** boy
uno scolaro	**a** pupil
una riunione	**a** meeting
un'amica	**a** girlfriend

C'erano **dei** ragazzini qua fuori.	There were **some** kids out here.
Incontrava **degli** amici.	She was meeting **some** friends.
Avresti **delle** graffette?	Have you got **any** clips?

To say *some* bread, *some* pasta and so on (i.e. *some* + a noun in the singular), in Italian you can use **del** (or **dello**), **della** (or **dell'**).

C'è ancora **del** pane, se vuoi.	There's still **some** bread left, if you'd like it.
Potremmo avere **dell'**acqua, per piacere?	Could we have **some** water, please?

Italian uses the definite article much more than English does. As a rule of thumb, Italian sentences rarely start with a noun that has no article.

La Toscana è molto bella.	Tuscany is very beautiful.
La mamma arriva subito.	Mum is coming.
Non mi piace **il** riso.	I don't like rice.

In Italian you use the article before *my, your, his* etc.

Quella è **la mia** macchina.	That's **my** car.

With body parts in Italian you can use the article instead of *my*, *your*, *his* etc.

| Dammi **la** mano. | Give me **your** hand. |

PRONOUNS

Subject pronouns

Subject pronouns are words such as *I*, *he*, *she* and *they* which perform the action expressed by the verb.

io	I
tu (*informal, singular*)	you
lui (*masculine*)	he, it
lei (*feminine; polite form*)	she, it; You
noi	we
voi (*plural*)	you
loro	they

BUONO A SAPERSI!
The pronouns **egli** (*he*), **ella** (*she*), **esso/essa** (*it*), and **essi** (*they*) are still used in literary and formal written Italian, so you may well come across them. However, they are not generally used in spoken Italian.

When do you use subject pronouns in Italian?

Italian pronouns are rarely used in Italian, as the verb ending makes it clear who the subject is. However, you must use them:

• when there is no verb in Italian:

| Chi è il più bravo? – **Lui**. | Who is the best? – **He** is. |

• for emphasis, contrast or clarity:

| Pago **io**! | **I**'ll get this! |
| **Io** vado, e tu? | **I**'m going, what about you? |

• after **anche** (*too*) or **neanche** (*neither* or *either*):

| Vengo **anch'io**. | I'm coming **too**. |
| **Neanche lui** lo sa. | **He** doesn't know **either**. |

How do you say *you* in Italian?

In English we have only one way of saying *you*. In Italian there are three words: **tu**, **lei** and **voi**.

- Use **tu** when you are speaking to a person you know well, or to a child.
- Use **lei** when speaking to strangers, or anyone you're not on familiar terms with.
- Use **voi** if *you* in English refers to more than one person.

As personal pronouns are rarely spelt out in Italian, you'll need to infer which form is being used from the verb ending. As in the rest of the text, in the examples that follow a lower case *you* signals that **tu** is being implied in the Italian example sentence, *You* alerts you to the implied use of the polite form **lei**, and *you* to the plural form **voi**:

Mi presti un CD?	Will **you** lend me a CD?
Mi ripete il nome, per favore?	Could **You** repeat Your name, please?
Venite?	Are **You** coming?

BUONO A SAPERSI!

If you are in doubt as to which form of *you* to use, it is safest to use **lei** and you will not offend anyone.

Direct object pronouns

Direct object pronouns are words such as *me*, *him*, *us* and *them*, which are used instead of a noun. They stand in for the person or thing most directly affected by the action of the verb. In Italian they are:

mi	me
ti (*informal, singular*)	you
lo (*masculine*)	him, it
la (*feminine; polite form*)	her, it; You
ci	us
vi (*plural*)	you
li	them

Unlike English, you usually put Italian direct object pronouns before the verb.

Mi ha chiamato Maria.	Maria called **me**.
Ho preso il giornale. **Lo** vuoi leggere?	I've bought the paper. Do You want to read **it**?

In some cases, for instance when you use the imperative in Italian, the pronoun is joined onto the verb.

Chiama**mi** domani.	Call **me** tomorrow.

The pronoun can also be joined onto the verb when you use the infinitive, although in this case, you can also keep the pronoun separate from the verb.

Posso aiutar**ti**?	Can I help **you**?
Ti posso aiutare?	Can I help **you**?

Indirect object pronouns

An indirect object pronoun is used instead of a noun to show the person or thing the action is intended to benefit, for example the word *me* in *He did it for me*. Here are the Italian indirect object pronouns:

mi	me, to me, for me
ti (*informal, singular*)	you, to you, for you
gli (*masculine*)	him, to him, for him; it, to it, for it
le (*feminine; polite form*)	her, to her, for her; it, to it, for it
	You, to You, for You
ci	us, to us, for us
vi (*plural*)	<u>you</u>, to <u>you</u>, for <u>you</u>
gli/loro	them, to them, for them

Unlike English, you usually put the pronoun before the verb.

Me l'ha dato Francesca.	Francesca gave it **to me**.
Gli ho dato la cartina.	I gave **him** the map.
Ho chiesto **loro** di restare.	I've asked **them** to stay.

> **BUONO A SAPERSI!**
> Although **gli** is also commonly used to translate *for them/to them* etc., the grammatically correct word is **loro**, which is still used, although generally in writing or in more formal speech.

Stressed object pronouns

These are pronouns used instead of a noun when you want to emphasize something, for example the word *me* in *Is this for me?* They are exactly the same as the subject pronouns, except that **me** and **te** are used instead of **io** and **tu**.

me	I, me
te (*informal, singular*)	you
lui (*masculine*)	he, him, it
lei (*feminine; polite form*)	she, her, it; You
noi	we, us
voi (*plural*)	<u>you</u>
loro	they, them

Stressed object pronouns are mostly used after a preposition or for emphasis and contrast.

Vieni con **me**.	Come with **me**.
Non guardava **me**, guardava **lei**.	He wasn't looking at **me**, he was looking at **her**.

Using si

In English *you* and *one* are used in general statements and questions such as *Can you park here?*; *One has to be careful*. For these kinds of statements and questions in Italian, use the impersonal form of the verb with **si**.

Si può nuotare qui?	Can you swim here?

ADJECTIVES

Agreement of adjectives

In Italian you need to know how to change adjectives to make them agree with the noun or pronoun they are describing. Here are some general rules:

To make an adjective feminine:

• if the masculine adjective ends in **–o**, change **–o** to **–a**:

un ragazzo **simpatico**	a **nice** boy
una ragazza **simpatica**	a **nice** girl

You don't change the ending for the feminine:

• if the masculine adjective ends in **–e**
• in the case of some colours
• if the adjective ends with a consonant

un treno **veloce**	a **fast** train
una macchina **veloce**	a **fast** car
un tappeto **blu**	a **blue** carpet
una tovaglia **blu**	a **blue** tablecloth
un gruppo **pop**	a **pop** group
la musica **pop**	**pop** music

To make an adjective plural:

• if the masculine singular adjective ends in **–o**, change **–o** to **–i**:

un fiore **rosso**	a **red** flower
dei fiori **rossi**	**red** flowers

• if the feminine singular adjective ends in **–a**, change **–a** to **–e**:

una gonna **nera**	a **black** skirt
delle gonne **nere**	**black** skirts

• if the adjective ends in **–e**, change **–e** to **–i** for both masculine and feminine plural:

un esercizio **difficile**	a **difficult** exercise
degli esercizi **difficili**	**difficult** exercises
una storia **triste**	a **sad** story
delle storie **tristi**	**sad** stories

Some adjectives don't change in the plural.

una macchina **blu**	one **blue** car
due macchine **blu**	two **blue** cars

BUONO A SAPERSI!
Note that when you're describing a couple consisting of a man and a woman or a group of people, you should use a masculine plural adjective unless the group consist entirely of females (in which case you should use a feminine plural adjective).

Word order with adjectives

Italian adjectives usually go after the noun, especially adjectives describing colours, shapes or nationalities.

la cucina **italiana**	**Italian** food
delle cravatte **rosse**	**red** ties

There are some very common expressions where the adjective goes before the noun.

una **bella** giornata	a **lovely** day
Buona fortuna!	**Good** luck!

Some adjectives can either go before or after the noun, but their meaning changes depending on where they go.

una casa **vecchia**	an **old** house
un mio **vecchio** amico	an **old** friend of mine (*long-standing*)
Cara Maria	**Dear** Maria
un ristorante **caro**	an **expensive** restaurant

The following adjectives always precede the noun they refer to:

• **mio**, **tuo**, **suo** etc (*my, your, his* etc)

mio fratello	**my** brother

• **questo**, **quello** etc (*this, that* etc)

questa strada	**this** street
quei ragazzi	**those** boys

• **ogni** (*each, every*), **qualche** (*some*) and **nessuno** (*no*)

ogni giorno	**every** day
qualche errore	**some** mistakes
nessuna chiamata	**no** calls

• **quale**, **quanto** etc in questions (*which, what, how much*)

Quanta pasta vuoi?	**How much** pasta do you want?
Quali programmi hai?	**What** plans do you have?

If two adjectives are used with a noun and they both come after it, they are joined together by **e** (*and*).

una persona interessante **e** divertente	an interesting, funny person

Comparisons

To say that something is bigger, more beautiful and so on, put **più** (*more*) before the adjective. To say that something is less important, less expensive and so on, put **meno** (*less*) before the adjective. *than* is translated by **di**, which can become **del**, **dello**, **della**, **dell'**, **dei**, **degli** or **delle** when used with the definite article (**il**, **lo**, **la**, **l'**, **i**, **gli**, **le**).

Emma è **più** alta **di** te.	Emma is tall**er than** you.
La mia stanza è **meno** spaziosa **della** tua.	My room is **less** spacious **than** yours.

If you want to say *the most* ...use **il più/la più** ... etc.

la più bella città del mondo *or* **la** città **più** bella del mondo	**the most** beautiful city in the world

Possessive adjectives

In English a possessive adjective is one of the words *my, your, his, her, its, our* or *their* used with a noun to show that one person or thing belongs to another.

	with masculine singular nouns	with feminine singular nouns	with plural nouns masculine/feminine
my	**mio**	**mia**	**miei/mie**
your	**tuo**	**tua**	**tuoi/tue**
his; her; its; Your *(polite form)*	**suo**	**sua**	**suoi/sue**
our	**nostro**	**nostra**	**nostri/nostre**
your	**vostro**	**vostra**	**vostri/vostre**
their	**loro**	**loro**	**loro**

Possessive adjectives agree with the noun they describe, not with the person who owns that thing. For example **sua** can mean *his, her, its* and *Your (polite form)*, but can only be used with a feminine noun. Note that in Italian you use the article before **mio**, **tuo** etc.

I miei genitori sono in pensione. **La sua macchina** è dal meccanico.	**My** parents are retired. **His** *or* **her** *or* **Your** car is at the garage.

The article is not used when **mio**, **tuo** etc are immediately followed by nouns referring to relatives (*mother, father* etc).

Mio fratello si chiama Leo.	**My** brother is called Leo.

BUONO A SAPERSI!
You must use the article, however, where you describe a relative using an adjective, for example, **la mia cara nonna** (*my dear grandmother*).

QUESTIONS

How to ask a question in Italian

There are several ways of asking a question in Italian.

• If you are expecting the answer *yes* or *no* keep the word order as it would be in an ordinary sentence, but turn it into a question by making your voice go up at the end of the sentence.

Prendi un caffè?	**Would you like** a coffee?

• You can also ask a question by changing the word order in the sentence.

È bella **la Calabria**?	Is **Calabria** nice?

In Italian, you can answer with a simple **sì** or **no**, when in English you would tend to add a short phrase.

Sa nuotare? – **Sì.**	Can he swim? – **Yes, he can.**

If you wish to use a fuller phrase, in Italian you need to repeat the whole verb.

Sa nuotare? – **Sì, sa nuotare.**	Can he swim? – **Yes, he can.**

NEGATIVES

Making sentences negative

In Italian, if you want to make a statement negative, you generally use **non**. Note that **non** comes in front of the verb. There is no equivalent in Italian to the English *don't/doesn't* as used in questions.

Non fumo.	I **don't** smoke.
Jeremy **non** abita più qui.	Jeremy **doesn't** live here anymore.

neanch'io or nemmeno io are interchangeable and are the equivalent of English phrases like *me neither, neither do I, neither was I,* and so on. You can use it in all situations without worrying about the tense of the verb.

Non sono mai stata in Spagna. – **Neanch'io**.	I've never been to Spain. – **Neither have I**.
Non lo conosco. – **Nemmeno io**.	I don't know him. – **Neither do I**.
Io non ci vado, e **neanche lui**.	I'm not going and **neither is he**.

Word order with negatives

If there are words such as **mi**, **ti**, **ci**, **vi**, **li** or **le** in front of the verb, **non** goes immediately in front of them.

Marco **non mi** ha telefonato.	Marco **didn't** phone **me**.
Non l'ho vista.	I **didn't** see her.

In phrases like *not now, not yet* etc, **non** comes before the other word.

non ancora	**not now**
non sempre	**not always**

You use **no** instead of **non** in certain phrases:

sempre **no**, ma qualche volta	**not** always, but sometimes
Credo di **no**.	I **don't** think so.
Ha detto di **no**.	He said **no**.
Vieni o **no**?	Are you coming or **not**?

In English you only use one negative word in a sentence: *I haven't ever seen him*, as opposed to *I haven't never seen him*. In Italian you can use two negatives, i.e. **non** and another word such as **niente** (*nothing*), **mai** (*never*) and so on.

Non hanno fatto **niente**.	They have**n't** done **anything**.
Non la vedo **mai**.	I **never** see her.
Non c'era **nessuno**.	There was **nobody** there.

If the sentence begins with a negative word, such as **niente** or **nessuno**, do not use **non** with the verb that comes after it.

Nessuno è venuto.	**Nobody** came.

SOME COMMON TRANSLATION DIFFICULTIES

Often you can't translate Italian into English and English into Italian word for word. The next section points out some common translation difficulties to watch out for.

Prepositions

English phrasal verbs, for example, *to run away*, *to fall down*, are often translated by one word in Italian.

scappare	to run away
cadere	to fall down

Sentences which contain a verb and preposition in English might not contain a preposition in Italian, and vice versa.

ascoltare qualcosa	to listen **to** something
telefonare **a** qualcuno	to call somebody

The same Italian preposition may be translated into English in different ways, and vice versa.

Sono **in** treno.	I'm **on** the train.
Vado a Milano **in** treno.	I'm going to Milan **by** train.
dipinto **da** un grande artista	painted **by** a great artist

Singular and plural nouns

A word which is singular in English may not be in Italian, and vice versa.

i bagagli (*plural*)	luggage
la gente (*singular*)	people

The verb *to be*

The verb *to be* is generally translated by **essere**.

Sono sposati.	They **are** married.

When you are talking about location, **trovarsi** can also be used.

Mi trovavo a Milano.	**I was** in Milan.

In certain set phrases which describe how you are feeling or a state you are in, the verb **avere** is used.

avere caldo	**to be** warm
avere freddo	**to be** cold
avere fame	**to be** hungry
avere sete	**to be** thirsty
avere paura	**to be** afraid
avere ragione	**to be** right
avere torto	**to be** wrong

When you are talking about someone's age, use the verb **avere**.

Quanti anni **hai**?	How old **are** you?
Ho quindici anni.	I**'m** fifteen.

stare is used for *to be* in some common contexts:

Come **stai**?	How **are** you?
Sto benissimo.	I**'m** very well.
Vuole **stare** solo.	He wants to **be** alone.
Stai zitto.	**Be** quiet.

stare is also used to make continuous tenses.

Stava studiando.	She **was** studying.

BUONO A SAPERSI!
The continuous form *to be...-ing* is often translated in Italian with a simple tense, for example, **Arrivo**. (*I'm coming*.).

When you are talking about the time, use **è** or **sono**.

Che ora **è**? *or* Che ore **sono**?	What time **is it**?
È l'una.	It**'s** one o'clock.
Sono le sette.	It**'s** seven o'clock.

can, to be able

If you want to talk about someone's physical ability to do something, use **potere** *or* **riuscire**.

Puoi fare dieci chilometri a piedi?	**Can** you walk ten kilometres?
Non **riesco a** uscire.	I **can**'t get out.

If you want to say that you know how to do something, use **sapere**.

Non **sa** nuotare.	She **can't** swim.
Non **so** guidare.	I **can't** drive.

Showing possession

In English, you can use 's and s' to show who or what something belongs to. In Italian, you have to use **di**.

la macchina **di** mio fratello	my brother**'s** car
la camera **delle** bambine	the girls**'** bedroom

VERBS

Introduction to verbs

Verbs are usually used with a subject: a noun, or a pronoun such as *I*, *you* or *he*, or with somebody's name. They can relate to the present, the past and the future – this is called their tense.

Verbs can be either:

• Regular: their forms follow the normal rules
• Irregular: their forms do not follow the normal rules

Regular English verbs have a base form (the form without any endings added to it, for example, *walk*). The base form can have *to* in front of it, for example, *to walk* – this is called the **infinitive**.

Italian verbs also have an infinitive, which generally ends in **–are**, **–ere**, or **–ire**, for example, **parlare** (*to speak*), **credere** (*to believe*), **dormire** (*to sleep*).

As well as the base form and the infinitive, English verbs have forms ending in *–s* (*walks*), *–ing* (*walking*), and *–ed* (*walked*). Italian verbs have many more forms than this, which are made by adding endings to a stem. The stem of a regular verb can be worked out from its infinitive.

Italian verb endings change, depending on who you are talking about: **io** (*I*), **tu** (*you*) **lui/lei/Lei** (*he/she/You*), in the singular, or **noi** (*we*), **voi** (*you*) and **loro** (*they*) in the plural. Italian verbs also have different forms depending on whether you are referring to the present, the past or the future.

In English, pronouns such as I, you and he are very often used as the subject of a verb. In Italian, pronouns are used much less often because the form of the verb itself shows who the subject is.

Irregular verbs

Some verbs in Italian do not follow the normal rules and are called irregular verbs. These include some very common and important verbs like **avere** (to have), **essere** (to be), **fare** (to do or to make) and **andare** (to go). The most common irregular verbs are shown in the verb tables, along with a number of others that you may need to use. For more detailed information on all the most important irregular verbs in Italian, use *Collins Easy Learning Italian Verbs*.

A few common irregular verbs have infinitives endings in **–rre**. For example:

comporre	to compose	**condurre**	to lead
porre	to put	**produrre**	to produce
proporre	to propose	**ridurre**	to reduce
supporre	to suppose	**tradurre**	to translate

Regular verbs

There are three main groups of regular verbs:

* **–are** verbs: verbs that end in **–are** like **parlare** (shown in full on page 275)
* **–ere** verbs: verbs that end in **–ere** like **credere** (shown in full on page 276)
* **–ire** verbs: verbs that end in **–ire** like **dormire** (shown in full on page 277)

These are called regular verbs because they follow set patterns. When you have learned these patterns you will be able to form any regular verb.

To form the stem of the verb for the present, future, conditional, imperfect, imperative or subjunctive of any regular verb, take the infinitive minus the last three letters, for example, **parlare → parl–**; **credere → cred–**; **dormire → dorm–**, and add the appropriate ending.

There are sets of endings for regular **–are** verbs, for regular **–ere** verbs and for regular **–ire** verbs. Verb endings for regular verbs are highlighted in orange in the verb tables on the following pages.

One group of regular **–ire** verbs take the same endings as **dormire**, but add **isc** to the stem in the **io**, **tu**, **lui/lei/Lei** and **loro** present and present subjunctive forms. Important examples of this type of **–ire** verb are **capire** (to understand), **preferire** (to prefer), and **finire** (to finish).

preferisco	I prefer
preferiamo	we prefer
capisce	he understands
capite tutti	<u>you</u> all understand
finisci	you finish
finiscono	they are finishing

To form the **perfect tense** of any regular verb, you need:

• to know the present tense forms of **avere** and *essere* (see pages 279 and 282)
• to be able to form the past participle

To form the past participle of regular verbs, take the infinitive minus the last three letters, for example, **parlare** → **parl–**; **credere** → **cred–**; **dormire** → **dorm–**, and add the appropriate ending **–ato**, **–uto**, or **–ito**. The past participles of **parlare**, **credere** and **dormire** are therefore **parlato**, **creduto**, and **dormito**.

Some verbs are irregular in some forms and not in others. **avere** (*to have*), **andare** (*to go*), **volere** (*to want*), **dovere** (*to have to*), **sapere** (*to know*) and **potere** (*to be able*), for example, all have regular past participles: **avuto**, **andato**, **voluto**, **dovuto**, **saputo** and **potuto**.

Common irregular past participles

Many verbs that are regular in most of their forms have irregular past participles. Here are some important examples:

aprire, aperto	to open, opened
chiedere, chiesto	to ask, asked
chiudere, chiuso	to close, closed
decidere, deciso	to decide, decided
leggere, letto	to read, read
mettere, messo	to put, put
offrire, offerto	to offer, offered
prendere, preso	to take, taken
rimanere, rimasto	to stay, stayed
scendere, sceso	to get off, got off
scrivere, scritto	to write, written

Reflexive verbs

Reflexive verbs are used with reflexive pronouns such as *myself*, *yourself* and *herself* in English, for example *I washed myself; he shaved himself*. Italian reflexive verbs are shown in the dictionary as infinitives with their final **e** replaced by **si** (*oneself*), for example **divertirsi** (*to enjoy oneself*), **chiamarsi** (*to be called*).

Many verbs are reflexive in Italian, but not in English:

accomodarsi	to sit down
addormentarsi	to go to sleep
alzarsi	to get up
annoiarsi	to get bored
chiamarsi	to be called
incontrarsi	to meet
perdersi	to get lost
preoccuparsi	to worry
ricordarsi	to remember
sedersi	to sit down
sbrigarsi	to hurry
sposarsi	to get married
svegliarsi	to wake up
trovarsi	to meet
vestirsi	to get dressed

To use a reflexive verb in Italian, you need to decide which reflexive pronoun to use. Here are the Italian reflexive pronouns:

subject pronoun	reflexive pronoun	meaning
io	**mi**	myself
tu	**ti**	yourself
lui		himself
lei	**si**	herself
Lei		Yourself
noi	**ci**	ourselves
voi	**vi**	yourselves
loro	**si**	themselves

The reflexive pronoun is added onto the end of infinitives, but otherwise it generally comes before the verb:

Dove vuole seder**si**?	Where would You like to sit?
Mi chiamo Silvia.	My name's Silvia.
Quando **vi** sposate?	When are <u>you</u> getting married?
Va bene se **ci** incontriamo là?	Does it suit you okay if we meet there?

VERB TENSES

The present tense

The present tense is used to talk about what is true at the moment, what happens regularly and what is happening now, for example, *I'm a student*; *he works as a consultant*; *I'm studying Italian*.

There are two present tense forms in English, with different meanings. For example, you can say *I speak* or *I'm speaking*. In Italian both meanings can be expressed by **parlo**:

Parlo un pessimo italiano.	**I speak** terrible Italian.
Parlo troppo veloce?	**Am I speaking** too fast?

It is possible to use another form: **sto parlando**, which is the exact equivalent of *I am speaking*, but this form is much less common in Italian than in English. It is used to stress that something is happening right now:

Stanno arrivando!	**They're coming**!
Cosa **stai facendo**?	What **are you doing**?

In English you can also use the present to talk about something that is going to happen in the near future. You can do the same in Italian.

Parto domani alle undici.	**I'm leaving** tomorrow at eleven.
Arriva la settimana prossima.	**She's coming** next week.

The future tense

The future tense is used to talk about something that will happen or will be true. There are several ways to express the future tense in English: you can use the future tense (*I'll ask him on Tuesday*), the present tense (*I'm not working tomorrow*), or *going to* followed by an infinitive (*she's going to study in Italy for a year*). In Italian you can use the future tense or the present tense.

Quando **saranno** pronti i documenti?	When **will** the documents **be** ready?
Se non le dispiace **ripasso** sabato.	If You don't mind **I'll come back** on Saturday.
Vedo Gianni giovedì.	**I'm seeing** Gianni on Thursday.
Pensi di rivederlo?	**Are you going to** see him again?

The imperfect tense

The imperfect tense is used to talk about the past, especially in descriptions, and to say what used to happen, for example *I used to work in Manchester*; *it was sunny yesterday*.

Ieri mi **sentivo** bene.	I **felt** fine yesterday.
Quanto **pensava** di spendere?	How much **were You thinking** of spending?
Tu gli hai detto che **andava** bene, no?	You told him it **was** okay, didn't you?
Ci trovavamo ogni venerdì.	**We used to meet** every Friday.

The perfect tense

In English the perfect tense is made with the verb *have* and the past participle: *I have done; he has gone*. This form has a different meaning from the simple past (*I did; he went*).

In Italian the perfect tense is also made up of two parts: the present tense of **avere** or **essere**, and the past participle. To find out how to form the past participle of any regular verb in Italian, see page 269.

Both the English perfect (*I have done*), and the English simple past (*I did*) are translated by the Italian perfect.

Ma insomma! Te l'**ho** appena **detto**!	But I **have** just **told** you!
Te l'**ho detto** ieri.	I **told** you yesterday.

Most verbs form the perfect tense with **avere**. There are two main groups of verbs which form their perfect tense with **essere** instead of **avere**: all reflexive verbs (see page 269) and a group of verbs that are mainly used to talk about movement or a change of some kind, including:

andare	to go
venire	to come
succedere	to happen
partire	to leave, to go
scendere	to go down, to come down, to get off
salire	to go up, to come up
entrare	to go in, to come in
uscire	to go out, to come out
morire	to die
nascere	to be born
divenire	to become
restare	to stay
cadere	to fall

Si è rotto una gamba.	He's broken his leg.
Com'è andata la vacanza?	How was your holiday?
Sono partita prima di lui.	I left before him.

The imperative

The imperative is a verb form used to give orders and instructions, for example, *Be quiet!*, *Don't do that!*, *Please fill in this form*.

In Italian, you give instructions or orders to someone by adding the appropriate endings to the verb stem, depending on whether the infinitive ends in **–are**, **–ere**, or **–ire**.

To make suggestions (*let's*; *shall we?*), the **noi** form of the imperative is used.

Parlami del tuo nuovo ragazzo.	Tell me about your new boyfriend.
Compili questo modulo, per cortesia.	Please fill in this form.
Aiutatemi!	Help me!
Prendiamo prima un aperitivo?	Shall we have a drink first?

To tell someone not to do something, **non** is used with the imperative, except in the case of a person you call **tu**, when **non** is used with the infinitive.

| Non dimenticate ragazzi. | Don't forget children. |
| Non preoccuparti! | Don't worry! |

The subjunctive

The present subjunctive is a verb form that is often used after **che**.

| Vuole **che parli** più piano? | Do You want me to speak more slowly? |
| Bisogna **che** tu **vada** di persona. | You must go in person. |

The imperfect subjunctive is used after **E se ...?** to make a suggestion.

| E se passassimo la notte qui? | How about spending the night here? |
| E se ci andassimo in traghetto? | How about going there by ferry? |

The conditional

The conditional is used to talk about things that would happen or that would be true under certain conditions, for instance, *I would help you if I could*. It is also used to say what you would like or need, for example, *Could you give me the bill?*

Mi piacerebbe rivederti.	**I'd like** to see you again.
Quando ti **andrebbe** bene?	When **would be** a good time for you?
Portrebbe portarci i caffè?	**Could You** bring us our coffee?

The conditional of **preferire** is followed by **che** and the imperfect subjunctive to say what you'd like someone to do.

Preferirei che mi rimborsasse.	**I'd rather** You gave me my money back.
Preferirei che spedisse la pratica via email.	**I'd rather** You sent the file by email.

to speak

present

(io)	par**lo**
(tu)	par**li**
(lui/lei/Lei)	par**la**
(noi)	par**liamo**
(voi)	par**late**
(loro)	par**lano**

present subjunctive

(io)	par**li**
(tu)	par**li**
(lui/lei/Lei)	par**li**
(noi)	par**liamo**
(voi)	par**liate**
(loro)	par**lino**

perfect

(io)	**ho** par**lato**
(tu)	**hai** par**lato**
(lui/lei/Lei)	**ha** par**lato**
(noi)	**abbiamo** par**lato**
(voi)	**avete** par**lato**
(loro)	**hanno** par**lato**

imperfect

(io)	par**lavo**
(tu)	par**lavi**
(lui/lei/Lei)	par**lava**
(noi)	par**lavamo**
(voi)	par**lavate**
(loro)	par**lavano**

future

(io)	par**lerò**
(tu)	par**lerai**
(lui/lei/Lei)	par**lerà**
(noi)	par**leremo**
(voi)	par**lerete**
(loro)	par**leranno**

conditional

(io)	par**lerei**
(tu)	par**leresti**
(lui/lei/Lei)	par**lerebbe**
(noi)	par**leremmo**
(voi)	par**lereste**
(loro)	par**lerebbero**

imperative

par**la**/par**liamo**
par**late**

past participle

par**lato**

gerund

par**lando**

---

example phrases

Pronto, chi **parla**?	Hello, who**'s speaking**?
Di cosa **parla** quel libro?	What **is** that book **about**?
Lascia che gli **parli** io.	Let me **talk** to him.

CREDERE

to believe

	present		**present subjunctive**
(io)	cred**o**	(io)	cred**a**
(tu)	cred**i**	(tu)	cred**a**
(lui/lei/Lei)	cred**e**	(lui/lei/Lei)	cred**a**
(noi)	cred**iamo**	(noi)	cred**iamo**
(voi)	cred**ete**	(voi)	cred**iate**
(loro)	cred**ono**	(loro)	cred**ano**
	perfect		**imperfect**
(io)	**ho** cred**uto**	(io)	cred**evo**
(tu)	**hai** cred**uto**	(tu)	cred**evi**
(lui/lei/Lei)	**ha** cred**uto**	(lui/lei/Lei)	cred**eva**
(noi)	**abbiamo** cred**uto**	(noi)	cred**evamo**
(voi)	**avete** cred**uto**	(voi)	cred**evate**
(loro)	**hanno** cred**uto**	(loro)	cred**evano**
	future		**conditional**
(io)	cred**erò**	(io)	cred**erei**
(tu)	cred**erai**	(tu)	cred**eresti**
(lui/lei/Lei)	cred**erà**	(lui/lei/Lei)	cred**erebbe**
(noi)	cred**eremo**	(noi)	cred**eremmo**
(voi)	cred**erete**	(voi)	cred**ereste**
(loro)	cred**eranno**	(loro)	cred**erebbero**

imperative	**past participle**
cred**i**/cred**iamo**	cred**uto**
cred**ete**	

gerund
cred**endo**

example phrases

Non ci **credo**!	I don't **believe** it!
Non dirmi che **credi** ai fantasmi!	Don't tell me you **believe** in ghosts!
Non voglio che lei **creda** che sono un bugiardo.	I don't want her to **think** I'm a liar.

to sleep

	present			**present subjunctive**
(io)	dormo		*(io)*	dorma
(tu)	dormi		*(tu)*	dorma
(lui/lei/Lei)	dorme		*(lui/lei/Lei)*	dorma
(noi)	dormiamo		*(noi)*	dormiamo
(voi)	dormite		*(voi)*	dormiate
(loro)	dormono		*(loro)*	dormano

	perfect			**imperfect**
(io)	**ho** dormito		*(io)*	dormivo
(tu)	**hai** dormito		*(tu)*	dormivi
(lui/lei/Lei)	**ha** dormito		*(lui/lei/Lei)*	dormiva
(noi)	**abbiamo** dormito		*(noi)*	dormivamo
(voi)	**avete** dormito		*(voi)*	dormivate
(loro)	**hanno** dormito		*(loro)*	dormivano

	future			**conditional**
(io)	dormirò		*(io)*	dormirei
(tu)	dormirai		*(tu)*	dormiresti
(lui/lei/Lei)	dormirà		*(lui/lei/Lei)*	dormirebbe
(noi)	dormiremo		*(noi)*	dormiremmo
(voi)	dormirete		*(voi)*	dormireste
(loro)	dormiranno		*(loro)*	dormirebbero

imperative
dormi/dormiamo
dormite

gerund
dormendo

past participle
dormito

example phrases

Era così stanco che **dormiva** in piedi.	He was so tired he **was asleep** on his feet.
Dormivo e non ti ho sentita entrare.	I **was asleep** and didn't hear you come in.
Sta **dormendo**.	She**'s sleeping**.

ANDARE

to go

	present		present subjunctive
(io)	**vado**	(io)	**vada**
(tu)	**vai**	(tu)	**vada**
(lui/lei/Lei)	**va**	(lui/lei/Lei)	**vada**
(noi)	andiamo	(noi)	andiamo
(voi)	andate	(voi)	andiate
(loro)	**vanno**	(loro)	**vadano**

	perfect		imperfect
(io)	sono andato/a	(io)	andavo
(tu)	sei andato/a	(tu)	andavi
(lui/lei/Lei)	è andato/a	(lui/lei/Lei)	andava
(noi)	siamo andati/e	(noi)	andavamo
(voi)	siete andati/e	(voi)	andavate
(loro)	sono andati/e	(loro)	andavano

	future		conditional
(io)	**andrò**	(io)	**andrei**
(tu)	**andrai**	(tu)	**andresti**
(lui/lei/Lei)	**andrà**	(lui/lei/Lei)	**andrebbe**
(noi)	**andremo**	(noi)	**andremmo**
(voi)	**andrete**	(voi)	**andreste**
(loro)	**andranno**	(loro)	**andrebbero**

imperative
vai/andiamo
andate

past participle
andato

gerund
andando

example phrases

Su, **andiamo**!	Come on, **let's go**!
Come **va**? – bene, grazie!	How **are** you? – fine thanks!
La mamma vuole che tu **vada** a fare la spesa.	Mum wants you to **go** and do the shopping.

to have

	present			present subjunctive
(io)	**ho**		(io)	*a*bbia
(tu)	**hai**		(tu)	*a*bbia
(lui/lei/Lei)	**ha**		(lui/lei/Lei)	*a*bbia
(noi)	**abbiamo**		(noi)	abbiamo
(voi)	avete		(voi)	abbiate
(loro)	**hanno**		(loro)	*a*bbiano

	perfect			imperfect
(io)	ho avuto		(io)	avevo
(tu)	hai avuto		(tu)	avevi
(lui/lei/Lei)	ha avuto		(lui/lei/Lei)	aveva
(noi)	abbiamo avuto		(noi)	avevamo
(voi)	avete avuto		(voi)	avevate
(loro)	hanno avuto		(loro)	avevano

	future			conditional
(io)	**avrò**		(io)	**avrei**
(tu)	**avrai**		(tu)	**avresti**
(lui/lei/Lei)	**avrà**		(lui/lei/Lei)	**avrebbe**
(noi)	**avremo**		(noi)	**avremmo**
(voi)	**avrete**		(voi)	**avreste**
(loro)	**avranno**		(loro)	**avrebbero**

imperative
abbi/abbiamo
abbiate

past participle
avuto

gerund
avendo

example phrases

All'inizio **ha avuto** un sacco di problemi.	He **had** a lot of problems at first.
Ho già mangiato.	**I've** already eaten.
Ha la macchina nuova.	She**'s got** a new car.

DARE

to give

	present			present subjunctive
(io)	do		(io)	**dia**
(tu)	**dai**		(tu)	**dia**
(lui/lei/Lei)	**dà**		(lui/lei/Lei)	**dia**
(noi)	diamo		(noi)	diamo
(voi)	date		(voi)	diate
(loro)	**danno**		(loro)	**diano**

	perfect			imperfect
(io)	ho dato		(io)	davo
(tu)	hai dato		(tu)	davi
(lui/lei/Lei)	ha dato		(lui/lei/Lei)	dava
(noi)	abbiamo dato		(noi)	davamo
(voi)	avete dato		(voi)	davate
(loro)	hanno dato		(loro)	davano

	future			conditional
(io)	**darò**		(io)	**darei**
(tu)	**darai**		(tu)	**daresti**
(lui/lei/Lei)	**darà**		(lui/lei/Lei)	**darebbe**
(noi)	**daremo**		(noi)	**daremmo**
(voi)	**darete**		(voi)	**dareste**
(loro)	**daranno**		(loro)	**darebbero**

imperative
dai or **da'**/diamo
date

past participle
dato

gerund
dando

example phrases

Gli **ho dato** un libro.	I **gave** him a book.
Può **darsi** che sia malata.	She **may** be ill.
La mia finestra **dà** sul giardino.	My window **looks** onto the garden.

to have to

present

(io)	**devo**
(tu)	**devi**
(lui/lei/Lei)	**deve**
(noi)	**dobbiamo**
(voi)	dovete
(loro)	devono

present subjunctive

(io)	**debba**
(tu)	**debba**
(lui/lei/Lei)	**debba**
(noi)	**dobbiamo**
(voi)	**dobbiate**
(loro)	**debbano**

perfect

(io)	ho dovuto
(tu)	hai dovuto
(lui/lei/Lei)	ha dovuto
(noi)	abbiamo dovuto
(voi)	avete dovuto
(loro)	hanno dovuto

imperfect

(io)	dovevo
(tu)	dovevi
(lui/lei/Lei)	doveva
(noi)	dovevamo
(voi)	dovevate
(loro)	dovevano

future

(io)	**dovrò**
(tu)	**dovrai**
(lui/lei/Lei)	**dovrà**
(noi)	**dovremo**
(voi)	**dovrete**
(loro)	**dovranno**

conditional

(io)	**dovrei**
(tu)	**dovresti**
(lui/lei/Lei)	**dovrebbe**
(noi)	**dovremmo**
(voi)	**dovreste**
(loro)	**dovrebbero**

imperative

—

past participle

dovuto

gerund

dovendo

example phrases

Ora **devo** proprio andare.	I**'ve** really **got** to go now.
Devi finire i compiti prima di uscire.	You **must** finish your homework before you go out.
Dev'essere tardi.	It **must** be late.

to be

	present		present subjunctive
(io)	sono	*(io)*	sia
(tu)	sei	*(tu)*	sia
(lui/lei/Lei)	è	*(lui/lei/Lei)*	sia
(noi)	siamo	*(noi)*	siamo
(voi)	siete	*(voi)*	siate
(loro)	sono	*(loro)*	siano

	perfect		imperfect
(io)	sono **stato/a**	*(io)*	ero
(tu)	sei **stato/a**	*(tu)*	eri
(lui/lei/Lei)	è **stato/a**	*(lui/lei/Lei)*	era
(noi)	siamo **stati/e**	*(noi)*	eravamo
(voi)	siete **stati/e**	*(voi)*	eravate
(loro)	sono **stati/e**	*(loro)*	erano

	future		conditional
(io)	sarò	*(io)*	sarei
(tu)	sarai	*(tu)*	saresti
(lui/lei/Lei)	sarà	*(lui/lei/Lei)*	sarebbe
(noi)	saremo	*(noi)*	saremmo
(voi)	sarete	*(voi)*	sareste
(loro)	saranno	*(loro)*	sarebbero

imperative
sii/siamo
siate

past participle
stato

gerund
essendo

example phrases

Sono italiana.	I'm Italian.
Mario **è** appena partito.	Mario **has** just left.
Siete mai **stati** in Africa?	**Have** you ever **been** to Africa?

to do, to make

	present		**present subjunctive**
(io)	**faccio**	(io)	**faccia**
(tu)	**fai**	(tu)	**faccia**
(lui/lei/Lei)	fa	(lui/lei/Lei)	**faccia**
(noi)	**facciamo**	(noi)	**facciamo**
(voi)	fate	(voi)	**facciate**
(loro)	**fanno**	(loro)	**facciano**

	perfect		**imperfect**
(io)	ho **fatto**	(io)	**facevo**
(tu)	hai **fatto**	(tu)	**facevi**
(lui/lei/Lei)	ha **fatto**	(lui/lei/Lei)	**faceva**
(noi)	abbiamo **fatto**	(noi)	**facevamo**
(voi)	avete **fatto**	(voi)	**facevate**
(loro)	hanno **fatto**	(loro)	**facevano**

	future		**conditional**
(io)	**farò**	(io)	**farei**
(tu)	**farai**	(tu)	**faresti**
(lui/lei/Lei)	**farà**	(lui/lei/Lei)	**farebbe**
(noi)	**faremo**	(noi)	**faremmo**
(voi)	**farete**	(voi)	**fareste**
(loro)	**faranno**	(loro)	**farebbero**

imperative
fai or **fa'**/
faciamo/fate

gerund
facendo

past participle
fatto

example phrases

Due più due **fa** quattro.	Two and two **makes** four.
Fa il medico.	He **is** a doctor.
Fa caldo.	It**'s** hot.

POTERE

to be able

	present		present subjunctive
(io)	posso	(io)	possa
(tu)	puoi	(tu)	possa
(lui/lei/Lei)	può	(lui/lei/Lei)	possa
(noi)	possiamo	(noi)	possiamo
(voi)	potete	(voi)	possiate
(loro)	possono	(loro)	possano

	perfect		imperfect
(io)	ho potuto	(io)	potevo
(tu)	hai potuto	(tu)	potevi
(lui/lei/Lei)	ha potuto	(lui/lei/Lei)	poteva
(noi)	abbiamo potuto	(noi)	potevamo
(voi)	avete potuto	(voi)	potevate
(loro)	hanno potuto	(loro)	potevano

	future		conditional
(io)	potrò	(io)	potrei
(tu)	potrai	(tu)	potresti
(lui/lei/Lei)	potrà	(lui/lei/Lei)	potrebbe
(noi)	potremo	(noi)	potremmo
(voi)	potrete	(voi)	potreste
(loro)	potranno	(loro)	potrebbero

imperative
—

past participle
potuto

gerund
potendo

example phrases

Si **può** visitare il castello tutti i giorni dell'anno.	You **can** visit the castle any day of the year.
Può aver avuto un incidente.	She **may** have had an accident.
Speriamo che voi **possiate** aiutarci.	We hope you **can** help us.

to want

	present		present subjunctive
(io)	**voglio**	(io)	**voglia**
(tu)	**vuoi**	(tu)	**voglia**
(lui/lei/Lei)	**vuole**	(lui/lei/Lei)	**voglia**
(noi)	**vogliamo**	(noi)	**vogliamo**
(voi)	volete	(voi)	**vogliate**
(loro)	**vogliono**	(loro)	**vogliano**

	perfect		imperfect
(io)	ho voluto	(io)	volevo
(tu)	hai voluto	(tu)	volevi
(lui/lei/Lei)	ha voluto	(lui/lei/Lei)	voleva
(noi)	abbiamo voluto	(noi)	volevamo
(voi)	avete voluto	(voi)	volevate
(loro)	hanno voluto	(loro)	volevano

	future		conditional
(io)	**vorrò**	(io)	**vorrei**
(tu)	**vorrai**	(tu)	**vorresti**
(lui/lei/Lei)	**vorrà**	(lui/lei/Lei)	**vorrebbe**
(noi)	**vorremo**	(noi)	**vorremmo**
(voi)	**vorrete**	(voi)	**vorreste**
(loro)	**vorranno**	(loro)	**vorrebbero**

imperative
—

past participle
voluto

gerund
volendo

example phrases

Voglio comprare una macchina nuova.	I **want** to buy a new car.
Devo pagare subito o posso pagare domani? – Come **vuole**.	Do I have to pay now or can I pay tomorrow? – As You **prefer**.

A

a, an un, una, uno
able to be able to essere capace di
about (*relating to*) su; (*approximately*) circa; **What is it about?** Di che cosa tratta?; **I don't know anything about it** Non ne so niente; **at about 10 o'clock** verso le dieci
above sopra; **above the bed** sopra il letto
abroad all'estero
abscess l'ascesso *m*
accelerator l'acceleratore *m*
accent l'accento *m*
to accept accettare; **Do you accept credit cards?** Accettate carte di credito?
access l'accesso *m*
wheelchair access l'accesso per disabili
accident l'incidente *m*
accident & emergency department il pronto soccorso
accommodation l'alloggio *m*
according to secondo; **according to him** secondo lui
account (*bank*) il conto in banca
account number il numero del conto
to ache fare male; **My head aches** Mi fa male la testa; **It aches** Fa male
across (*on the other side*) dall'altra parte di
ad l'annuncio *m*
address l'indirizzo *m* **Here's my address** Ecco il mio indirizzo
admission charge il biglietto d'ingresso
to admit to admit to hospital ricoverare in ospedale
adult l'adulto, l'adulta; **for adults** per adulti
advance in advance in anticipo

advice il consiglio
to advise consigliare
A&E il pronto soccorso
aeroplane l'aeroplano *m*
afraid to be afraid of avere paura di
after dopo
afternoon il pomeriggio; **in the afternoon** nel pomeriggio; **this afternoon** questo pomeriggio; **tomorrow afternoon** domani pomeriggio
afterwards dopo
again di nuovo; **I won't go there again** Non ci torno più
against contro; **I'm against the idea** Sono contrario all'idea
age l'età *f*
agency l'agenzia *f*
ago a week ago una settimana fa; **a month ago** un mese fa
to agree essere d'accordo
agreement l'accordo *m*
air aria; **by air** in aereo
air bed il materassino gonfiabile
air-conditioning l'aria *f* condizionata
air-conditioning unit il condizionatore
air freshener il deodorante per ambienti
airline la linea aerea
air mail by airmail per posta aerea
airplane l'aeroplano *m*
airport l'aeroporto *m*
aisle il corridoio
alarm l'allarme *m*
alarm clock la sveglia
alcohol l'alcol *m*
alcoholic (*drink*) alcolico(a)
all tutto(a); **all day** tutto il giorno; **all the books** tutti i libri
allergic allergico(a); **I'm allergic to ...** Sono allergico a...
to allow permettere; **It's not allowed** Non è permesso

all right (*agreed*) va bene; **to be all right** andare bene; (*person*) stare bene; **Are You all right?** Sta bene?
almost quasi
alone solo(a)
along lungo; **along the beach** lungo la spiaggia
alphabet l'alfabeto *m*
Alps le Alpi
already già
also anche
altogether in tutto; **20 euros altogether** 20 euro in tutto
always sempre
am del mattino; **at 4 am** alle quattro del mattino
ambulance l'ambulanza *f*
America l'America *f*
American americano(a)
among tra
amount (*quantity*) la quantità; (*total*) la somma
anchovies le acciughe
and e
angry arrabbiato(a)
animal l'animale *m*
ankle la caviglia
to annoy dare fastidio
another un altro, un'altra; **Another beer, please** Un'altra birra, per favore
answer la riposta
to answer rispondere
answering machine la segreteria telefonica
answerphone la segreteria telefonica
antibiotic l'antibiotico *m*
antifreeze l'antigelo *m*
antihistamine l'antistaminico *m*
antique shop il negozio d'antiquariato
antiseptic l'antisettico *m*
any qualche; (*whichever*) qualsiasi; **I haven't got any** Non ne ho; **I don't play tennis any more** Non gioco più a tennis
anyone (*in questions*) qualcuno; (*in negative sentences*) nessuno

anything (*in questions*) qualcosa; (*in negative sentences*) niente

anyway comunque

anywhere (*in questions*) da qualche parte; (*in negative sentences*) da nessuna parte; **You can buy them almost anywhere** Li puoi comprare quasi dappertutto

apart from a parte; **Apart from that ...** A parte questo...

apartment l'appartamento *m*

apple la mela

application form il modulo di domanda

appointment l'appuntamento *m* **I have an appointment** Ho un appuntamento

approximately circa

apricot l'albicocca *f*

April aprile *m*

arm il braccio

to arrange sistemare

to arrive arrivare

art l'arte *f*

art gallery la galleria d'arte

arthritis l'artrite *f*

as come; (*when*) quando; (*since*) dato che; **as if** come se

ashtray il portacenere

to ask chiedere; **to ask for something** chiedere qualcosa; **I'd like to ask you a question** Vorrei farti una domanda

aspirin l'aspirina *f*

asthma l'asma *f* **I have asthma** Ho l'asma

at a; **at home** a casa; **at 8 o'clock** alle 8; **at once** subito; **at night** di notte

attractive attraente

aubergine la melanzana

August agosto

aunt la zia

Australia l'Australia *f*

Australian australiano(a)

automatic automatico(a)

automatic car la macchina con cambio automatico

autumn l'autunno *m*

available disponibile

avocado l'avocado *m*

B

baby il bambino, la bambina

baby food gli alimenti per bambini

baby milk (*formula*) il latte per bambini

baby's bottle il biberon

babysitter il/la babysitter

back (*of body*) la schiena

back (*of body*) la schiena; (*not front*) la parte posteriore; **to go back** tornare indietro

backpack lo zaino

backpacker il saccopelista

bad (*weather, news*) brutto(a); (*food, mood*) cattivo(a)

bag la borsa

baggage i bagagli

baggage allowance il peso consentito di bagaglio

baggage reclaim il ritiro bagagli

baker's la panetteria

ball la palla; (*large: football, rugby*) il pallone; (*small: golf, tennis*) la pallina

banana la banana

band (*rock music*) il gruppo

bandage la fascia

bank (*for money*) la banca

bank account il conto in banca

banknote la banconota

bar (*pub*) il bar; **a bar of chocolate** la tavoletta di cioccolato

barbecue il barbecue; **to have a barbecue** fare una grigliata

barber's il barbiere

basil il basilico

basket il cestino

bath il bagno; (*bathtub*) la vasca; **to have a bath** fare un bagno

bathroom il bagno; **with bathroom** con bagno

battery (*for car*) la batteria; (*for radio, camera*) la pila

to be essere; **I'm cold** Ho freddo; **I'm fine** Sto bene

beach la spiaggia; **on the beach** sulla spiaggia

bean il fagiolo

beard la barba

beautiful bello(a)

because perché

become diventare; **to become ill** ammalarsi

bed il letto; **double bed** il letto matrimoniale; **single bed** il letto a una piazza; **twin beds** i letti gemelli

bed and breakfast (*place*) la pensione familiare; **How much is it for bed and breakfast?** Quanto viene la camera con la prima colazione?

bedroom la camera da letto

beef il manzo

beer la birra

before prima di; **before we go** prima di andare; **I've seen this film before** Ho già visto questo film

to begin cominciare; **to begin doing** cominciare a fare

behind dietro a; **behind the house** dietro alla casa

beige beige

to believe credere

bell (*door*) il campanello; (*church*) la campana

to belong to appartenere a; (*club*) far parte di; **That belongs to me** È mio

below sotto

belt la cintura

beside accanto a; **beside the bank** accanto alla banca

best il/la migliore

better meglio; **better than** meglio di

between fra

bib (*baby's*) il bavaglino

bicycle la bicicletta; **by bicycle** in bicicletta

bicycle pump la pompa per bicicletta

big (*house, car*) grande; (*animal, book, parcel*) grosso(a)

bike (*pushbike*) la bici; (*motorbike*) la moto *f*

bikini il bikini
bill il conto
bin (*dustbin*) il bidone
bird l'uccello *m*
biro la biro *f*
birthday il compleanno;
  Happy birthday! Buon
  compleanno!; **my birthday
  is on ...** il mio compleanno
  è il...
birthday card il biglietto
  d'auguri di compleanno
biscuits i biscotti
bit **a bit (of)** un po' (di)
bitter amaro(a)
black nero(a)
black ice il ghiaccio sulla
  strada
blanket la coperta
to bleed sanguinare; **My
  nose is bleeding** Ho sangue
  di naso
blind (*for window*) la
  tapparella
blind (*person*) cieco(a)
blister la vescica
block of flats il palazzo
blocked ostruito(a); **The
  sink is blocked** Il lavandino
  è ostruito; **I have a blocked
  nose** Ho il naso chiuso
blog il blog
to blog scrivere un blog
blond (*person*) biondo(a)
blood il sangue
blood group il gruppo
  sanguigno
blood pressure la pressione
  sanguigna
blouse la camicetta
blow-dry la messa in piega
  a phon
blue azzurro(a); **dark blue**
  blu; **light blue** azzurro(a)
to board (*bus, train*) salire
  su; (*ship, plane*) imbarcarsi
  su; **What time are we
  boarding?** A che ora è
  l'imbarco?
boarding card la carta
  d'imbarco
boat la barca; (*rowing*) la
  barca a remi
boat trip la gita in battello
body il corpo
boiler la caldaia
bone l'osso *m* (*fish*) la lisca
bonnet (*of car*) il cofano

book il libro
to book prenotare
booking la prenotazione
booking office l'ufficio *m*
  prenotazioni
bookshop la libreria
boot (*of car*) il bagagliaio
boots (*knee-high*) gli stivali;
  (*of soldier, for hiking*) gli
  scarponi
bored **I'm bored** Mi annoio
boring **It's boring** È noioso
born **I was born in Rome**
  Sono nato a Roma
to borrow **Can I borrow
  Your map?** Mi presta la
  cartina?
boss il capo
both entrambi; **I'd like
  both T-shirts** Mi piacciono
  entrambe le magliette; **We
  both went** Ci siamo andati
  entrambi
bottle la bottiglia; **a bottle
  of wine** una bottiglia di
  vino; **a half-bottle of ...**
  una mezza bottiglia di...
bottle opener l'apribottiglie
  m
bottom il fondo
box la scatola
box office il botteghino
boy il ragazzo; (*small*) il
  bambino; (*son*) il figlio
boyfriend il ragazzo
bra il reggiseno
bracelet il braccialetto
brake il freno
to brake frenare
brake fluid il liquido dei freni
brake lights gli stop
brake pads le pastiglie dei
  freni
branch (*of bank*) la filiale
brand (*make*) la marca
bread il pane; **wholemeal
  bread** il pane integrale;
  (*French stick*) il filoncino;
  sliced bread il pancarré
to break rompere
breakdown (*car*) il guasto
breakdown van il carro-
  attrezzi
breakfast la colazione
to breathe respirare
bride la sposa
bridegroom lo sposo
bridge il ponte

briefcase la cartella
to bring portare
Britain la Gran Bretagna
British britannico(a)
broadband l'ADSL *m*
broccoli i broccoli
brochure l'opuscolo *m*
broken rotto(a); **My leg is
  broken** Ho una gamba rotta
broken down (*car*)
  guasto(a)
brooch la spilla
brother il fratello
brother-in-law il cognato
brown marrone
bucket il secchio
buffet car (*train*) il vagone
  ristorante
building l'edificio *m*
bulb (*light*) la lampadina
bumper (*on car*) il paraurti
bunch **a bunch of flowers**
  un mazzo di fiori; **a bunch
  of grapes** un grappolo d'uva
bureau de change l'ufficio
  m cambi
burger l'hamburger *m*
burglar il ladro, la ladra
burglar alarm l'allarme *m*
  antifurto
burnt (*food*) bruciato(a)
bus l'autobus *m* (*coach*) la
  corriera; **by bus** in autobus
  (*o* in corriera)
bus pass la tessera
  dell'autobus
bus station la stazione delle
  corriere
bus stop la fermata
  dell'autobus
business gli affari; **He's
  got his own business** Ha
  un'attività in proprio
business card il biglietto
  da visita
business class business
  class
businessman l'uomo d'affari
businesswoman la donna
  d'affari
business trip il viaggio
  d'affari
busy impegnato(a);
  He's very busy È molto
  impegnato
but ma
butcher's la macelleria
butter il burro

button il bottone
to buy comprare
by (*beside*) accanto a;
(*cause, agent*) da; (*in time expressions*) entro; **by the church** accanto alla chiesta; **a painting by Picasso** un quadro di Picasso; **They were caught by the police** Sono stati catturati dalla polizia; **I have to be there by 3 o'clock** Devo essere lì entro le tre; **by car** in macchina

C
cab il taxi
cablecar la funivia
café il bar
cake (*large*) la torta; (*small*) il pasticcino
cake shop la pasticceria
call (*telephone*) la telefonata; **a long distance call** una chiamata interurbana
to call (*speak, phone*) chiamare
camera la macchina fotografica
camera shop il negozio di ottica
to camp campeggiare
camping gas il gas da campeggio
camping stove il fornellino da campeggio
campsite il campeggio
can (*to be able to*) potere; (*to know how to*) sapere; **I can't do that** Non posso farlo; **I can swim** So nuotare
can (*of beans*) la scatola; (*of beer*) il barattolo
can opener l'apriscatole *m*
Canada il Canada
Canadian canadese
to cancel (*booking, appointment*) disdire
candle la candela
canoeing to go canoeing andare in canoa
capital (*city*) la capitale
cappuccino il cappuccino
car la macchina; **to go by car** andare in macchina
car alarm l'antifurto *m*
car hire l'autonoleggio *m*

car insurance l'assicurazione *f* della macchina
car park il parcheggio
carafe la caraffa
caravan la roulotte
carburettor il carburatore
card (*greetings*) il biglietto d'auguri; (*business*) il biglietto da visita; **playing cards** le carte da gioco
cardigan il cardigan
careful attento(a); **Be careful!** Stai attento!
carriage (*on train*) il vagone
carrot la carota
to carry portare
case (*suitcase*) la valigia; **in any case** in ogni caso
cash i contanti
to cash (*cheque*) incassare
cash desk la cassa
cash dispenser (*ATM*) il Bancomat®
cashpoint il Bancomat®
castle il castello
casualty department il pronto soccorso
cat il gatto
to catch (*bus, train, plane*) prendere
cathedral il duomo
Catholic cattolico(a)
cauliflower il cavolfiore
CD il CD
CD player il lettore CD
CD-ROM il CD-ROM
ceiling il soffitto
cent il centesimo
centimetre il centimetro
central The hotel is very central L'albergo è in posizione molto centrale
central heating il riscaldamento autonomo
central locking la chiusura centralizzata
centre il centro
century il secolo
cereal i cereali
certificate il certificato
chair la sedia
chairlift la seggiovia
chalet (*in the mountains*) lo chalet; (*in resort*) il bungalow
chambermaid la cameriera
change gli spiccioli; **I**

haven't got any change Non ho spiccioli; **Can You give me change for ten euros?** Può cambiarmi dieci euro?; **Keep the change** Tenga il resto
to change cambiare; **to change 50 euros** cambiare 50 euro; **to change trains in Paris** cambiare treno a Parigi
changing room lo spogliatoio
Channel (*English*) Il Canale della Manica
charge (*fee*) la tariffa; **to be in charge** essere responsabile
to charge (*money*) far pagare; (*battery, phone*) caricare; **Please charge it to my account** Lo metta sul mio conto, per favore; **I need to charge my phone** Dovrei caricare il telefonino
charter flight il volo charter
chatroom la chat
cheap economico(a)
cheaper più economico(a)
to check (*oil, level, amount*) controllare
to check in (*at airport*) fare il check-in; (*at hotel*) fare la registrazione
check-in (*desk*) il banco accettazione
cheers! (*toast*) Cin-cin!
cheese il formaggio
chemist's la farmacia
cheque l'assegno *m*
cherry la ciliegia
chewing gum la gomma di masticare
chicken il pollo
child il bambino, la bambina
children i bambini; **for children** per bambini
chilli il peperoncino
chips le patatine fritte
chiropodist il/la pedicure
chocolate la cioccolata
to choose scegliere
chop (*meat*) la cotoletta
Christian name il nome di battesimo
Christmas il Natale; **Merry Christmas!** Buon Natale!

Christmas card il biglietto d'auguri natalizi
Christmas Eve la vigilia di Natale
church la chiesa
cigar il sigaro
cigarette la sigaretta
cigarette lighter l'accendino *m*
cinema il cinema *m*
circle (*theatre*) la galleria
city la città
city centre il centro
class la classe; **first-class** di prima classe; **second-class** di seconda classe
clean pulito(a)
to clean pulire
cleaner (*person*) l'addetto(a) alle pulizie
clear (*explanation*) chiaro(a)
clever intelligente
client il/la cliente
climate il clima *m*
to climb (*mountain*) scalare; **to go climbing** fare roccia
clinic la clinica
cloakroom il guardaroba *m*
clock l'orologio *m*
close close by vicino(a)
to close chiudere
closed chiuso(a)
clothes i vestiti
clothes shop il negozio d'abbigliamento
club il club
clutch (*in car*) la frizione
coach (*bus*) il pullman
coach trip la gita in pullman
coal il carbone
coast la costa
coat il cappotto
coat hanger la gruccia
cockroach lo scarafaggio
cocktail il cocktail
code il codice; (*dialling code*) il prefisso
coffee il caffè; **white coffee** il caffellatte; **black coffee** il caffè americano; **decaffeinated coffee** il decaffeinato
Coke® la Coca
cold freddo(a); **I'm cold** Ho freddo; **It's cold** Fa freddo; **cold water** acqua fredda
cold (*illness*) il raffreddore; **I have a cold** Ho il raffreddore

collar il colletto
colleague il/la collega
to collect (*someone*) andare a prendere
colour il colore
colour film (*for camera*) la pellicola a colori
comb il pettine
to come venire; (*to arrive*) arrivare
to come back tornare
to come in entrare; **Come in!** Avanti!
comfortable comodo(a)
company (*firm*) la ditta
compartment (*on train*) lo scompartimento
compass la bussola
to complain presentare un reclamo; **We're going to complain to the manager** Presenteremo un reclamo al direttore
complaint (*in shop, hotel*) il reclamo
complete completo(a)
compulsory obbligatorio(a)
computer il computer
concert il concerto
concert hall la sala concerti
concession la riduzione
conditioner il balsamo
condom il preservativo
conductor (*on bus, train*) il bigliettaio
conference la conferenza
to confirm confermare; **Please confirm** La prego di inviare conferma
confirmation (*flight, booking*) la conferma
congratulations! congratulazioni!
connection (*train, plane*) la coincidenza
consulate il consolato
to consult consultare
to contact mettersi in contatto con; **Where can we contact You?** Dove possiamo contattarla?
contact lens le lenti a contatto
contact lens cleaner il liquido per lenti a contatto
to continue continuare
contraceptive il contraccettivo

contract il contratto
convenient Is it convenient? Va bene?
to cook cucinare
cooker il fornello
cookies i biscotti
cool (*place*) fresco(a)
copy (*duplicate*) la copia
to copy copiare; (*photocopy*) fotocopiare
cork il tappo
corkscrew il cavatappi
corner l'angolo *m* **the shop on the corner** il negozio all'angolo
cornflakes i cornflakes
corridor il corridoio
cost il costo
to cost costare; **How much does it cost?** Quanto costa?
cot il lettino
cotton il cotone
cotton wool il cotone idrofilo
cough la tosse
to cough tossire
cough mixture lo sciroppo per la tosse
counter (*shop, bar*) il banco
country (*not town*) la campagna; (*nation*) il paese; **I live in the country** Vivo in campagna
couple (*two people*) la coppia; **a couple of ...** un paio di...
courgette la zucchina
courier service il corriere
course (*of meal*) la portata; **first course** il primo piatto; **main course** il piatto forte
cousin il cugino, la cugina
cover charge (*in restaurant*) il coperto
crab il granchio
crash (*car*) lo scontro
crash helmet il casco
cream (*food*) la panna; (*lotion*) la crema
credit il credito
credit card la carta di credito
crisps le patatine
croissant la brioche
to cross (*road*) attraversare
crowded affollato(a)
cruise la crociera
cucumber il cetriolo

cufflinks i gemelli
cup la tazza
cupboard l'armadio *m*
current (*air, water*) la corrente
customs (*at border*) la dogana
to cut tagliare
cut il taglio
to cycle andare in bicicletta
cycle track la pista ciclabile
cycling il ciclismo

D

daily (*each day*) ogni giorno
dairy products i latticini
damage i danni
damp umido(a)
to dance ballare
dangerous pericoloso(a)
dark (*colour*) scuro(a)
date la data
date of birth la data di nascita
daughter la figlia
daughter-in-law la nuora
day il giorno; **every day** ogni giorno; **it costs 50 euros per day** costa 50 euro al giorno
dead morto(a)
deaf sordo(a)
dear (*expensive, in letter*) caro(a)
decaffeinated decaffeinato(a)
December dicembre *m*
deckchair la sedia a sdraio
deep profondo(a)
deep freeze il congelatore
delay il ritardo; **How long is the delay?** Di quant'è il ritardo?
delayed in ritardo
delicatessen il negozio di specialità gastronomiche
delicious delizioso(a)
dental floss il filo interdentale
dentist il/la dentista
dentures la dentiera
deodorant il deodorante
department il reparto
department store il grande magazzino
departure lounge la sala partenze
departures le partenze

desk (*in hotel, airport*) il banco
desktop il desktop
dessert il dolce
details personal details le generalità
detergent il detersivo
to develop (*photos*) sviluppare
diabetic diabetico(a); **I'm diabetic** Sono diabetico
to dial (*a number*) comporre
dialling code il prefisso telefonico
dialling tone il segnale di libero
diapers i pannolini
diarrhoea la diarrea
dictionary il dizionario
diesel il gasolio; **a diesel car** una macchina diesel
diet la dieta; **I'm on a diet** Sono a dieta
different diverso(a)
difficult difficile
digital camera la fotocamera digitale
dining room la sala da pranzo
dinner (*evening meal*) la cena; **to have dinner** cenare
direct (*train, flight*) diretto(a)
directions to ask for directions chiedere la strada
directory phone directory l'elenco *m* telefonico
directory enquiries il servizio informazioni
dirty sporco(a)
disabled disabile
to disagree non essere d'accordo
discount lo sconto
dish il piatto
dishwasher la lavastoviglie
disinfectant il disinfettante
disk il disco
to dislocate (*joint*) lussarsi
disposable usa e getta
district (*of town*) il quartiere; (*of country*) la zona
divorced divorziato(a)
dizzy I feel dizzy Mi gira la testa

to do fare; **How are You doing?** Come va?; **How do You do?** Piacere
doctor il medico
documents i documenti
dog il cane
dollar il dollaro
domestic domestic flight il volo interno
door la porta
double doppio(a); **double bed** il letto matrimoniale; **double room** la camera doppia
down giù; **to go down the stairs** scendere le scale
to download scaricare
downstairs dabbasso; **the flat downstairs** l'appartamento *m* al piano di sotto
draught there's a draught c'è corrente d'aria
draught lager la birra alla spina
drawing il disegno
dress il vestito
to dress vestirsi
dressed to get dressed vestirsi
drink la bibita
to drink bere
drinking water l'acqua *f* potabile
to drive guidare
driver l'autista *m/f*
driving licence la patente
dry (*weather, wine*) secco(a); (*clothes, paint*) asciutto(a)
to dry asciugare
dry-cleaner's il lavasecco
due When is the rent due? Quando bisogna pagare l'affitto?; **When is the train due to arrive?** Quando è previsto l'arrivo del treno?
during durante
dust la polvere
duster lo straccio
duty-free esente da dazio
duvet il piumino
DVD il DVD
DVD player il lettore DVD

E

each ogni
ear l'orecchio *m*

earache il mal *m* d'orecchi **I have earache** Ho mal d'orecchi

earlier più presto; **I saw him earlier** L'ho già visto; **Is there an earlier flight?** C'è un volo che parte prima?

early presto

earphones le cuffie

earrings gli orecchini

east l'est *m*

Easter la Pasqua

easy facile

to eat mangiare

e-book il libro elettronico

ecological ecologico(a)

e-commerce il commercio elettronico

egg l'uovo *m* **fried eggs** le uova al tegame; **hard-boiled egg** l'uovo sodo; **scrambled eggs** le uova strapazzate; **soft-boiled egg** l'uovo alla coque

eggplant la melanzana

either **I've never been to Corsica – I haven't either** Non sono mai stato in Corsica – Neanch'io

elastoplast® il cerotto

electric elettrico(a)

electric razor il rasoio elettrico

electrician l'elettricista *m/f*

electric point la presa di corrente

electronic elettronico(a)

elevator l'ascensore *m*

e-mail la e-mail; **to e-mail somebody** mandare una e-mail a qualcuno

e-mail address l'indirizzo *m* e-mail

embassy l'ambasciata *f*

emergency l'emergenza *f*

empty vuoto(a)

end la fine

engaged (*to be married*) fidanzato(a); (*phone, toilet etc*) occupato(a)

engine il motore

England l'Inghilterra *f*

English inglese; (*language*) l'inglese *m*

Englishman an Englishman un inglese

Englishwoman an Englishwoman un'inglese

to enjoy **to enjoy oneself** divertirsi; **I enjoy swimming** Mi piace nuotare; **Enjoy your meal!** Buon appetito!

enough abbastanza; **I haven't got enough money** Non ho abbastanza soldi; **That's enough** Basta così

enquiry desk il banco informazioni

to enter (*to get in*) entrare in

entrance l'ingresso *m*

entrance fee il biglietto d'ingresso

envelope la busta

equipment l'attrezzatura *f*

escalator la scala mobile

essential essenziale

estate agent's l'agenzia *f* immobiliare

euro l'euro *m*

euro cent il centesimo

Europe l'Europa *f*

European europeo(a)

even anche; **even on Sundays** anche di domenica; **even though, even if** anche se; **even if it rains** anche se piove

evening la sera; **this evening** stasera; **tomorrow evening** domani sera; **in the evening** di sera; **at 7 o'clock in the evening** alle sette di sera

evening meal la cena

every ogni; **every time** ogni volta

everyone tutti

everything tutto

everywhere dappertutto

examination (*school, medical*) l'esame *m*

example esempio; **for example** per esempio

excellent ottimo(a)

except for eccetto; **except for me** eccetto me

exchange **in exchange for** in cambio di

to exchange scambiare

exchange rate il tasso di cambio

excursion l'escursione *f*

excuse **Excuse me!** Mi scusi!; (*to get by*) Permesso!

exhaust pipe il tubo di scappamento

exhibition la mostra

exit l'uscita *f*

expensive caro(a)

to expire (*ticket, passport*) scadere

to explain spiegare

express (*train*) l'espresso *m* **to send a letter express** mandare una lettera espresso

extra (*in addition*) supplementare; **Can you give me an extra blanket?** Posso avere una coperta in più?; **There's an extra charge** C'è un supplemento

eye l'occhio *m*

eyeliner l'eyeliner *m*

eye shadow l'ombretto *m*

F

fabric la stoffa

face il viso

fair (*hair*) biondo(a); **That's not fair** Non è giusto

fair (*funfair*) il luna park; **a trade fair** una fiera

fake falso(a)

fall (*autumn*) l'autunno *m*

to fall over cadere; **He fell over** È caduto

family la famiglia

famous famoso(a)

fan (*handheld*) il ventaglio; (*electric*) il ventilatore; (*of football club, band*) il/la fan; (*of music*) il patito, la patita

far lontano(a); **Is it far?** È lontano?; **How far is it?** Quanto dista?

farm la fattoria

farmhouse la fattoria

fashionable alla moda

fast veloce; **too fast** troppo veloce

fat (*plump*) grasso(a); (*in food, on person*) il grasso

father il padre

father-in-law il suocero

fault (*defect*) il difetto; **It's not my fault** Non è colpa mia

favourite preferito(a)

fax il fax; **by fax** via fax

to fax (*document*) mandare via fax; **to fax someone** mandare un fax a qualcuno

February febbraio
to feed dare da mangiare a
to feel sentirsi; **I don't feel well** Non mi sento bene; **I feel sick** Ho la nausea
ferry il traghetto
festival il festival
to fetch andare a prendere
few pochi; **few tourists** pochi turisti; **with a few friends** con alcuni amici
fiancé il fidanzato
fiancée la fidanzata
fig il fico
file (*computer*) il file
to fill riempire
to fill in (*form*) riempire
to fill up Fill it up please! (*car*) Il pieno per favore!
fillet il filetto
filling (*in tooth*) l'otturazione *f*
film (*at cinema*) il film; (*for camera*) la pellicola
to find trovare
fine (*to be paid*) la multa
fine bene; **I'm fine** Sto bene; **The weather is fine** Il tempo è bello
finger il dito
to finish finire
finished finito(a)
fire (*electric, gas*) il fornello; (*open*) il fuoco; (*accidental*) l'incendio *m*
fire alarm l'allarme *m* antincendio
firm la ditta
first primo(a)
first aid il pronto soccorso
first class la prima classe; **to travel first class** viaggiare in prima classe
first name il nome di battesimo
fish (*food*) il pesce
to fish pescare
fishing la pesca
fishmonger's la pescheria
to fit (*clothes*) andare bene; **It doesn't fit me** Non mi va bene
fitting room il camerino
to fix (*repair*) aggiustare
fizzy gassato(a); **fizzy water** acqua gassata
flash (*for camera*) il flash
flask il thermos

flat l'appartamento *m*
flat (*battery*) scarico(a); (*beer*) svampito(a)
flat tyre la gomma a terra
flavour (*taste*) il sapore; (*of ice cream*) il gusto; **Which flavour?** A che gusto?
flaw il difetto
fleas le pulci
flesh la carne
flex (*electrical*) il filo
flight il volo
flippers le pinne
floor (*of room*) il pavimento; (*of building*) il piano; **Which floor?** A che piano?; **on the ground floor** al pianterreno; **on the first floor** al primo piano
floppy disk il dischetto
flour la farina
flower il fiore
flu l'influenza *f*
fly la mosca
to fly (*person, bird*) volare
fly sheet il telo esterno
fog la nebbia
foggy It's foggy C'è nebbia
food il cibo
foot il piede; **to go on foot** andare a piedi
football il calcio
football match la partita di calcio
for per; **for me** per me; **for five euros** per cinque euro; **I've been here for two weeks** Sono qui da due settimane; **She'll be away for a month** Starà via per un mese
foreign straniero(a)
foreigner lo straniero, la straniera
forever per sempre
to forget dimenticare; **to forget to do** dimenticare di fare
fork (*for eating*) la forchetta
form (*document*) il modulo
fortnight due settimane
forward avanti
four-wheel drive vehicle una macchina a quattro ruote motrici
free (*not occupied*) libero(a); (*costing nothing*) gratis; **Is**

this seat free? È libero questo posto?
freezer il congelatore
French francese; (*language*) il francese
French fries le patatine fritte
frequent frequente
fresh fresco(a)
Friday il venerdì
fridge il frigorifero
fried fritto(a)
friend l'amico, l'amica
friendly amichevole
frog la rana
from da; **Where are You from?** Di dove è?; **from nine o'clock** dalle nove in poi
front davanti; **in front of** davanti a
frozen (*food*) surgelato(a)
fruit la frutta
fruit juice il succo di frutta
fruit salad la macedonia
frying-pan la padella
fuel (*petrol*) la benzina
fuel tank il serbatoio della benzina
full (*tank, glass*) pieno(a); (*restaurant, hotel*) al completo
full board la pensione completa
funfair il luna park
funny divertente
furnished ammobiliato(a)
furniture i mobili

G

gallery la galleria
game il gioco
garage (*for petrol*) la stazione di servizio; (*for parking*) il garage; (*for repair*) l'officina *f*
garden il giardino
garlic l'aglio *m*
gas il gas
gas cooker il fornello a gas
gas cylinder la bombola del gas
gate il cancello; (*at airport*) l'uscita *f*
gay (*person*) gay
gear la marcia; **first gear** la prima; **reverse gear** la retromarcia

gearbox il cambio
gents (*toilet*) la toilette (degli uomini)
genuine autentico(a)
to get (*to receive*) ricevere; (*to fetch*) prendere
to get in (*vehicle*) salire in
to get out (*vehicle*) scendere da
gift il regalo
gift shop il negozio di articoli da regalo
girl la ragazza; (*small*) la bambina
girlfriend la ragazza
to give dare
to give back restituire
glass (*for drinking*) il bicchiere; (*material*) il vetro; **a glass of water** un bicchiere d'acqua
glasses (*spectacles*) gli occhiali
gloves i guanti
to go andare; **to go home** tornare a casa
to go back ritornare
to go in entrare
to go out uscire
God Dio
goggles (*for swimming*) gli occhialini da piscina; (*for skiing*) gli occhiali da sci
golf il golf
golf ball la pallina da golf
golf clubs le mazze da golf
golf course il campo da golf
good (*idea, food*) buono(a); (*film, book*) bello(a); (*student*) bravo(a); **good afternoon** buongiorno; **good evening** buona sera; **good morning** buongiorno; **good night** buona notte
goodbye arrivederci
good-looking bello(a)
gram il grammo
grandchildren i nipoti
granddaughter la nipote
grandfather il nonno
grandmother la nonna
grandparents i nonni
grandson il nipote
grapefruit il pompelmo
grapes l'uva *f*
grated (*cheese*) grattugiato(a)
greasy grasso(a)

great (*wonderful*) fantastico(a)
Great Britain la Gran Bretagna
green verde
greengrocer's il fruttivendolo
grey grigio(a)
grill (*part of cooker*) la griglia
grilled alla griglia
grocer's il negozio di alimentari
ground floor il pianterreno; **on the ground floor** al pianterreno
groundsheet il telone impermeabile
group il gruppo
guarantee la garanzia
guesthouse la pensione
guide (*person, book*) la guida
guidebook la guida
guided tour la visita guidata
guitar la chitarra
gums (*in mouth*) le gengive
gym (*gymnasium*) la palestra
gynecologist il ginecologo, la ginecologa

H

hair i capelli
haircut il taglio di capelli
hairdresser la parrucchiera
hairdryer l'asciugacapelli *m*
half la metà; **half of the cake** mezza torta; **half an hour** mezz'ora
half board la mezza pensione
ham (*cooked*) il prosciutto cotto; (*cured*) il prosciutto crudo
hamburger l'hamburger *m*
hand la mano *f*
handbag la borsetta
hand luggage il bagaglio a mano
handicapped disabile
handlebars il manubrio
handsome bello(a)
hangover i postumi della sbornia
to hang up (*telephone*) riattaccare
to happen succedere; **What happened?** Cos'è successo?

happy felice; **Happy birthday!** Buon compleanno!
harbour il porto
hard (*not soft*) duro(a); (*not easy*) difficile
hardly **I've hardly got any money** Ho pochissimi soldi
hardware shop il negozio di ferramenta
hat il cappello
to have avere; **I have ...** Ho...; **I don't have ...** Non ho...; **to have to** dovere; **I've done it** L'ho fatto; **I'll have a coffee** Prendo un caffè
hay fever il raffreddore da fieno
he lui
head la testa
headache il mal di testa; **I have a headache** Ho mal di testa
headlights i fari
headphones la cuffia
to hear sentire
heart il cuore
heart attack l'infarto *m*
heartburn il bruciore di stomaco
heater il termosifone
heating il riscaldamento
heavy pesante
heel il tallone
hello salve; (*on telephone*) pronto
helmet il casco
help! Aiuto!
to help aiutare; **Can You help me?** Può aiutarmi?
her la; le; lei; (*belonging to her*) il suo, la sua; **I saw her last night** L'ho vista ieri sera; **I don't know her** Non la conosco; **I gave her the book** Le ho dato il libro; **with her** con lei; **I'm older than her** Sono più vecchio di lei; **her passport** il suo passaporto; **her room** la sua camera; **her suitcases** la sue valigie
here qui; **here is ...** ecco...; **Here's my passport** Ecco il mio passaporto
Hi! Salve!
high alto(a)

hill la collina
hill-walking il trekking
him lui; lo; gli; **I saw him last night** L'ho visto ieri sera; **I don't know him** Non lo conosco; **I gave him the letter** Gli ho dato la lettera; **with him** con lui
hip (part of the body) il fianco; (bone) l'anca f
hire car hire l'autonoleggio m **bike hire** il noleggio bici; **boat hire** il noleggio barche; **ski hire** il noleggio sci
to hire noleggiare
hired car la macchina a noleggio
his il suo, la sua; **his passport** il suo passaporto; **his room** la sua camera; **his suitcases** le sue valigie
historic storico(a)
hobby l'hobby m
to hold tenere; (contain) contenere; **Please hold** Resti in linea per favore
hole il buco
holiday la vacanza; (public) la festa; **on holiday** in vacanza
home la casa; **at home** a casa
homeopathic omeopatico(a)
honey il miele
honeymoon la luna di miele
to hope sperare; **I hope so** Spero di sì; **I hope not** Spero di no
hors d'œuvre l'antipasto m
horse racing l'ippica f
horse-riding l'equitazione f
hospital l'ospedale m
hostel (youth hostel) l'ostello m
hot caldo(a); **hot water** acqua calda; **I'm hot** Ho caldo; **It's hot** (weather) Fa caldo
hotel l'albergo m
hour l'ora f **half an hour** mezz'ora
house la casa
house wine il vino della casa
how (in what way) come; **how much?** quanto(a)?; **how many?** quanti(e)?; **How are You?** Come sta?

hungry to be hungry avere fame
hurry I'm in a hurry Ho fretta
to hurt fare male; **My back hurts** Mi fa male la schiena; **That hurts** Fa male; **Have You hurt Yourself?** Si è fatto male?
husband il marito

I
I io
ice il ghiaccio; **ice cube** il cubetto di ghiaccio; **with/ without ice** con/senza ghiaccio
ice box (for picnics) la borsa termica; (in fridge) il freezer
ice cream il gelato
ice lolly il ghiacciolo
idea l'idea f
if se
ignition l'accensione f
ignition key la chiave dell'accensione
ill malato(a)
illness la malattia
immediately subito
immersion heater lo scaldabagno a immersione
immobilizer (on car) l'immobilizer m
to import importare
important importante
impossible impossibile
to improve migliorare
in in; **in Italy** in Italia; **in London** a Londra; **in the hotel** in albergo; **in ten minutes** tra dieci minuti; **in front of** davanti a
included compreso(a)
indicator (in car) la freccia
indigestion l'indigestione f
infection l'infezione f
information le informazioni
information desk il banco informazioni
inhaler (for medication) l'inalatore m
injection l'iniezione f
injured ferito(a)
injury la ferita
inn la locanda
inquiry desk il banco informazioni
insect l'insetto m

insect repellent l'insettifugo
inside dentro
instant instant coffee il caffè solubile
instead instead of invece di
insulin l'insulina f
insurance l'assicurazione f
insurance certificate il certificato di assicurazione
to insure assicurare
insured assicurato(a)
intend to intend to avere intenzione di
interesting interessante
international internazionale
internet Internet m **on the internet** in Internet; **Do you have internet access?** Avete un accesso a Internet?
interpreter l'interprete m/f
interval (theatre) l'intervallo m
into in; **to get into a car** salire in macchina; **to go into the cinema** entrare al cinema; **to go into town** andare in città
to introduce presentare
invitation l'invito m
to invite invitare
invoice la fattura
Ireland l'Irlanda f
Irish irlandese
iron (for clothes) il ferro da stiro
to iron stirare
ironing board l'asse f da stiro
ironmonger's il negozio di ferramenta
island l'isola f
it esso, essa; lo, la
Italian italiano(a); (language) l'italiano m
Italy l'Italia f
to itch prudere

J
jack (for car) il cric
jacket la giacca; **waterproof jacket** il giaccone impermeabile
jam (food) la marmellata
jammed bloccato(a)
January gennaio
jar (honey, jam) il vasetto

jeans i blue jeans
jelly (*dessert*) la gelatina
jet ski l'acquascooter *m*
jeweller's la gioielleria
jewellery i gioielli
Jewish ebreo(a)
job il lavoro
to jog fare jogging
to join (*club*) iscriversi a
journey il viaggio
juice il succo; **a carton of juice** un cartone di succo di frutta
July luglio
jumper il maglione
jump leads i cavi per far partire la macchina
June giugno
just solo; **just two** solo due; **I've just arrived** Sono appena arrivato
to keep (*retain*) tenere

K

kettle il bollitore
key la chiave
kid (*child*) il bambino
kidneys i reni
kilo(gram) il chilo(grammo)
kilometre il chilometro
kind (*person*) gentile
kind (*sort*) il tipo; **What kind?** Di che tipo?
to kiss baciare
kitchen la cucina
knee il ginocchio
knickers le mutandine
knife il coltello
to know (*facts*) sapere; (*person, place*) conoscere; **I don't know** Non lo so; **I don't know Rome** Non conosco Roma; **to know how to swim** saper nuotare

L

label l'etichetta *f*
lace (*fabric*) il pizzo
ladies (*toilet*) la toilette (per signore)
lady la signora
lager la birra (bionda); **bottled lager** la birra in bottiglia; **draught lager** la birra alla spina
lake il lago
lamb l'agnello *m*
lamp la lampada

to land atterrare
landlady la padrona di casa
landline il telefono fisso
landlord il padrone di casa
landslide la frana
lane la stradina; (*of motorway*) la corsia
language la lingua
language school la scuola di lingue
laptop il computer portatile
large grande
last ultimo(a); **the last bus** l'ultimo autobus; **last time** l'ultima volta; **last week** la settimana scorsa; **last year** l'anno scorso; **last night** (*evening*) ieri sera; (*night-time*) ieri notte
late tardi; **The train is late** Il treno è in ritardo; **Sorry we are late** Scusi il ritardo
later più tardi
to laugh ridere
launderette la lavanderia automatica
laundry service il servizio lavanderia
lavatory la toilette
lavender la lavanda
lawyer l'avvocato *m*
lead (*electric*) il filo
leak la perdita
to leak perdere; **It's leaking** Perde
to learn imparare
lease (*rental*) l'affitto *m*
least at least almeno
leather la pelle
to leave (*a place*) partire; (*to leave behind*) lasciare; **I left it at home** L'ho lasciato a casa; **What time does the train leave?** Quando parte il treno?
leek il porro
left on/to the left a sinistra
left-luggage office il deposito bagagli
left-luggage locker l'armadietto *m* per i bagagli
leg la gamba
legal legale
leisure centre il centro ricreativo
lemon il limone
lemonade la limonata

to lend prestare; **Can You lend me Your biro?** Può prestarmi la biro?
lens (*of camera*) l'obiettivo *m* (*contact lens*) la lente a contatto
less meno; **less than me** meno di me; **A bit less, please** Un po' di meno, per favore
lesson la lezione
to let (*to allow*) permettere; (*to hire out*) affittare
letter la lettera
letterbox la cassetta delle lettere
lettuce la lattuga
licence (*for car*) la patente; (*for fishing*) la licenza
to lie down sdraiarsi
lift (*elevator*) l'ascensore *m* **Can You give me a lift to the party?** Può darmi un passaggio per andare alla festa?
lift pass (*skiing*) lo ski pass
light (*not heavy*) leggero(a)
light la luce; **Have You got a light?** Ha da accendere?
light bulb la lampadina
lighter l'accendino *m*
lighthouse il faro
lightning il fulmine
like (*similar to*) come; **a city like Florence** una città come Firenze
to like **I like coffee** Mi piace il caffè; **I don't like ...** Non mi piace...; **I'd like to ...** Vorrei...
lilo® il materassino
lime (*fruit*) il lime
line (*row, queue*) la fila; (*telephone*) la linea
linen il lino
lingerie la biancheria intima da donna
lips le labbra
lipstick il rossetto
to listen to ascoltare
litre il litro
little piccolo(a); **a little** un po' di
to live (*in a place*) abitare; **I live in London** Vivo a Londra
liver il fegato
living room il salotto

loaf la pagnotta
lobster l'astice *m*
local locale
lock (*on door, box*) la serratura
to lock chiudere a chiave
locker (*for luggage*) l'armadietto *m*
locksmith il fabbro
log (*for fire*) il ceppo
lollipop il lecca lecca
London Londra; **to/in London** a Londra
long lungo(a); **for a long time** per molto tempo
long-sighted presbite
to look after prendersi cura di
to look at guardare
to look for cercare
loose (*not fastened*) slegato(a); **It's come loose** (*unscrewed*) Si è allentato; (*detached*) Si è staccato
lorry il camion
to lose perdere
lost (*object*) perso(a); **I've lost ...** Ho perso...; **I'm lost** Mi sono perso
lost property office l'ufficio *m* oggetti smarriti
lot a lot of, lots of molto(a); **a lot of people** molta gente; **a lot of friends** molti amici
lotion la lozione
loud forte
loudspeaker l'altoparlante *m*
lounge (*in hotel*) la hall; (*at airport*) la sala d'attesa
love l'amore *m*
to love amare; **I love you** Ti amo; **I love swimming** Mi piace nuotare
lovely bellissimo(a)
low basso(a)
lucky fortunato(a)
luggage i bagagli
luggage allowance il peso consentito di bagaglio
luggage rack il portabagagli
luggage tag l'etichetta *f* del bagaglio
luggage trolley il carrello
lump (*swelling*) il bernoccolo
lunch il pranzo

lung il polmone
luxury di lusso

M
mad matto(a)
magazine la rivista
maid (*in hotel*) la cameriera
maiden name il nome da ragazza
mail la posta; **by mail** per posta
main principale
main course (*of meal*) il piatto forte
main road la strada principale
make (*brand*) la marca
to make fare; **made of wood** fatto(a) di legno
make-up il trucco
man l'uomo *m*
to manage riuscire; (*to be in charge of*) dirigere
manager il direttore, la direttrice
manicure il/la manicure
manual manuale
many molti(e)
map (*of region, country*) la carta geografica; (*of town*) la piantina; **road map** la carta stradale; **street map** la cartina della città
March marzo
margarine la margarina
marina il porticciolo
mark (*stain*) la macchia
market il mercato; **When is the market?** Quando c'è il mercato?
marmalade la marmellata d'arance
married sposato(a); **I'm married** Sono sposato; **Are You married?** È sposato?
mass (*in church*) la messa
massage il massaggio
to message messaggiare
match (*game*) la partita
matches i fiammiferi
material (*cloth*) il tessuto
to matter importare; **It doesn't matter** Non importa; **What's the matter?** Cosa c'è?
mattress il materasso
May maggio
mayonnaise la maionese

mayor il sindaco
maximum il massimo
me me; mi; **Can You hear me?** Mi sente?; **It's me** Sono io; **without me** senza di me; **with me** con me
meal il pasto
to mean voler dire; **What does this mean?** Cosa vuol dire?
meat la carne
medicine la medicina
Mediterranean Sea il Mar Mediterraneo
medium (*size*) medio(a)
medium rare (*meat*) a media cottura
medium sweet non troppo zuccherato
to meet (*by chance, arrangement*) incontrare; **I'm meeting her tomorrow** La vedo domani; **Pleased to meet You** Piacere di conoscerla
meeting la riunione; (*by chance*) l'incontro *m*
melon il melone
member (*of club*) il socio, la socia
to mend riparare
menu il menù; **set menu** il menù a prezzo fisso
message il messaggio
to message messaggiare
metal il metallo
meter il contatore
metre il metro
microwave oven il forno a microonde
midday il mezzogiorno; **at midday** a mezzogiorno
middle il mezzo; **in the middle of the street** in mezzo alla strada; **in the middle of May** a metà maggio
middle-aged di mezz'età
midge il moscerino
midnight la mezzanotte; **at midnight** a mezzanotte
migraine l'emicrania *f* **I have a migraine** Ho l'emicrania
mild (*weather*) mite; (*cheese*) dolce; (*curry*) non piccante
milk il latte; **with/without milk** con/senza latte; **fresh**

milk il latte fresco; **hot milk** il latte caldo; **long-life milk** il latte a lunga conservazione; **powdered milk** il latte in polvere; **soya milk** il latte di soia
milkshake il frappè
millimetre il millimetro
mince (*meat*) la carne macinata
to mind dispiacere; **Do You mind if I ...?** Le dispiace se...?; **I don't mind** Non mi dà fastidio
mineral water l'acqua *f* minerale
minidisc il minidisco
minimum il minimo
minute il minuto
mirror lo specchio; (*in car*) lo specchietto
to miss (*train, flight*) perdere
Miss Signorina
missing (*disappeared*) scomparso(a); **My son is missing** Mio figlio è scomparso
mistake l'errore *m*
to mix mescolare
mobile number numero di cellulare
mobile phone il cellulare
modem il modem
modern moderno(a)
moisturizer la crema idratante
moment momento; **at the moment** al momento; **just a moment** un momento
monastery il monastero
Monday il lunedì
money i soldi
month il mese; **this month** questo mese; **last month** il mese scorso; **next month** il mese prossimo
moped il motorino
more più; **more expensive** più caro; **more than before** più di prima; **more than 10** più di dieci; **Do You want some more tea?** Vuole ancora un po' di tè?; **There isn't any more** Non ce n'è più
morning la mattina; **in the morning** di mattina;

this morning stamattina; **tomorrow morning** domani mattina
mosque la moschea
mosquito la zanzara
mosquito repellent l'insettifugo *m*
most the most interesting il più interessante; **most of the time** per gran parte del tempo; **most people** gran parte della gente
mother la madre
mother-in-law la suocera
motor il motore
motorbike la moto *f*
motorboat il motoscafo
motorway l'autostrada *f*
mountain la montagna
mountain bike la mountain bike
mountaineering l'alpinismo *m*
mouse (*animal*) il topo; (*computer*) il mouse
mouth la bocca
to move muoversi
movie il film
Mr Signor; **Mr Rossi** il Signor Rossi
Mrs Signora; **Mrs Bianchi** la Signora Bianchi
Ms Signora
much molto; **too much** troppo; **too much money** troppi soldi; **I feel much better** Mi sento molto meglio
mugging lo scippo
museum il museo
mushrooms i funghi
music la musica
Muslim mussulmano(a)
mussels le cozze
must dovere
mustard la senape
my il mio, la mia; **my passport** il mio passaporto; **my room** la mia camera; **my suitcases** le mie valigie

N

nail (*metal*) il chiodo; (*finger*) l'unghia *f*
nail file la limetta per le unghie
name il nome; **My name is** Mi chiamo; **What is Your**

name? Come si chiama?
nanny la bambinaia
napkin il tovagliolo
nappy il pannolino
narrow stretto(a)
nationality la nazionalità
natural naturale
nature reserve la riserva naturale
navy blue blu scuro
near vicino a; **near the bank** vicino alla banca; **Is it near?** È vicino?
necessary necessario(a)
neck il collo
necklace la collana
nectarine la nocepesca
to need avere bisogno di; **I need** Ho bisogno di; **We need to phone** Abbiamo bisogno di telefonare
needle l'ago *m* **a needle and thread** ago e filo
negative (*photo*) la negativa
neighbours i vicini
nephew il nipote
net the Net Internet *m*
never mai; **I never drink wine** Non bevo mai vino
new nuovo(a)
news (*TV, radio*) il notiziario
newsagent's il giornalaio
newspaper il giornale
news stand l'edicola *f*
New Year il Capodanno; **Happy New Year!** Buon Anno!
New Year's Eve l'ultimo *m* dell'anno
New Zealand la Nuova Zelanda
next prossimo(a); **the next train** il prossimo treno; **next week** la prossima settimana; **next Monday** lunedì prossimo; **next to** accanto a; **What did you do next?** Cos'hai fatto dopo?
nice (*kind*) gentile; (*pretty*) carino(a); (*good*) buono(a)
niece la nipote
night (*night-time*) la notte; (*evening*) la sera; **at night** di notte; **per night** a notte; **last night** (*evening*) ieri sera; (*night-time*) ieri notte;

tomorrow night (*evening*) domani sera; (*night-time*) domani notte
nightclub il nightclub
no no; (*without*) senza; **no thanks** no, grazie; **no smoking** vietato fumare; **no problem** non c'è problema; **no ice** senza ghiaccio; **no sugar** senza zucchero; **There's no hot water** Non c'è acqua calda
nobody nessuno; **Nobody came** Non è venuto nessuno
noise il rumore
noisy rumoroso(a); **It's very noisy** C'è molto rumore
non-alcoholic analcolico(a)
none nessuno(a)
non-smoking (*seat, compartment*) per non-fumatori
normally normalmente
north il nord
Northern Ireland l'Irlanda f del Nord
nose il naso
nosebleed to have a nosebleed avere sangue di naso
not non; **I am not going** Non ci vado
note (*banknote*) la banconota; (*written*) il biglietto
note pad il bloc-notes
nothing niente; **nothing else** nient'altro
notice l'avviso m
November novembre m
now adesso; **now and then** ogni tanto
number il numero; **phone number** il numero di telefono; **a large number of people** moltissima gente
numberplate (*of car*) la targa
nurse l'infermiera, l'infermiere
nursery slope la pista per principianti
nuts (*to eat*) la frutta secca

O
to obtain ottenere
occasionally ogni tanto

occupation (*work*) il lavoro
October ottobre m
of di; **a glass of wine** un bicchiere di vino; **made of cotton** fatto(a) di cotone
off (*light, heater*) spento(a); (*tap, gas*) chiuso(a); (*milk*) andato(a) a male; **I'm off** Vado
office l'ufficio m
often spesso; **How often do you go to the gym?** Quante volte vai in palestra?
oil l'olio m
oil gauge l'indicatore m del livello dell'olio
OK! va bene!
old vecchio(a); **How old are You?** Quanti anni ha?; **I'm ... years old** Ho... anni
old-age pensioner il pensionato, la pensionata
olive l'oliva f
olive oil l'olio m d'oliva
on (*TV, light, engine*) acceso(a); (*tap, gas*) aperto(a)
on su; **on the table** sulla tavola; **on the TV** alla TV; **on the 2nd floor** al secondo piano; **on Friday** venerdì; **on Fridays** di venerdì; **on time** in orario
once una volta; **once a week** una volta alla settimana; **at once** subito
onion la cipolla
only solo; **We only want to stay for one night** Vogliamo fermarci solo una notte; **the only day I'm free** l'unico giorno in cui sono libero
open aperto(a)
to open aprire
opening hours l'orario m di apertura
opera l'opera f
operation (*surgical*) l'operazione f
operator (*phone*) il/la centralinista
opposite di fronte a; **opposite the bank** di fronte alla banca; **quite the opposite** al contrario
optician l'ottico m
or o; **Tea or coffee?** Tè o

caffè?; **I don't eat meat or fish** Non mangio né carne né pesce
orange (*fruit*) l'arancia f (*colour*) arancione
orange juice il succo d'arancia
order out of order fuori servizio
to order (*in restaurant*) ordinare; **I'd like to order** Vorrei ordinare
organic biologico(a)
to organize organizzare
ornament il soprammobile
other l'altro(a); **the other car** l'altra macchina; **the other one** l'altro(a); **Have you any others?** Ce ne sono altri?
ought dovere
our il nostro, la nostra; **our room** la nostra stanza; **our passports** i nostri passaporti; **our baggage** i nostri bagagli
out (*light*) spento(a); **She's out** È fuori; **He lives out of town** Vive fuori città
outdoor (*pool*) all'aperto
outside fuori; **It's outside** È fuori; **outside the house** fuori dalla casa
oven il forno
over (*on top of*) sopra; **over here** qua; **over there** là; **over the holidays** durante le vacanze; **It's over** È finito
to overcharge far pagare troppo
overdone (*food*) troppo cotto
to owe dovere; **I owe You ...** Le devo...
own It's his own company È la sua ditta; **on my own** da solo
to own possedere
owner il proprietario, la proprietaria
oxygen l'ossigeno m
oyster l'ostrica

P
pacemaker il pacemaker
to pack (*luggage*) fare la valigia
package tour il viaggio

organizzato
packet il pacchetto
paid pagato(a)
pain il dolore
painful doloroso(a)
painkiller l'analgesico *m*
to paint dipingere
painting (*picture*) il quadro
pair il paio
palace il palazzo
pale (*person*) pallido(a);
  pale blue celeste
pan (*saucepan*) la pentola;
  (*frying pan*) la padella
panniers (*for bike*) il cestino
panties le mutandine
pants (*mens' underwear*) le
  mutande
panty liner il proteggislip
paper la carta
paragliding il parapendio
parcel il pacco
pardon? Scusi?; **I beg Your**
  pardon? Scusi?
parents i genitori
park il parco
to park parcheggiare
parking meter il
  parchimetro
partner (*business*) il socio,
  la socia; (*boy/girlfriend*) il
  compagno, la compagna
party (*group*) la comitiva;
  (*celebration*) la festa
pass (*bus, train*) la tessera;
  (*mountain*) il passo
to pass passare; **Can You**
  pass me the salt, please?
  Mi passa il sale per favore?
passenger il passeggero, la
  passeggera
passport il passaporto
password la password
pasta la pasta
pastry (*cake*) il pasticcino
path il sentiero
patient (*in hospital*) il/la
  paziente
to pay pagare; **I'd like to**
  pay Vorrei pagare; **Where**
  do I pay? Dove devo pagare?
payment il pagamento
payphone il telefono
  pubblico
peach la pesca
peanut la nocciolina
  americana
pear la pera

peas i piselli
pedalo il pedalò
pedestrian il pedone
to peel sbucciare
peg (*for clothes*) la molletta;
  (*for tent*) il picchetto
pen la penna
pencil la matita
pensioner il pensionato, la
  pensionata
people la gente
pepper (*spice*) il pepe;
  (*vegetable*) il peperone
per a; **per day** al giorno;
  per person a persona;
  per cent per cento
performance (*in theatre*) la
  rappresentazione; (*in cinema*)
  lo spettacolo
perfume il profumo
perhaps forse
perm la permanente
permit il permesso
person la persona
petrol la benzina; **unleaded**
  petrol la benzina senza
  piombo
petrol pump la pompa della
  benzina
petrol station la stazione di
  servizio
petrol tank il serbatoio della
  benzina
pharmacy la farmacia
phone il telefono; **by phone**
  per telefono
to phone telefonare;
  to phone somebody
  telefonare a qualcuno
phonebook l'elenco *m*
  telefonico
phone call la telefonata
photo la foto *f* **to take a**
  photo fare una foto
photocopy la fotocopia
to photocopy fotocopiare
to pick (*choose*) scegliere
pickpocket il borseggiatore
picnic il picnic; **to have a**
  picnic fare un picnic
picture (*painting*) il quadro;
  (*photo*) la foto *f*
pie (*fruit*) la torta; (*meat*) il
  pasticcio
piece il pezzo
pig il maiale
pill la pillola
pillow il cuscino

pilot il pilota
pin lo spillo
pineapple l'ananas *m*
pink rosa
pipe (*drains*) il tubo
pity What a pity! Che
  peccato!
pizza la pizza
place il luogo
place of birth il luogo di
  nascita
plain (*yogourt*) naturale
plan (*of town*) la piantina;
  What are Your plans for
  tonight? Che programmi ha
  per stasera?
plane (*aircraft*) l'aereo *m*
plaster (*sticking plaster*) il
  cerotto; (*for broken limb, on*
  wall) il gesso
plastic (*made of*) di plastica
plastic bag il sacchetto di
  plastica
plate il piatto
platform (*railway*) il binario;
  Which platform? A che
  binario?
play (*theatre*) la commedia
to play (*games*) giocare;
  (*instrument*) suonare
please per favore
pleased Pleased to meet
  You! Piacere di conoscerla!
plug (*electrical*) la spina; (*for*
  sink) il tappo
to plug in attaccare
plum la prugna
plumber l'idraulico *m*
pm del pomeriggio; **at**
  4 pm alle quattro del
  pomeriggio
poached (*egg*) in camicia;
  (*fish*) bollito(a)
pocket la tasca
policeman il poliziotto
policewoman la donna
  poliziotto
police station il
  commissariato
polish (*for shoes*) il lucido
polite educato(a)
pool la piscina
poor povero(a)
popular popolare
pork la carne di maiale
porter (*hotel*) il portiere; (*at*
  station) il facchino
portion la porzione

possible possibile
post la posta; **by post** per posta
to post imbucare
postbox la buca delle lettere
postcard la cartolina
postcode il codice postale
poster il poster
postman/woman il postino, la postina
post office l'ufficio *m* postale
pot (*for cooking*) la pentola
potato la patata; **baked potato** la patata al forno; **boiled potatoes** le patate lesse; **fried potatoes** le patate fritte; **mashed potatoes** il purè di patate; **roast potatoes** le patate arrosto
potato salad l'insalata *f* di patate
pottery la terracotta
pound (*money*) la sterlina
powder la polvere
powdered in polvere
power (*electricity*) l'elettricità
pram la carrozzina
prawn il gamberetto
to prefer preferire
pregnant incinta; **I'm pregnant** Sono incinta
to prepare preparare
prescription la ricetta
present (*gift*) il regalo
president il/la presidente
pressure la pressione
pretty carino(a)
price il prezzo
price list il listino prezzi
priest il prete
print la stampa
to print stampare
printer la stampante
printout la stampa
private privato(a)
probably probabilmente
problem il problema *m*
programme (*TV, radio*) il programma *m*
to promise promettere
to pronounce pronunciare; **How's it pronounced?** Come si pronuncia?
public pubblico(a)

public holiday la festa nazionale
pudding il dessert
to pull tirare
pullover il pullover
pulse il legume
pump (*for bike*) la pompa; **petrol pump** la pompa di benzina
puncture to have a puncture forare
purple viola
purpose scopo; **on purpose** apposta
purse il borsellino
to push spingere
pushchair il passeggino
to put (*place*) mettere

Q

quality la qualità
quantity la quantità
quarter il quarto; **a quarter of an hour** un quarto d'ora
question la domanda; **to ask a question** fare una domanda
queue la coda
to queue fare la coda
quick veloce
quickly velocemente
quiet (*place*) tranquillo(a)
quilt la trapunta
quite (*rather*) abbastanza; **quite good** non male; **quite expensive** abbastanza caro(a); **I'm not quite sure** Non sono proprio sicuro; **quite a lot** un bel po'

R

racket la racchetta
radiator il radiatore
radio la radio *f* **car radio** l'autoradio *f*
railway la ferrovia
railway station la stazione ferroviaria
rain la pioggia
to rain it's raining piove
raincoat l'impermeabile *m*
rare (*uncommon*) raro(a); (*steak*) al sangue
raspberry il lampone
rat il ratto
rate (*price*) la tariffa

rate of exchange il tasso di cambio
rather piuttosto; **rather expensive** piuttosto caro(a); **I'd rather stay in tonight** Preferirei restare a casa stasera
raw crudo(a)
razor il rasoio
razor blades le lamette
to read leggere
ready pronto(a)
real vero(a)
really veramente
receipt la ricevuta
reception desk la reception
receptionist il/la receptionist
to recharge (*battery*) ricaricare
recipe la ricetta
to recognize riconoscere
to recommend raccomandare
red rosso(a)
refill il ricambio
refund il rimborso
region la regione
to register (*at hotel*) registrarsi
registered (*letter*) raccomandata
registration form il modulo d'iscrizione
relation (*family*) il/la parente
relationship il rapporto
to remain restare
to remember ricordare; **I don't remember** Non mi ricordo
remote control il telecomando
rent l'affitto *m*
to rent (*house*) affittare; (*car, bike*) noleggiare
rental (*house*) l'affitto *m* (*car, bike*) il noleggio
to repair riparare
to repeat ripetere
to reply rispondere
to require richiedere
to rescue salvare
reservation la prenotazione
to reserve prenotare
reserved prenotato(a)

resident (*in country*) il/ la residente; (*in street*) l'abitante *m/f* (*in hostel*) l'ospite *m/f*

rest (*relaxation*) il riposo; (*remainder*) il resto; **the rest of the money** il resto dei soldi

to rest riposarsi

restaurant il ristorante

restaurant car il vagone ristorante

retired in pensione

to return ritornare

return ticket il biglietto di andata e ritorno

retweet il retwit

to retweet retwittare

to reverse fare marcia indietro; **to reverse the charges** fare una telefonata al carico del destinatario

reverse gear la retromarcia

rice il riso

rich (*person, food*) ricco(a)

to ride (*on horseback*) cavalcare; **to ride a bike** andare in bicicletta

right (*correct*) giusto(a); **to be right** avere ragione; **You're right** Ha ragione; **That's right** È giusto; **on/ to the right** a destra

right of way la precedenza

ring (*on finger*) l'anello *m* (*telephone*) lo squillo

ripe maturo(a)

river il fiume

road la strada

roast arrosto(a)

roll (*bread*) il panino

roof il tetto

room (*in house*) la stanza; (*in hotel*) la camera; (*space*) lo spazio; **double room** la camera doppia; **single room** la camera singola; **family room** la camera per famiglia

room number il numero di camera

room service il servizio in camera

rosé wine il vino rosé

rotten (*fruit etc*) marcio(a)

row (*line, theatre*) la fila

rubber (*material*) la gomma; (*eraser*) la gomma da cancellare

rubbish la spazzatura

rucksack lo zaino

to run correre

rush hour l'ora *f* di punta

S

sad triste

saddle la sella

safe (*for valuables*) la cassaforte

safe sicuro(a); **Is it safe?** È sicuro?

safety belt la cintura di sicurezza

safety pin la spilla di sicurezza

to sail (*sport, leisure*) andare in barca

sailboard la tavola da windsurf

sailing (*sport*) la vela

sailing boat la barca a vela

salad l'insalata *f* **green salad** l'insalata verde; **mixed salad** l'insalata mista; **salad dressing** il condimento per l'insalata

sales (*reductions*) i saldi

sales assistant il commesso, la commessa

salesman il commesso

saleswoman la commessa

sales rep il/la rappresentante

salmon il salmone

salt il sale

salt water l'acqua *f* salata

salty salato(a)

same stesso; **Have a good weekend! – The same to you!** Buon weekend! – Anche a te!

sand la sabbia

sandals i sandali

sandwich il tramezzino; **toasted sandwich** il toast

sanitary towels gli assorbenti

sardines le sardine

satellite dish l'antenna *f* parabolica

satellite TV la televisione via satellite

Saturday il sabato

sauce la salsa

saucepan la pentola

saucer il piattino

sausage la salsiccia

savoury salato(a)

to say dire

scarf (*headscarf*) il foulard; (*woollen*) la sciarpa

scenery il paesaggio

schedule Is the flight on schedule? Il volo è in orario?

school la scuola; **at school** a scuola; **to go to school** andare a scuola; **after school** dopo la scuola; **primary school** la scuola elementare

scissors le forbici

score (*of match*) il punteggio; **What's the score?** Qual è il punteggio?; **to score a goal** segnare un gol

Scotland la Scozia

Scottish scozzese

screen (*on computer, TV*) lo schermo

screw la vite

screwdriver il cacciavite

scuba diving le immersioni subacquee

sea il mare

seafood i frutti di mare

seaside at the seaside al mare

season (*of year*) la stagione; **high season** l'alta stagione; **in season** di stagione

season ticket l'abbonamento *m*

seat (*chair*) la sedia; (*in bus, train*) il posto

seatbelt la cintura di sicurezza

second secondo(a); **a second** un secondo

second class la seconda classe

secretary il segretario, la segretaria

to see vedere

self-service il self-service

to sell vendere

Sellotape® lo Scotch®

to send inviare

senior citizen il pensionato, la pensionata

sensible (*person*) ragionevole; (*shoes etc*) pratico(a)

separated separato(a)
**separately to pay
separately** pagare
separatamente
September settembre *m*
serious (*accident, problem*)
grave
to serve servire
service (*in restaurant,
shop*) il servizio; (*church*)
la funzione; **Is service
included?** Il servizio è
incluso?; **service charge** il
servizio; **service station** la
stazione di servizio
to service (*car, washing
machine*) revisionare
serviette il tovagliolo
set menu il menù a prezzo
fisso
several diversi(e); **several
times** diverse volte
shade l'ombra *f* **in the
shade** all'ombra
shallow basso(a)
shampoo lo shampoo
to share dividere
to shave farsi la barba
shaver il rasoio
shaving cream la crema da
barba
she lei
sheet (*for bed*) il lenzuolo
sherry lo sherry
ship la nave
shirt la camicia
shock absorber
l'ammortizzatore *m*
shoe la scarpa
shoelaces i lacci delle scarpe
shoe polish il lucido per
scarpe
shoe shop il negozio di
calzature
shop il negozio
shop assistant il
commesso, la commessa
shopping la spesa; **to go
shopping** (*for pleasure*) fare
compere; (*for food*) fare la
spesa
shopping centre il centro
commerciale
shop window la vetrina
short corto(a)
shorts i calzoncini corti
short-sighted miope
shoulder la spalla

show lo spettacolo
to show mostrare
shower (*bath*) la doccia;
(*rain*) l'acquazzone *m* **to
take a shower** fare la
doccia
shower gel il docciaschiuma
m
shrimp il gamberetto
shut (*closed*) chiuso(a)
to shut chiudere
shutters (*outside*) le
imposte
shuttle service il servizio
navetta
sick (*ill*) malato(a); **I feel
sick** Mi sento male
side il lato
side dish il contorno
**sightseeing to go
sightseeing** fare un giro
turistico
to sign firmare
signature la firma
silk la seta
silver l'argento *m*
SIM card la SIM card
similar similar to simile
a; **They're similar** Si
assomigliano
since da; **since 1974** dal
1974; **since you're not
Italian** dato che non siete
italiani
to sing cantare
single (*unmarried*) non
sposato(a); (*bed, room*)
singolo(a)
single ticket il biglietto di
sola andata
sister la sorella
sister-in-law la cognata
to sit sedersi; **Sit down,
please!** Prego, si accomodi!
site (*website*) il sito
size (*clothes*) la taglia;
(*shoes*) il numero
to skate pattinare
skateboard lo skateboard
skis gli sci
to ski sciare
ski boots gli scarponi da sci
skiing sciare
ski instructor il maestro di
sci, la maestra di sci
ski lift lo ski-lift
ski pass lo skipass
ski pole/stick il bastoncino

ski run/piste la pista
to skid scivolare
skimmed skimmed milk il
latte scremato
skin la pelle
skirt la gonna
to sleep dormire; **to go to
sleep** andare a dormire
sleeper (*on train*) la
cuccetta
sleeping bag il sacco a pelo
sleeping car il vagone letto
sleeping pill il sonnifero
slice (*bread, cake, ham*) la
fetta
sliced bread il pancarrè
slide (*photograph*) la
diapositiva
slightly leggermente
slow lento(a)
slowly lentamente
small piccolo(a); **smaller
than** più piccolo di
smell l'odore *m* **a bad smell**
un cattivo odore; **a nice
smell** un buon odore
to smile sorridere
to smoke fumare; **I don't
smoke** Non fumo; **Can I
smoke?** Posso fumare?
SMS il SMS
snack lo spuntino; **to have
a snack** fare uno spuntino
snow la neve
to snow nevicare; **It's
snowing** Nevica
**snowboarding to go
snowboarding** andare a
fare snowboard
snow chains le catene da
neve
so così; **It's not so
expensive as the other one**
Non è caro come l'altro; **So
do I** Anch'io; **so much/so
many ...** tanto/tanti...; **I
think so** Penso di sì; **So
what?** E allora?
soap il sapone
socket (*for plug*) la presa
socks i calzini
soda water il selz
sofa bed il divano letto
soft drink la bibita
software il software
sole (*shoe*) la suola
some un po' di; **Would You
like some bread?** Vuole del

pane?; **some books** un po' di libri; **some of them** alcuni di loro
someone qualcuno
something qualcosa
sometimes qualche volta
son il figlio
son-in-law il genero
song la canzone
soon presto; **as soon as possible** il più presto possibile
sore to have a sore throat avere il mal di gola
sorry Sorry! Mi scusi!; **I'm sorry!** Mi dispiace!
sort il tipo
soup la minestra
sour aspro(a)
south il sud
souvenir il souvenir
space lo spazio
spade la pala
spare parts i pezzi di ricambio
spare tyre la gomma di scorta
spare wheel la ruota di scorta
sparkling sparkling water l'acqua gassata; **sparkling wine** il vino frizzante
to speak parlare; **Do You speak English?** Parla inglese?
speaker (*loudspeaker*) l'altoparlante *m*
special speciale
speciality la specialità
speedboat il motoscafo
speed limit il limite di velocità
speedometer il tachimetro
to spell How is it spelt? Come si scrive?
to spend (*money*) spendere
spicy piccante
spinach gli spinaci
spirits (*alcohol*) i liquori
spite in spite of nonostante
spoon il cucchiaio
sport lo sport
sports centre il centro sportivo
sports shop il negozio di articoli sportivi
spring (*season*) la primavera
square (*in town*) la piazza

squash lo squash
squid il calamaro
stadium lo stadio
stain la macchia
stairs le scale
stalls (*in theatre*) la platea
stamp il francobollo
to stand stare in piedi
start inizio; **at the start of the film** all'inizio del film; **from the start** fin dall'inizio
to start cominciare; **What time does it start?** A che ora comincia?; **The car won't start** La macchina non parte
starter (*in meal*) l'antipasto *m*
station la stazione
stationer's la cartoleria
stay il soggiorno; **Enjoy your stay!** Buona permanenza!
to stay (*remain*) rimanere; **I'm staying at the... hotel** Alloggio all'albergo ...; **to stay the night** fermarsi per la notte; **We stayed in Venice for a few days** Ci siamo fermati a Venezia per alcuni giorni
steak la bistecca
to steal rubare
steamed al vapore
steering wheel il volante
stepdaughter la figliastra
stepfather il patrigno
stepmother la matrigna
stepson il figliastro
stereo lo stereo
sterling la sterlina
steward (*on plane*) lo steward
stewardess (*on plane*) la hostess
sticking-plaster il cerotto
still still water acqua naturale
sting la puntura
to sting pungere
stockings le calze
stomach lo stomaco; **He's got stomach-ache** Ha mal di pancia
stone la pietra
stop bus stop la fermata dell'autobus

to stop fermarsi; **Do You stop at the station?** Ferma alla stazione?; **to stop doing** smettere di fare; **to stop smoking** smettere di fumare
store (*shop*) il negozio
storey il piano
straightaway subito
straight straight on diritto
strange strano(a)
straw (*for drinking*) la cannuccia
strawberry la fragola
street la strada
street map la piantina
strike lo sciopero; **to be on strike** essere in sciopero
striped a strisce
stroke (*medical*) l'ictus *m*
strong forte
stuck It's stuck È bloccato
student lo studente, la studentessa
student discount lo sconto per studenti
stuffed farcito(a)
stupid stupido(a)
subway (*train*) la metropolitana; (*passage*) il sottopassaggio
suddenly all'improvviso
suede la pelle scamosciata
sugar lo zucchero
to suggest proporre
suit (*man's*) l'abito *m* (*woman's*) il tailleur
suitcase la valigia
summer l'estate *f*
summer holidays le vacanze estive
sun il sole
to sunbathe prendere il sole
sunblock la protezione solare totale
sunburn la scottatura solare
suncream la crema solare
Sunday la domenica
sunglasses gli occhiali da sole
sunny It's sunny C'è il sole
sunroof il tettuccio apribile
sunscreen (*lotion*) la crema solare protettiva
sunshade l'ombrellone *m*
sunstroke l'insolazione *f*
suntan l'abbronzatura *f*

suntan lotion la crema abbronzante

supermarket il supermercato

supplement il supplemento

to surf fare surf; **to surf the Net** navigare in Internet

surfboard la tavola da surf

surname il cognome

surprise la sorpresa; **What a surprise!** Che sorpresa!

sweater il maglione

sweatshirt la felpa

sweet (*not savoury*) dolce; (*dessert*) il dolce; **sweets** le caramelle

to swim nuotare

swimming pool la piscina

swimsuit il costume da bagno

swing (*for children*) l'altalena *f*

switch l'interruttore *m*

to switch off spegnere

to switch on accendere

swollen gonfio(a)

T

table la tavola

tablecloth la tovaglia

table tennis il ping pong

tablet (*medicine*) la pastiglia; (*computer*) il tablet

tailor's la sartoria

to take prendere; (*take with you*) portare; (*exam*) dare; (*subject at school*) scegliere; **Do You take sugar?** Vuole zucchero?; **I'll take You to the airport** La porterò all'aeroporto; **How long does it take?** Quanto tempo ci vuole?; **It takes about one hour** Ci vuole circa un'ora; **We take credit cards** Accettiamo carte di credito

take away (*food*) il cibo da asporto

to take off (*plane*) decollare; (*clothes*) togliere

to take out tirar fuori

to talk to talk to parlare a

tall alto(a)

tampons gli assorbenti interni

tangerine il mandarino

tank petrol tank il serbatoio

tap il rubinetto

tap water l'acqua *f* del rubinetto

tart la crostata

taste il sapore

to taste assaggiare; **Can I taste some?** Ne posso assaggiare un po'?

taxi il taxi

taxi driver il/la tassista

taxi rank il posteggio dei taxi

tea il tè; **herbal tea** la tisana; **lemon tea** il tè al limone; **tea with milk** il tè al latte

teabag la bustina di tè

teapot la teiera

teaspoon il cucchiaino

to teach insegnare

teacher l'insegnante *m/f*

team la squadra

teenager il/la teenager

teeth i denti

telephone il telefono

to telephone telefonare; **to telephone somebody** telefonare a qualcuno

telephone call la telefonata

telephone number il numero di telefono

television la televisione

to tell dire

temperature la temperatura; **to have a temperature** avere la febbre

tenant l'inquilino, l'inquilina

tennis il tennis

tennis ball la pallina da tennis

tennis court il campo da tennis

tennis racket la racchetta da tennis

tent la tenda

tent peg il picchetto

terminal (*airport*) il terminal

terrace la terrazza

to test (*to try out*) provare

to text mandare un messaggino; **I'll text you** Ti manderò un messaggino

text message il messaggino

than di; **Diana sings better than me** Diana canta meglio di me; **more than you** più di te; **more than five** più di cinque

thank you grazie; **Thank you very much** Molte grazie

that quel, quella, quello; **that cat** quel gatto; **that man** quell'uomo; **that one** quello là; **to think that ...** pensare che...

the (*sing*) il, lo, la; (*plural*) i, gli, le

theatre il teatro

their (*sing*) il/la loro; (*plural*) i/le loro; **their car** la loro macchina; **their children** i loro bambini

them loro; li; le; **I didn't know them** Non li conoscevo; **I gave them some brochures** Ho dato loro alcuni depliant; **It's for them** È per loro

there (*over there*) lì; **there is, there are** c'è, ci sono; **there was** c'era; **there'll be** ci sarà

therefore quindi

thermometer il termometro

these questi, queste; **these ones** questi qui

they loro

thick (*not thin*) spesso(a)

thief il ladro, la ladra

thin (*person*) magro(a)

thing la cosa

to think pensare

thirsty I'm thirsty Ho sete

this questo, questa; **this cat** questo gatto; **this woman** questa donna; **this one** questo(a)

those quei, quelle, quegli; **those ones** quelli(e)

throat la gola

through attraverso; **to go through Milan** attraversare Milano; **a through train** un treno diretto; **from May through to September** da maggio a settembre

Thursday il giovedì

ticket il biglietto; **a single ticket** un biglietto di (sola) andata; **a return ticket** un

biglietto di andata e ritorno; **a book of tickets** un blocchetto di biglietti
ticket collector il controllore
ticket office la biglietteria
tide (*sea*) la marea; **low tide** la bassa marea; **high tide** l'alta marea
tidy ordinato(a)
tie la cravatta
tight (*fitting*) stretto(a)
tights i collant; (*woollen*) la calzamaglia
till (*cash desk*) la cassa
till (*until*) fino a; **till 2 o'clock** fino alle due
time il tempo; **this time** questa volta; **What time is it?** Che ore sono?; **on time** in orario
timetable l'orario *m*
tin (*can*) la scatola
tin-opener l'apriscatole *m*
tip (*to waiter*) la mancia
tipped (*cigarette*) con il filtro
tired stanco(a)
tissues i fazzoletti di carta
to a; (*with name of country*) in; **to London** a Londra; **to Italy** in Italia; **to the airport** all'aeroporto; **from nine o'clock to three** dalle dieci alle tre; **something to drink** qualcosa da bere
toast il pane tostato
tobacconist's il tabaccaio
today oggi
toe il dito del piede
together insieme
toilet la toilette
toilet paper la carta igienica
toiletries gli articoli da toletta
toll (*motorway*) il pedaggio
tomato il pomodoro; **tinned tomatoes** i pelati
tomato soup la zuppa di pomodoro
tomorrow domani; **tomorrow morning** domani mattina; **tomorrow afternoon** domani pomeriggio; **tomorrow evening** domani sera
tongue la lingua
tonic water l'acqua *f* tonica

tonight (*evening*) stasera; (*night-time*) stanotte
too (*also*) anche; (*excessively*) troppo; **My sister came too** È venuta anche mia sorella; **The water's too hot** L'acqua è troppo calda; **too late** troppo tardi; **too much** troppo(a); **too much noise** troppo rumore; **too many** troppi(e); **too many people** troppa gente
tooth il dente
toothache il mal di denti
toothbrush lo spazzolino da denti
toothpaste il dentifricio
toothpick lo stuzzicadenti
top **the top floor** l'ultimo piano *m*
top (*of bottle, pen*) il tappo; (*of pyjamas, bikini*) la parte di sopra; (*of hill, mountain*) la cima; **on top of** sopra di
total (*amount*) il totale
to touch toccare
tough (*meat*) duro(a)
tour (*trip*) il giro; (*of museum*) la visita; **guided tour** la visita guidata
tour guide la guida turistica
tour operator l'operatore *m* turistico
tourist il/la turista
tourist information office l'ufficio *m* turistico
towel l'asciugamano *m*
tower la torre
town la città; **town centre** il centro città; **town plan** la piantina
toy il giocattolo
toyshop il negozio di giocattoli
traffic il traffico
traffic jam l'ingorgo *m*
traffic lights il semaforo
traffic warden il vigile
train il treno; **by train** in treno; **the next train** il prossimo treno; **the first train** il primo treno; **the last train** l'ultimo treno
trainers le scarpe da ginnastica
tranquillizer il tranquillante
to translate tradurre

to travel viaggiare
travel agent's l'agenzia *f* di viaggi
travel guide la guida
travel insurance l'assicurazione *f* di viaggi
travel sickness (*in car*) il mal *m* d'auto; (*on ship*) il mal *m* di mare
traveller's cheque i traveller's (cheque)
tray il vassoio
treatment la cura
tree l'albero *m*
trip la gita
trolley (*for luggage, shopping*) il carrello
trousers i pantaloni
truck il camion
true vero(a)
trunk (*luggage*) il baule
trunks **swimming trunks** i calzoncini da bagno
to try provare
to try on (*clothes, shoes*) provare
t-shirt la maglietta
Tuesday il martedì
tuna il tonno
to turn girare
to turn off (*light, cooker, TV*) spegnere; (*tap*) chiudere
to turn on (*light, cooker, TV*) accendere; (*tap*) aprire
turquoise (*colour*) turchese
tweet il twit
to tweet twittare
twice due volte; **twice a week** due volte alla settimana
twin-bedded room camera a due letti
twins i gemelli, le gemelle
tyre la gomma
tyre pressure la pressione delle gomme

U

ugly brutto(a)
ulcer l'ulcera *f* **mouth ulcer** l'afta *f*
umbrella l'ombrello *m*
uncle lo zio
uncomfortable scomodo(a)
under sotto; **children under 10** i bambini sotto i dieci anni
undercooked poco cotto(a)

underground la
metropolitana
underpants (*man's*) le
mutande
to understand capire;
I don't understand
No capisco; **Do You
understand?** Capisce?
underwear la biancheria
intima
unfortunately purtroppo
United Kingdom il Regno
Unito
United States gli Stati Uniti
university l'università *f*
unleaded petrol la benzina
senza piombo
unlikely improbabile
to unlock aprire
to unpack disfare le valigie
unpleasant sgradevole
up su; **up here** quassù; **up
there** lassù; **What's up?**
Cosa succede?; **up to 50**
fino a 50; **up to now** fino
adesso
upstairs di sopra; **the
people upstairs** gli inquilini
del piano di sopra
urgent urgente
us ci; noi; **Can You help us?**
Ci aiuta?; **with us** con noi
USA gli USA
to use usare
useful utile
usual solito(a)
usually di solito

V
vacancy (*in hotel*) la camera
libera
vacant libero(a)
vacation la vacanza
vacuum cleaner
l'aspirapolvere *m*
valid valido(a)
valuable di valore
value il valore
VAT l'IVA *f*
veal la carne di vitello
vegan vegano(a)
vegetables le verdure
vegetarian vegetariano(a);
I'm vegetarian Sono
vegetariano
very molto; **very much**
moltissimo; **I like it very
much** Mi piace moltissimo

vest la canottiera
via via
video (*machine*) il video;
(*cassette*) la videocassetta
video camera la
videocamera
video recorder il
videoregistratore
view la vista
village il paese
vinegar l'aceto *m*
vineyard la vigna
virus il virus
visa il visto
visit la visita
to visit visitare
visiting hours l'orario *m*
delle visite
visitor il visitatore, la
visitatrice
voicemail il servizio di
messaggeria vocale
voucher il buono

W
waist la vita
to wait for aspettare
waiter il cameriere
waiting room la sala
d'aspetto
waitress la cameriera
to wake up svegliarsi
Wales il Galles
walk la passeggiata; **to go
for a walk** andare a fare una
passeggiata
to walk passeggiare; (*go on
foot*) andare a piedi
walking boots gli
scarponcini
walking stick il bastone
wall il muro
wallet il portafoglio
to want volere
ward (*hospital*) il reparto
wardrobe l'armadio *m*
warehouse il magazzino
warm caldo(a); **It's warm
outside** Fa caldo fuori
to warm up (*milk, food*)
riscaldare
to wash lavare
washing machine la
lavatrice
washing powder il
detersivo in polvere
washing-up bowl la
bacinella

washing-up liquid il
detersivo per i piatti
wasp la vespa
waste bin il bidone della
spazzatura
watch l'orologio *m*
to watch (*look at*)
guardare
water l'acqua *f* **bottled
water** l'acqua in bottiglia;
cold water l'acqua fredda;
drinking water l'acqua
potabile; **hot water** l'acqua
calda; **sparkling water**
l'acqua gassata; **still water**
l'acqua naturale
water heater lo
scaldabagno
watermelon l'anguria *f*
to waterski fare sci d'acqua
watersports gli sport
acquatici
waves (*on sea*) le onde
way in l'entrata *f*
way out l'uscita *f*
we noi
weak (*coffee, tea*)
leggero(a); (*person*) debole
to wear portare
weather il tempo
weather forecast le
previsioni del tempo
web (*internet*) il web
website il sito web
wedding il matrimonio
wedding present il regalo di
matrimonio
Wednesday il mercoledì
week la settimana; **last
week** la settimana scorsa;
next week la prossima
settimana; **per week** alla
settimana; **this week**
questa settimana; **during
the week** durante la
settimana
weekday il giorno feriale
weekend il fine settimana;
next weekend il prossimo
fine settimana; **this
weekend** questo fine
settimana
to weigh pesare
weight il peso
Welcome! Benvenuto!
well bene; **I'm very well**
Sto molto bene; **He's not
well** Non sta bene

well done (*steak*) ben cotto(a)
Welsh gallese
west l'ovest *m*
wet bagnato(a); **wet weather** brutto tempo
wetsuit la muta
what? cosa?; **What colour is it?** Di che colore è?; **What is it?** Cos'è?; **I saw what happened** Ho visto cosa è successo; **Tell me what you did** Dimmi cos'hai fatto
wheel la ruota
wheelchair la sedia a rotelle
when? quando?
where? dove?
whether se; **I don't know whether to go or not** Non so se andarci o no
which? quale; **which one?** quale?; **which ones?** quali?
while mentre; **in a while** fra un po'; (*very soon*) fra poco
whisky il whisky
white bianco(a)
who? chi?
whole tutto
wholemeal bread il pane integrale
whose **Whose is it?** Di chi è?
why? perché?
wide largo(a)
widow la vedova
widower il vedovo
wife la moglie
wild (*animal*) selvatico(a)
to win vincere
window la finestra; (*in car, train*) il finestrino; **shop window** la vetrina

windscreen il parabrezza *m*
windscreen wipers il tergicristallo
to windsurf fare windsurf
windy **It's windy** C'è vento
wine il vino; **dry wine** il vino secco; **house wine** il vino della casa; **red wine** il vino rosso; **rosé wine** il vino rosé; **sparkling wine** il vino frizzante; **white wine** il vino bianco; **wine list** la lista dei vini
wing mirror lo specchietto laterale
winter l'inverno *m*
wireless senza fili
with con; **with ice** con ghiaccio; **with milk** con il latte
without senza; **without ice** senza ghiaccio; **without milk** senza latte
woman la donna
wonderful meraviglioso(a)
wood (*material*) il legno
wooden di legno
wool la lana
woollen di lana
word la parola
work il lavoro; **at work** al lavoro
to work (*person*) lavorare; (*machine, car*) funzionare; **It doesn't work** Non funziona
world il mondo
worried preoccupato(a)
worse peggio
worth **It's worth ...** Vale...
to wrap (*parcel*) incartare
wrapping paper la carta da regalo

wrist il polso
to write scrivere; **Please write it down** Lo scriva per favore
wrong sbagliato(a); **What's wrong?** Cosa c'è che non va?

X
X-ray la radiografia

Y
yacht lo yacht
year l'anno *m* **a year ago** un anno fa; **this year** quest'anno; **next year** l'anno prossimo; **last year** l'anno scorso
yearly annualmente
yellow giallo(a)
yes sì; **Yes please** Sì, grazie
yesterday ieri; **yesterday morning** ieri mattina
yet ancora; **not yet** non ancora
yoghurt lo yogurt; **plain yoghurt** lo yogurt naturale
yolk il tuorlo
you (*familiar*) tu; (*polite*) lei; (*plural*) voi
young giovane
your (*familiar sing*) il tuo, la tua; (*polite sing*) il suo, la sua; (*familiar plural*) il vostro, la vostra
youth hostel l'ostello

Z
zip la cerniera lampo
zoo lo zoo
zoom lens lo zoom
zucchini la zucchina